ROBERTO PALOMO-SILVA

SCRIPTA I

Roberto Palomo-Silva

SCRIPTA I

La Pereza Ediciones

R O B E R T O   P A L O M O - S I L V A

S C R I P T A   I

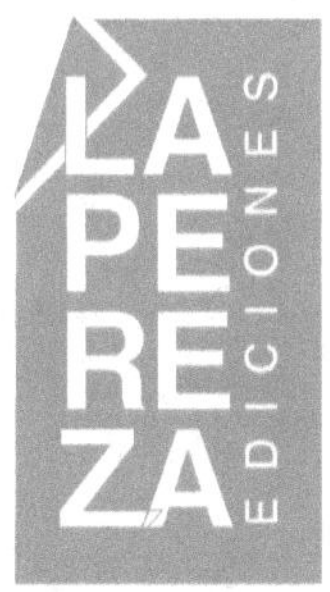

PREFACE

After returning from The Hague and whilst my Tour of Duty came to a close, my main concern fell on the question of how to deal with my time. For many years my duties as a diplomat kept me occupied with a series of matters and issues, and my ever-present intellectual or academic research had been forced to take a secondary role, not anymore, the return to my philosophical thinking and primary interest were slowly coming back. From Philosophy to International Law, two fields of knowledge that are not so far apart as it might seem, it was the opposite, the latter stages of my work as a diplomat brought me into the realm of "conflict resolution", "solution of controversies", "peaceful means to solve disputes" and some other intriguing concepts, principles, and notions. Being mainly focused on what the British call —most confess I deeply dislike the term—, continental philosophy, focussing primordially on methods of thinking and study, equipped me with certain tools and ways to approach that elusive field of confrontation of systems, history, and overall, instruments to comprehend, interpret and translate opposing or in a more difficult framework, legal and political colliding realities not only ideas or principles but the state of affairs that affected directly peoples and countries. Whilst at these crossroads, the grand questions at the beginning and end of these troubling realities, were how to overcome differences and solve confronted positions that were even hurting entire populations and nations as well as individuals, human beings, were gravely impacted by the lack of solutions, answers to sometimes unexplainable circumstances and ways of coexistence.

My dearest daughter Andrea travelled with me to most of my posts and had been extremely close to me, on many of my professional and personal duties, we bid farewell together as we departed The Hague, in what turned out to be my last diplomatic post. When we arrived back in the United States, Virginia and then moving to Boca Raton, where my final retirement took place, she gave me this intriguing idea about to start a post or a blog and continue writing and researching as I did during my academic years. Phenomenology, Hermeneutics, and the Theory of Controversies, that the late great Israeli thinker, Marcelo Dascal, developed throughout his life. During our years in Berlin, Marcelo was working on the extraordinary project of publishing Leibniz's works that were concluded and remain today as the main source of study of Leibniz's remarkable corpus, as just stated, we meat frequently discussed not only Leibniz's work —I am coming from the Heideggerian and Phenomenological tradition but early in my career got very attached to the *Kritische Theorie* and the works of Adorno, Marcuse, Benjamin and specially Horkheimer and the critical thinking rooted deeply on my ways of interpreting reality, and specially Pragmatics and how it influenced the birth of the Theory of Controversies. I had found new tools to study and gain deeper insights into the world of controversies an enormous task ahead and it touched the core of my main field of work, none other than solving controversies and the peaceful forms to overcome differences. From this horizon, my daughter's ideas found a form for my thinking and writing to become more fruitful and generate questions and sometimes answers, to these huge questions and open conflicts. That is the reason why the entire chapter is devoted to the Belize/Guatemalan controversy.

The blog was borne. This came to light with the first article that I published, "The San Francisco Giants", which I include at the end of this first volume. The first post is here presented as the last one. It marked a starting point, both emotionally and of a project that after all these years grew in depth and dimension. All here present *scripta* —*I* dare to choose the Latin word for writings— or strict sense, essays, vary in length and subject but conform to an internal unity. The first chapter occupies itself with a group of writings that deal with art and truth; the second one, with the subject of foreign policy, a dear matter that walked very close to me for so many years, alongside my professional and personal activities and still remains as an indispensable discipline to my endeavours; the third chapter, Books and Authors, is mainly constructed around a certain number of books that helped me immensely to introduce certain ideas, whilst I navigated the authors works, some of them, very dear to me and close to my personal view of the world; the fourth chapter bring us directly into the Belize/Guatemala controversies and currently a filed case before the International Court of Justice, they are all written in Spanish, one characteristic of the present volume, to write in different languages simultaneously, a recent and modern trend that will keep expanding and will be used more extensively; the last two chapters, are mainly an Addendum and are mostly in Spanish too, one touches on the extraordinary persons that I had the privilege to called my friends and whom both shaped and influence my life and thinking deeply and it is more than faire to reproduce here and finally a series of smaller and short texts dealing with matters pertain to my country of birth, Guatemala, that have had me troubled and concerned immensely, corruption, some political philosophy and reflections on the future and current states of affairs in Guatemala.

Roberto Palomo-Silva

To Andrea

CHAPTER I
ON ART AND THE SEARCH FOR TRUTH

1
ON AGE, TIME AND THE FORGOTTEN LANGUAGES

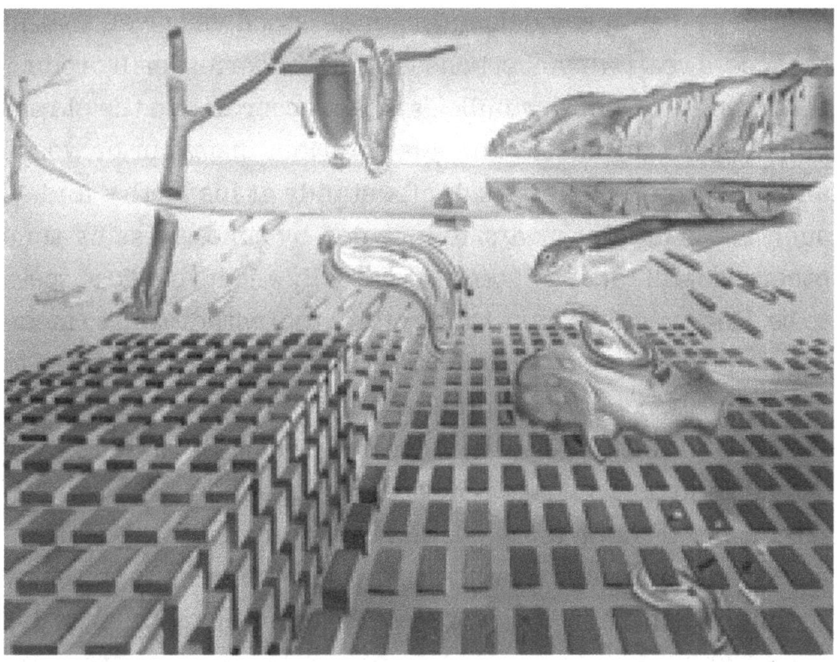

La Desintegración de la Persistencia de la Memoria, circa 1952-1954. Salvador Dalí. Saint Petersburg Museum, Florida. The Dalí Museum, Gift of A. Reynolds & Eleanor Morse.

Dalí was a master in many ways, his remarkable iconography is very well documented and the subject of a manifold of interpretations. Time, aging, and memory count among his preferred topics. Dreams and melting watches. The constant, never-ending passing of time to ultimately face Death, that great destructor of time. *La persistencia de la memoria* (The persistence of memory) and the famous quotation that watches are nothing more than *paranoiac-critical Camembert cheese of space and time...* and we know that he is shifting between Freudian psychoanalysis, surrealism onto quantum physics or quantum mechanics. We know that Camembert cheese is a very delicate outcome of the old art of making cheese and most likely Dalí, so close to French culture and culinary delicacies, understood very well that in essence, a real Camembert cheese is a wonderful small product that emerges from raw milk —at least according to the old art of hand-creating cheese and it is notorious disfavour or worst, an insult when pasteurized milk stands at his birth— and as such is essentially meant to be ruled by time, pressing time otherwise will rot and deteriorate rapidly and its magic success to be. However, Dalí links time or its actual withdrawal to memory. So, we have, first, *Persistency* and afterward, we come to *Disintegration,* not of time but curiously, memory. Memory thus persists but ultimately disintegrates, it carries a very heavy weight from the language of modern physics and non-Newtonian mechanics. From a more poetic term to an analytic one, from surrealism to quantum mechanics, is this the journey he is seeking by introducing newer or more permanent elements into his iconography of time and space, or is it a tribute to the mere decay of things and the subjective act of remembrance, memory, after all, disintegrates unless is turned into a collective expression, in Dalí's case, his persona brings us to his legacy, his art, and his unique work so, therefore, memory somehow survives in art and becomes a collective experience goes beyond his creator and establishes his own space and time, a world and earth. Art prevents and stops the inevitability of the withdrawal of memory, the subjective experience of decay and passing turns into a permanent persistence, and memory is not disintegrated. The telling of time through *Camembert cheese* leads us to a sensorial experience one that is perceived through the mystery of its decomposition. Re-telling this enormous complex process requires the deconstruction of common images and symbols to create a new narrative that speaks beyond the ambient of common meaning. So a clock disintegrates or melts even, so we can come into some sort of contact —mainly visual in this particular case— and re-leave the hidden meaning of these icons and symbols while being transformed from everyday objects into icons and symbols that tell us a tale of what surrounds us in its invisibility, none other than loss and decay and passing.

Currently, humanity as such is experiencing collectively —like the times of wars, when the winds of war blow— the fear and angst of Death. The silent, individual experience of the death of the other as our own, emerges from its darkness as an imminent threat. Pandemics, like the Great Pestilence, bring us as a collective *we* into the face of the kind of not seen menace, since the moments when the nuclear war could take place. The 1962 crisis of the Cuban missiles gave the American people a severe and bitter taste of the devastation of an imminent nuclear confrontation. But it wasn't an American revelation only, the response would generate apocalyptic destruction, the reality of world destruction, widespread pain and suffering, and the probability of a collapse of humanity as such. Plagues that emerge unexpectedly trigger the possibility of world annihilation. The end of times. The cursing of Gods or the unexplained evilness of mankind and its unending madding-driven thirst for wars and domination. We dwell in the vicinity of time and space, consumption, and destruction, all that is success to be. So, we are left with the power of memory and recollection, our extraordinary capacity —one that transcends most realms of human understanding— and mysterious skills that some individuals possess to create forms of perdurability that we call art, science, poetry, and thinking. With memory, we face and prevent the inevitability of decay and destruction by installing what will remain after our time and space disintegrate. The Greeks believed that αναμνησία is not only memory but a sort of previous knowledge that enables the knowledge of knowledge. Reminiscence. The recuperation of something that was known and lies in forgetfulness. Re-collecting that, that somehow was suppressed or set aside but remains latent, recapturing or bringing back this sort of original knowledge that enables or makes possible the current or actual knowledge. Anamnesía becomes Vorgriff. Not only is knowing a re-collection it is even a pre-apprehension, even more, memory as remembrance is also a celebration or commemoration, because the pre-apprehended leads us or drives us forward. The question is of course, from where to what or maybe from" where-to-where".

Remembering also is essentially linked to honouring. We bid farewell with honour and dignity. We value the life achievements and contributions of the other as well as we must acknowledge the previous generation for its dedication and commitment. But please, not so quickly and not so easily. The old ways of the previous generation might be losing their grip on the newer ones. Old systems of values might be considered outdated or not in agreement with the current ways. Nothing seems to be everlasting nor can withstand the passing of time. Some cultures and countries value their intellectuals, musicians, and artist much more than other countries though they might share the same cultural values and history even, sharing similar origins. Cultures and civilizations that stem and hold in high standard experience and the serenity that time brings, after enduring many battles through-out life, have a system of values that deeply respects an individual's life achievements, an artist or a writer's life-long work, sometimes the public recognition that a certain given person's body of work has transcended into levels of extraordinary manifestation deserves to be acknowledged into the broadness of the public view. Forms of kindness are a manifestation of a culture of generosity and openness to others despite differences and dissimilarities or profound disagreements and maybe because of these differences such a process of acceptance most at all costs, be conducted as a way of respect, humility, and dignity. Nowadays we face a constant threat against the pricing of extraordinary outcomes that can turn the face of the world and specifically, of a certain culture, into one of humanities highest expressions of acceptance and understanding, that is the fundamental reason we look up for a more embracing recognition of our core human values, namely those that help us stand with each other in forms of proximity and nearness, meaning reaching out to the other by means of admiration and celebration of the others success and brilliance, this an no other, is the pregnant meaning and significance of remembrance as honouring, recognition, the unique ability of mankind to see through the superficial differences to come before the extraordinary, the unique, the sacrifice and the suffering, the renunciation, to construct everlasting and changing forms of the highest expressions of the human soul: that is the deeper meaning of re-collection as a human alternative to the passing of time and the destruction of memory, not forgetting is nothing else but the enormous power of knowledge through memory.

Recognition is utterly relevant to establishing individual achievements and success, tough as discrete or private as the individual might have been in the ways his business was conducted, many individual contributions are never recognized and remain unknown, undiscovered, or ignored. In the brutal reality of absolute competition sometimes talent or even genius doesn't always suffice. Needless to point out that also in the realm where values and originality are weighed in currency non-profitability hampers and severely limits, even destroys, outstanding works of art from music to literature not no mention science and philosophical works, to quote a few. What's not markable or cannot be sold might ab initio be severed or cast away. Numerous examples can be cited regarding this criterion. Many great authors tell the stories of how their work was once rejected or consider not deemed to be published, exhibited, or heard by an audience because they wouldn't "sell" or worst, were not good enough. The old aesthetical idea that what endures the passing of time becomes a real work of art or a widely recognized novel, or musical success, has become outdated. Classicism rarely is invoked anymore. Success and recognition are measured under very different categories nowadays. In times past what has classically established a model, generated rules, transcended temporality, and became endurable? Everlasting, eternal so to speak. Time turns today into permanent present historicity seems to stop, halt, all that matters takes place in a constant *"now"*, the flow of times loses sense in the constant struggle to prevent it deliberately to contain its movement, the natural flow of time is quasi retained in the instant of the present that inexplicably rules and governs, despotically, the human existence and meaning of all there is.

We are dwelling in the existence of the constant present. We forget the question of the origins. We don't understand anymore the reasons why certain questions are asked and raised. The present becomes a presence and the tyranny of the *now* threaten our mere core and meaning. We define ourselves through achievements, reaching goals and of course, success, the sooner the better, we completely lose our ability and skills to understand past languages, not languages as such, here we're mainly referring to the written languages of the past, articulated to express conceptions, theories or build systems of thought. Thinkers engage constantly with other languages, some even not spoken anymore, whose written forms and expressions survive and still communicate from other times and moments. Probably one of the most difficult tasks one can face while recreating or fully understanding, not to say interpreting ancient constructions of thought, lies in the ability to recreate those long passed languages. Recapturing their hidden meaning and contextualizing them on their own accurate time construct from where they speak. Re-reading or grasping, unveiling all the secrets and frameworks, horizons, that shaped ideas, and conceptions. Words that are not employed anymore and their original meaning might be even difficult —sometimes impossible— to revisit and decode. Translating forgotten languages is a constant task and challenge for thinkers that search beyond the presence of the present. Origins hide somehow in forgotten languages and the effort to recapture ancient meanings and bring them up to a fully comprehensive current form of expression remains one very difficult endeavour. Necessary, utterly, and fundamentally demanding to restore the origins and be able to raise the questions of where we come from and from where thinking generated and came into being.

Salvador Dalí who also was a masterful sculptor, brought the idea of the *Camembert cheese* or the so-called melting watch, the futility of time measuring, the failed attempt at the telling of time, time itself consumes us, which is also the tale of the passing and never halting of the Great Punisher, on a late piece believed to be conceived around 1977 and the first cast circa 1997, however different versions of the melting watches were made, an extraordinary and beautiful masterwork, we choose to end this difficult reflection by returning to Dalí's iconography, where symbols speak much louder than words, invoking the sculpted vision of the melting timepiece, which he called, appropriately *Le Profil du Temps*. Let us allow the work of art to speak and while the symbols and images install an earth and a world, we follow the mystery of the decay of everything that is and fall to the mercy of the merciless grip of time. So, therefore, the human answer to the melting of the evanescence of all that is, cannot be anything else but the memory and honoring of remembrance. And that is how anamnesis, ἀνάμνησις, became Vorgriff with all that goes in between.

2
THE LIGHT AND THE DARKNESS

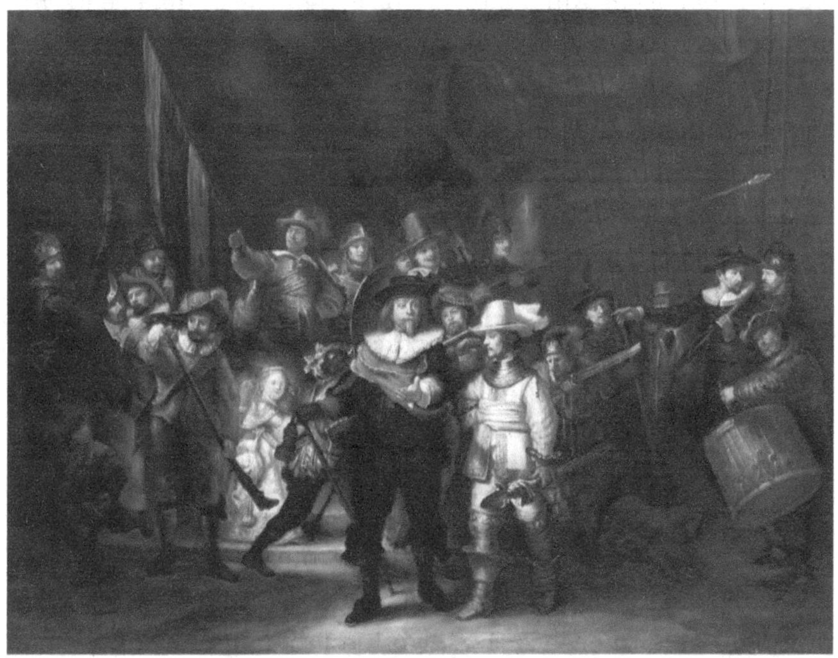

Officers and Men of the Company of Captain Frans Banning Cocq and Lieutenant Wilhelm van Ruytenburgh, known as the Night Watch, 1642, oil on canvas, 379.5 x 453.5 cm (Rijksmuseum, Amsterdam, Netherlands

The world is entering an age of darkness. The darkness is not a mere absence of light if we could still think in patristical terms. The old debate, about whether evil was the absence of goodness, and didn't have a being, as such but was thought of as a non-being. Evil doesn't have essential et existential and lacked an esse, quiddity, whatness you can say, we are very far away from this ancient debate, however, we seem to be in the heart of it inevitably, once again Maniqueism seems to be rebounding constantly. Nowadays we are witnessing manifestations of evilness all around us in different shapes, forms, languages, and actions, confusion reigns and we can affirm with a great deal of certainty that chaos is fighting to impose its will and power of destruction disguised, embossed and even not so subtly concealed. This calls for a *new order, solve et coagula,* the realm of lies and manipulation are gaining a strong grip over our cherished values. Noble institutions are under threat and assault, and we watch almost hopelessly irrationality and violence are not only instigated but fed through the channels and venues we so strongly fought to establish as grounding stones of an architecture meant to bring justice and a more human way of living together. The realm of confusion is imposing its dark seal on the sacred and the profane. Rembrandt understood probably, like very few great artists, the complexity and intricate linkage between light and darkness, and not only as an artistic technique but like most great artists it all comes from a deeper insight into the world, mankind, and faith. The great Dutch Masters were uniquely able to create this graphic language, which we call great art, to communicate and tell us stories and set up before our amazed eyes, the nature and essence of this struggle. The mystery of the encounter of light and darkness. The never-ending war between the *sons of light and the sons of darkness.*

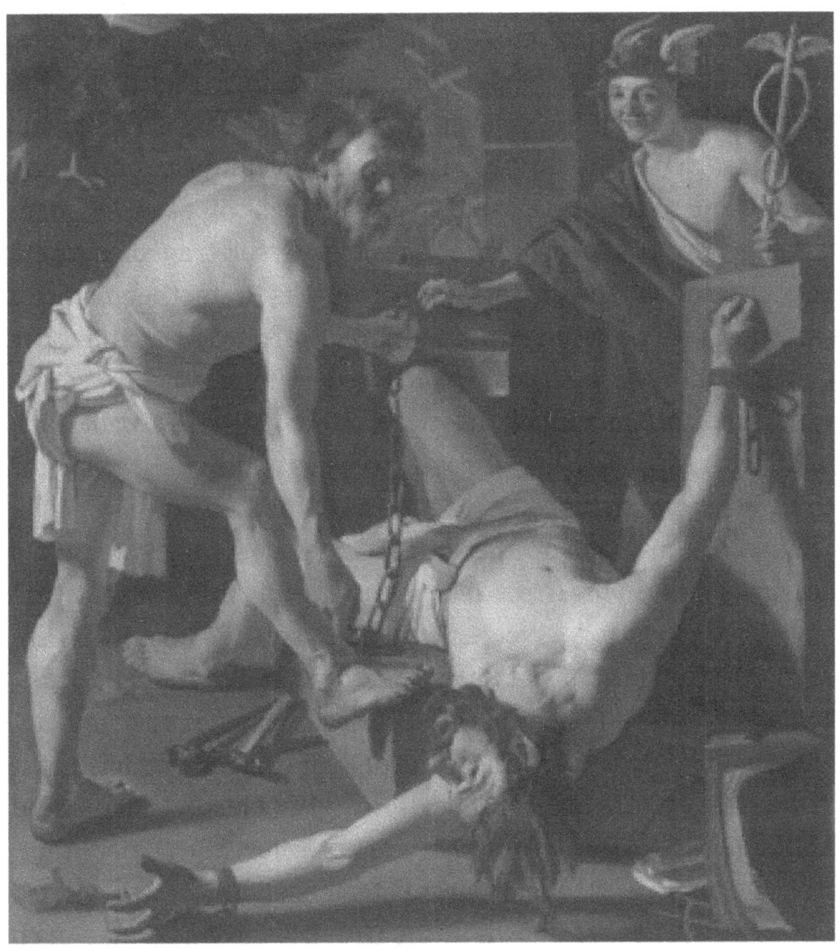

Dirk van Baburen, *Prometheus Being Chained by Vulcan*. Rijks Museum, 1623, on display in room 2.1

The great Dutch Masters are among the leading ones that penetrate and understand probably better than most, the mystery that the Italians introduced, on the interaction between dark and light. Chiaroscuro. Caravaggio immediately comes to mind. But the Dutch Masters go beyond the pure and sheer aesthetics of creation, there's a message always, a hidden maybe or undoubtedly, codified to use a more accurate term. Perhaps a public education service, invoking a rather —time not related— concept. Nonetheless serves a public function due to the nature of the message. In the present case, van Baburen speaks from the Greek world and its myths. Prometheus stands as one of the most discussed and analysed. On Aeschylus Prometheus Bound, which as we all know is part of a Trilogy, Greek tragedies would be presented as "three parts" sadly from the Prometheus Trilogy we only have one complete and fragments from others and other Greek authors as well, aside from the very famous story, where we encounter the dialogue between Hermes and Prometheus, filled with reprieves and threats, there is a line that stands for the ages, Prometheus refers to Time as the Teacher of all wisdom, Time who he also ages and he does, becomes even wiser, …*growing old turns Time in the Great Teacher of all things:* ἀλλ᾽ ἐκδιδάσκει πάνθ᾽ ὁ γηράσκων χρόνος, as we can find on line 981, there are so many translations but if we pick one that has endured Time, T.A. Buckley's rendering of the stanza comes close although not close enough, to the real meaning of Prometheus words, *Ay but Time, as he grows old, teaches all things.* (Philadelphia: David Mckay, 1897). Here Prometheus is not referring to his father, Kronos, but rather to another mysterious divine entity, named Chronos, Cronos, as shown in the Greek text, Time ruled even over the Gods themselves. He is the wisest of the wiser and the one who knows all things, but his knowledge comes precisely from becoming old. Profound knowledge emerges from enduring and suffering through endurance. Chronos was there even before the painful separation of Earth and Heaven, another remarkable story that requires further elaboration but bears no importance for our current discussions. The emphasis here is on the word ekdidasakei used in an older version by Aeschylus, if accepted loosely that the prefix ek carries a connotation of the origin or refers to origins and reaffirms instead of the classical example of the Alpha at the beginning of a word that might carry a negative affirmation, here it seems the verb didaskei is used and employed in a more original and pregnant meaning, it goes far beyond than its use or rendering as *education teaching* as the act of transmitting or giving knowledge, which acquired later on as it is used in the New Testament, although in some cases keeps the meaning of deliberate concussing and misguiding that can be found even on prophetical literature like Revelations or other pseudo-epigraphic texts.

This brings us to another notion that is intrinsically linked to the above just described. There are other sources of origin, but in Agamemnon line 176 the concept of πάθει μάθος, pathetic mathos, as utterly expressed, refers to the learning that comes or emerges through pain and or suffering. In Robert Browning's poetic rendition of the Aeschylus formula, ... *that suffering masterfully teach"* (London: Smith, Elder, and Co, 1889), the emphasis lays on that learning is achieved through enduring pain and suffering. On another, not as the well-known version of the Prometheus myth, when the Vulture asks the fallen Titan the reason why he accepts this terrible punishment —his liver being eaten every day— the reply is also the same again: πάθει μάθος. If there is such a rule, that Zeus imparted on mankind, of course, grounded on questionable principles, but that of divine selfishness and lack of empathy and compassion, ancient Greeks had this notorious feisty kind of relationship with their Gods, they were also constantly intervening on human affairs, and even more, mingling, guiding and conniving, lead to very destructive wars and even procreated —again for their selfish pleasure or obscure purposes'— with women, there's a long list of divine intervention in Greek literature of all these godly intrusions on Greek's everyday lives. So, to be mandated to suffer to learn or acquired knowledge leads to the second part of the process: the acquisition of this dearest and sought-after gift. So, enter Prometheus, the most generous of all divine creatures that bring and give freely what is probably the highest value amongst divinities, namely that of knowledge. Humans were originally forbidden or warned that severe punishments should rain down on them if they dare to acquire knowledge, both stories are very well known: from The Tree of Knowledge to Prometheus Fire in one an obscure character, a Serpent of sorts, mysteriously able to speak with the tung of the humans, deceives one and tricks her into violating the first mandate and on the other story, one of the original Gods or son of Gods, brings knowledge to humanity to bring her out of the deep darkness of ignorance. Pain and suffering enter the world of humans. If creation is bringing the light into the world by splitting or inserting the enormous power of illumination over the original great covering of its absence, the illuminating of all things has to have paired learning or maybe worded differently, an uncovering of all things being and that can only be done through the acquisition of knowledge so, therefore, the process begins, none other than that of learning and teaching in a more pregnant and original meaning.

As we endure and struggle to learn and understand this so-called *new normal*, while navigating through a sea of confusing information, given constantly to us by different means and ways, where science or one of the closest achievements mankind has that resembles knowledge in its pregnant meaning, so when politicians and journalist —the industry of information, that stands behind the quasi pontifices of truth— clashes to set us up in this chaotic world where understanding reality becomes even more complex as they generate layers to blind us and misguide us or split us up from truth and reality to which they seem to be devoted. However, this world of shadows into which we are thrown distances the seekers of truth from its source of origin. Knowledge carefully built by the means of research and investigation by highly educated individuals faces challenges from the quasi-fact-checkers, numbers of persons, and readers of the real whose mission are none other than to configure this dark world where we get lost and wonder hopelessly for the disappearing light. We dwell in language. Language is our house. Concealing and de-forming our sacred ways to relate to each other, turns us into blind slaves of this manipulative sense of deliberate concealment of the light, ultimately of truth, by ways and means to force us to read and see the shadows as light. Accept blindly the confusion and deceiving forms placed before us as pseudo-reality and quasi facts. We are thus caught up in the middle of this old struggle that takes nowadays the forms of suppressing real knowledge and placing before our at-hand given the false presentation of the mere shadows of truth. We might use a very old image, quoted countless times, discussed innu-merably ad aeternum, have we been able to leave the cave, or even worst, are we aware that we are dwelling in the cave, inha-bitants, of this dark world of shadows and mere appearances of truth and knowledge. We seem to be after more than two thousand years, in no position to answer this question.

3
THE SCIENTIST, THE POLITICIAN
AND THE JOURNALIST

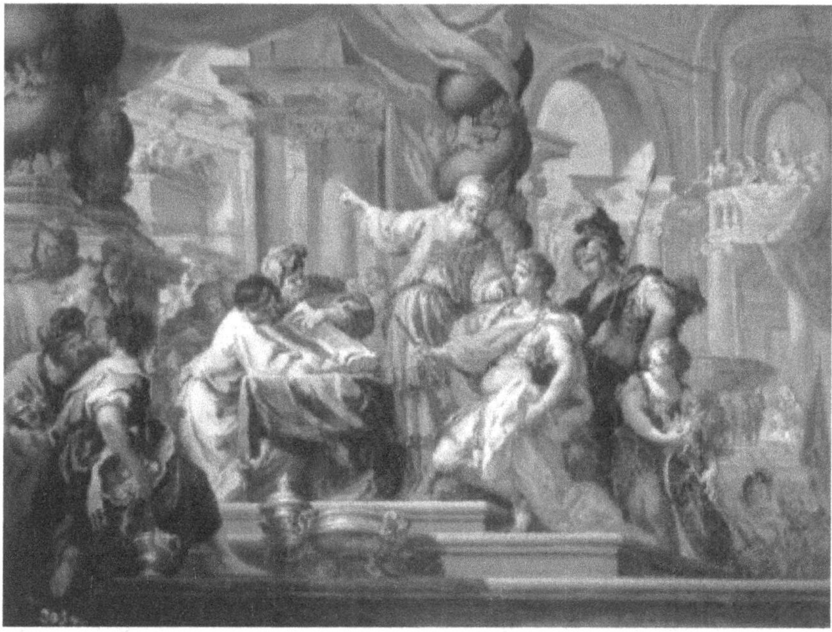

Alexander the Great in the Temple of Jerusalem (circa 1750), Sebastian Conca (1689-1764) The Prado Museum.

On the Talmud, *Tractate Tamid*, 33a, b, the story of the visit that Alexander the Great paid to the Elders of the Negev is told in a magnificent presentation. Much has been written about this quasi-mythological journey that Alexander took while expanding his empire throughout the Middle East and Africa. Tito Livius also tells a story about his entrance and meetings in Jerusalem with the Samaritans, the latter ones have been questioned and put into doubt as historical inaccuracies. Nonetheless, the extraordinary conversations between Alexander and the Elders as told in the Gemara and the Talmud, place us before one of the most fascinating conversations imaginable. From *Tractate Tamid* we extract the famous question, raised by Alexander to the Elders: *Alexander **said to** the Elders: Who **is** truly worthy of being called wise? They said to him, citing a tradition (see Avot 2:9):* **Who is** *the* **wise** *person? The one who sees and anticipates* **the consequences** *of his behaviour.* The wise man is the one who can anticipate, to see the consequences of his behaviour. To see or foresee what is about to come as a result of the actions taken by a leader of men, thus Alexander being one of the historical most notorious leaders amongst the ones that led men brings us directly into the idea of the virtues that leaders should possess to lead or better said *to guide.* Real leaders guide and especially during times of great despair or crisis, in the current usage, that the word bears in our ways of referring to *the worst of times.*

The ancient Greeks used two words to separate and distinguish two forms of organized knowledge, one is referred to as δόξα, which has many meanings, it comes from the verb δοκεῖν, that carries the meaning of appearing, seems like, and is generally equated to the notion of *opinion,* in the sense of expressing a not rigorously constructed form of knowledge, tends to confuse and portraits a seemly debatable reality. Has the shape of an appearance or even a shadowy idea, blurred and confusing to use the language employed by the late Plato while referring to all *that is not,* μή ὄv, has no being or the famous, idea of the nothingness, not true Knowledge is a form of not being. That which is false has no being. Is not. This of course leads to the false leader, the one that confuses, the one that deviates from his essential mission of *guiding with the truth.* Here we see the link to the sophists and their peculiar method, the anglers, those who draw up, the hunters of men, the fishers of men, the ones that carry a spear, a hook to be correct, to hook the ignorant, those that are at the mercy of the language of confusion and chaos, deliberately ignore and separate themselves from real knowledge, ἐπιστήμη, *epistńmń*, the hook is an instrument to fish for men, to capture by the language of misguiding and deliberate presenting reality twisted and reshape, according to obscure and sometimes, sinister motives. Once again, here we see the proximity of politicians and sophists. But politicians are not the only ones hunting for men, using the hook of language or false knowledge to submit the will of the weaker ones, the vulnerable. We must examine this phenomenon much closer. It presents itself in terrifying forms and even, where we least expect to erupt.

The present controversy existing amongst politicians, scientists, and journalists, as fascinating as it may be, carries within its innerness, some very old elements, that can even be traced back to the great times of the Greek thinkers. Plato's long debates against the sophists contained and constructed especially on his latter dialogues, specifically, those that carry the names of the most famous sophists namely, *Protagoras, Georgias*, and the one that is simply known by the generic name of the *Sophist*. We are not going to go into the details of the argumentations and complex philosophical discussions. Nonetheless, some concepts might be of exemplary use to illustrate the actual situation. If we could think like Plato and go through the original *experience of the Ancient Greek language*, probably the politician and the sophist would be hard to distinguish. So it seems nowadays. And we are precisely witnessing this case, emerge before our amazing view of the discussion, manipulations of words, and exchange of accusations to just mention a few of the astonishing ways and shapes that the interactions amongst the three of these powerful groups, present themselves while we struggle to understand what has engulfed all of us, on a global scale. Very few countries of the world, if any at all, seem to be immune to this other form of contagion. Mathematical and statistical models, algorithmic ones, became the language of expression and representation of reality. The colossal effort to bring to the comprehension and understanding of all human beings, how this total confusion took place, generated, and is acting, unravelling immense destruction and death everywhere and on all corners of the world. Notoriously we follow with the utmost astonishment, that is not —and is not clear nor have we gotten a clear and rational, scientifically grounded explanation to the reason for such disparities— to say with sheer disbelief how the numbers grow to levels that our phantasies wouldn't dare to fare. As we see staggering sums of human beings dying daily, the paradox of the need to save and rescue the economy starts to become a crude necessity, we also witness the dance of trillions and billions of dollars, euros, and other currencies, printed and offer to safeguard and safe the world economy from its destruction. We do not know what is going to come out of this explosion of numbers. But fear is rooted across the people of all countries.

In Plato's Sophist dialogue, where he not only discusses the meaning and scope of the sophist but defines his methods and tools as a *fisher of men*, which he also characterizes as an economical endeavour. The sophist acts underpayment, hired to introduce confusion and manipulation of the youth and others vulnerable to the *enchantment of words and lies*. His tools as an angler are none other than his spearing, drawing-up, hooking with the harpoon of his words all those susceptible to his bewitching craft. The Stranger uses a specific Greek word to describe his ways, says on one exchange with Theaetetus: *aspaleutikhe*, which is a form of παραδείγματα, although this Ancient Greek word is understood and used today in a different context and meaning, originally it refers to the education, that is why Plato on the Republic confronts, the two forms of Paideias, that of the poets and the one that he calls, παιδεία παραδηγματικά, the one built on values, virtues, and principles and of course, the ideals of a culture, the search for truth and good. An education that forms on the search and achievement of that which is central to a culture and to humans whose pursuit of the *idea of good takes central stage*. The so-called *aspaleutikhn* strives for nothing because it lacks a purpose and a goal, seeks only gratification in the form of that which is-not, motivated by the ambition to generate economical y financial advantages over the rest of humans by selling and buying a deformed presentation of reality. Sophists are for hire and sale. This is an old controversy and not entirely solved. Similarities are there and when a crisis of the current magnitude explodes all this angling and drawing-up emerges implacably. We have experienced on an everyday basis the current confrontations generated by the paradox installed by the pandemic.

There is an incredible journey that probably, started with *"the republic of letters"* to the reading public, the redactional society or editing sub-cultures, the so-called idea that *everyone is a journalist* has shaped into today's image-digital world of pseudo-information, commented *news* and the era of the cult of the anchor, this exceptional transformation has established an incredible complex subtextual and visually oriented presentation of reality. From the development of the field of critical cultural studies to the abandonment of the humanities as roots for the profile of the *journalist* —both terms *news* and *journalist,* intimately binned, are in desperate need of a very thorough and in-depth redefinition —in many or most of the leading schools of thought that educate and form journalists. This is a new age, and the written word is ceding its dominant place to the image or instant visual communicating message-sending information or interpretation process, a decoding and miscoding subculture. Written newspapers or critical commenting journals have been severely stricken and see a strong demise in favour of the quick and always manipulated and doctored virtually and digitally emitted messages/news. Is the era of the "spin doctor", whatever that might mean? It is true that as a discipline *cultural study (Hoggart)* probably inspired by its oldest predecessor, the *Kritishe Theorie* —the original Frankfurt Schule— probably through Adorno's vast work and also Walter Benjamin's influential legacy, had a very strong cultural component. But the emphasis was and still is on criticism. And thus, the critical journalist comes to life. News is not anymore, just merely presented, and old- although in major countries this is the dominant way— they are principally analysed and commented, redressed, and given in carefully crafted and constructed *doses* and overall, angels and perspectives. Images and words became tools to hook and capture innocent pray or nowadays called, uninformed individuals, hungry for information became vulnerable targets to the arts and ways of the huge *"news corporations"* or media, whose boards or even star anchors, fight personal agendas and ideological ones. Most of the time the person looking for "information" not only gets hooked, harpooned by the avid and skilful "fishers of men" —and here the resemblance becomes most evident— and joins without even imagining, a struggle for domination, power, and control. These secret wars catch us unprepared and turn out into naive victims of manipulative conflicts, where ideologies and mere financial or economic interests, masked and well hidden, clash for survival. These wars are cruel and fought without any kind of mercy or restraint. They are wars of destruction and annihilation. We, the silent witnesses. Sadly, this state of affairs contaminated the crucial war that humanity fights against a deadly virus, that spreads unmerciful all over the world. We are fed every day and from different fronts with false and misguiding information. We are being poorly led on a war that politicians decided they were to ones to lead the charge against the invisible enemy. Both journalists' politicians are not prepared to understand and fight this deadly enemy. The only ones —and they must be the conductors of the fight— are none others than *the scientists*, the epidemiologist, the real specialist assisted by all their peers, and soundly formed and highly educated professionals, some of which have spent their entire professional careers and lives, studying this phenomenon, to master the combat against this extraordinary malady are the scientist and not the politicians, nor the journalists, sometimes caught in other survival wars that are spilling over this most tenuous of times. Humanity is in the face of an engulfing catastrophe and the leaders of men this time, should lead if they are genuine guides, guiding the way the world to the ones that have the knowledge and master the ways to stop the spread of this evil decease. This post began with the quotation and retelling of the story that the Talmud and the Gomera left us, regarding the famous visit of Alexander the Great to the Elders of the Negev, the question raised then about "who is the wise man" and the reply by the Elders, stands as valid then and too, day, even more, *the wise man is the one who can anticipate*, those are the educated which are fully able to anticipate, thus being none others than the scientists and the real guider follows their words and advice. So, therefore, guiders-leaders only listen to their scientist and wise men to come out of this horrendous pandemic. We owe it to the victims and their grieving families.

4
ON DEATH, VIRUSES AND
THE GREAT PESTILENCE

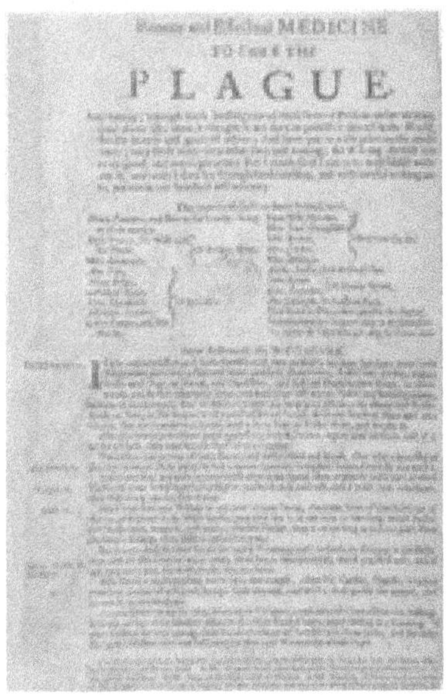

The best of times, the worst of times. The great pestilence. When Death becomes an everyday and habitual occurrence of our immediate existence, the old existentialist notion, of being thrown in the world and the meaning of our existence inhabits the very owners of being-towards-Death, Sein-Zum-Tode, which puts us in the presence of our historicity and temporality. But when the inevitability of Death starts to walk and parade in front of our eyes, panic, and terror, angst, wake from their ever-silent companionship. A war is being waged against humanity by an invisible enemy, powerful but not invincible, nonetheless. Leaders suddenly think of themselves as —or maybe are left without any other alternative— as military commanders that must rally their troops to face and destroy an unseen killer that hides in the invisibility of the very same old ones, that brought incredible punishment, pain, suffering without any announcement. No declaration of war whatsoever, jus ad Bellum, or chivalry gallantry play no role in this mysterious war against the hidden enemy, one that strikes unannounced and in the worst secrecy imaginable.

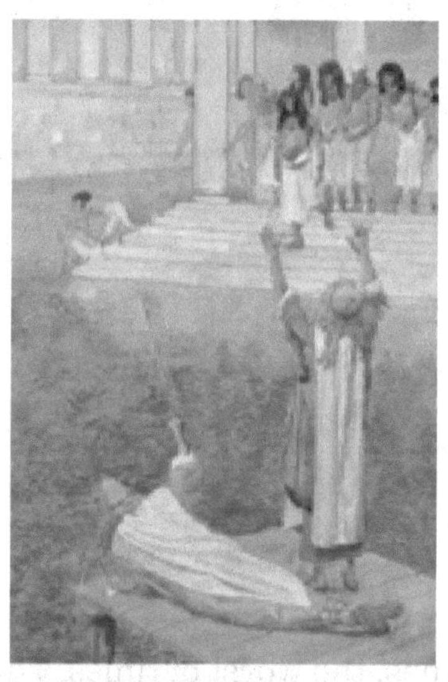

Probably the most famous reference to mankind in front of a great pestilence or plague comes from the Book of Exodus, שְׁמוֹת , Shemot or simply Names as in the names of the sons of Israel that came to Egypt with Joseph and their liberation from Pharaoh and guided, lead by Moses to Erezt Israel. Pharaoh and the Egyptians were forced to face and succumb to the plagues that were brought upon them for not allowing Joseph's descendants to leave Egypt. In the above painting by James Tissot, circa 1902, titled "Water is changed into blood", Moses uses Aaron's rod and turns the waters of Egypt into the blood. The story is told in The Book of Names, Exodus, Shemot, 7: 2-25.

Moses is commanded to take Aaron's rod —the same one that turned into a serpent and ate the rod-serpents of Pharaoh's magicians— and together they turn all the waters of Egypt into the blood and thereafter, the plagues were unleashed. There is an extraordinary ontological element in this story, whose implications are immense and transcendent to the limited scope of the present text, suffice it to say that we here refer to the following and respect certain practices and habits that mankind tends to forget or simply ignore. Here not only do we have the foundation of a nation emerging from diminished, severely diminished must be stressed, conditions, that of enslavement, to liberation and fulfilment of an alliance that will cover a whole people and the enormous punishment that carries and is inflicted on the leader that tyrannically wishes to continue the enslavement of the said people, the people of Israel, for the sole purpose of his selfish and egoistic wishes, not to mention that he thinks of himself as being a leaving god, something that history has it, can be retold many, many times more, from different individuals. The link here, this ontological link is none other than the one a genuine leader has with their people to provide them with morally and ethically encompassing leadership. Example with humility.

And from those times the plagues continue to unravel death and suffering to humanity like showing the limits of our dreams of conquering nature, transforming the world at large, and establishing man's domain over everything. During the times of the Enlightenment the idea that eventually scientifical knowledge will help a man become the ruler of all that is out there, created or not, gave birth also to the times of the great discoveries, the command over nature began its journey, poised by a blind faith on emerging technology and latter on, an industrial process that established the one-dimensional reality, one that will lead latter on to the construction of the global and interconnected world, one economy is deeply and secretly interwoven, in many shapes and forms, not all transparent and innocent, driven by the same blind idea that man can conquer and control all that is out there, even beyond the stars. And suddenly one day, when man was dreaming and planning to continue the exploration of space, even visiting again places where once a footprint and flag, were left and more daring, if at all possible, travel to Mars, beyond our undreamt dreams, take tourists to the Moon and some other working ideas in the process, out of silent silence, Nature reminded men, that the dialogue between both of them, has to be one of respect and mutual benefit, not the one generated by the language of domination and subjugation. Nature is not to be submitted, said the latter. Man must learn and understand that the need to coexist under certain principles is fundamental for both. So it spoke again, with its loud voice. A new plague strokes. Silently or voiceless. But with might that forces man to humble and rethink its essential relation with each other, the land, and the planet and listen again to the old voices that are being silenced by the obtuse thinking of never-ending domination. Even man's proudest domain was stroke by the irrationality of fear and angst. The global economy started to collapse, like a fragile construct before the silent eyes of the dominators. Nature is showing again man's limits. Once again, a very old tale must be retold, the plagues are present anew and with their silent power, forcing a man to reshape and maybe even understand and learn finally, to dwell well within his natural limits. The false dream is turning into a horrible nightmare, one that is so dark that has scared all the ruling powers that struggle to limit, prevent, and ultimately, if possible, contain the enormous damage generated. This plague like all the previous ones, will silently vanish and leave a trail of suffering and death. Man must pause and re-thing or engage in deep thinking and ask himself the fundamental questions, the meaning of life, and the way we leave with others.

The current state of affairs has constituted a so-called Black Swan event, to use a recent terminology that describes a situation or to partially invoke Nassim Nicholas Taleb's famous theory, what we face nowadays is none other than events beyond, well beyond, what could have been foreseen, although we begin to see that the science-oriented and educated minds begin to prevail over the crude politicians and global entrepreneurs, algorithmically or even statistical models undergo a very strenuous time gathering adequate and controllable data to predict the behaviour of the upcoming events, and needless to say that panic and the unknown —the very real fear of eminent Death or sickness— and its dark emotional prognosis, create this atmosphere of global collapse and the imminent destruction of the world as we know it. Corrupted data, fake news, uneducated guesses, and assumptions, mainly coming from leader's incapable of guiding through this terrible crisis or bi-dimensional reality that strikes not only globally, but on two fronts simultaneously, the economy and health. The newest form of the Blank Swan threatens us from this double dimension and the metaprobability of annihilation takes precedence. The recent and ongoing collapse of the financial markets touches on the domain of the algorithmic-digital reality that we leave in, or better said, the financial and global leaders, the owners of reality, and the shapers of this exclusive world of secrecy, that from a semi shadowy realm, rule most of our everyday reality, without the silent immense majorities being aware of its complexities and impacts on their everydayness and even more, on their livelihoods and even survival. Out of no comprehensible reasons —this is one of many groups of digital-algorithmic reality that is at risk here— employment, jobs and daily life suddenly turns into something not attainable, anymore. Dreams are shattered while politicians quarrel on different views or ideological positions, struggling to find ways to save multi-mega corporations —they employ enormous amounts of people— seem to face a very deep abyss before our own amazing eyes. The world and our being-in-the-world, namely our essential existence, to employ another old word, our Dasein is facing a terrible threat. The virus —and the malady generated has been named using a code and numbers, COVID-19— has infected the economy and by induction perhaps —just to recall that the original Black Swan dispute dealt with the nature of induction— has now infected our digital world, financial markets and all that evolves and revolves around them.

One final word about the current emerging controversy —it is, a very complex one we must underline—, addressing the monumental problem equipped with the tools of science is abundantly clear, beyond any dispute, the only strict approach. Resisting the temptation of politicization is of the utmost importance. But there is an essential aspect of the crisis that must be faced and openly stated, this is not a mere numbers game, this is not an algorithmic construct, behind these numbers, there are faces, human faces, stories, lives, tragedies, tears, and despair. Human beings are dying every day and comparing one pandemic to another doesn't suffice. This is a colossal human tragedy a drama of global proportions. Some of us, probably a small minority, dislike deeply the never-ending allusion to numbers, curves, and predicting when the curve will flatten or when this unending recounting of faceless, cold, and cruel numbers, will be replaced by words of empathy, consolation, and warmth. Again, the numbers hide human beings, with names and loved ones, families, dear ones, and friends that were inexplicably forced to come into the face of Death and her cruelty. Words of empathy and care must take precedence, so humanity shows his bright side, the luminous splendours of human nature, some of this we have seen, especially given the sacrifices and devotion with which physicians at all levels, nurses, health workers in general, the real front line of this war against the silent enemy, are enduring this terrible battle. The light will prevail at the end and a new world will emerge, let us hope it is going to be more human and fuller of generosity and care where the recognition and acceptance of the otherness of the other shall take central stage.

5
ON TRUTH AND LIGHT.
MUNDUS EST FABULA

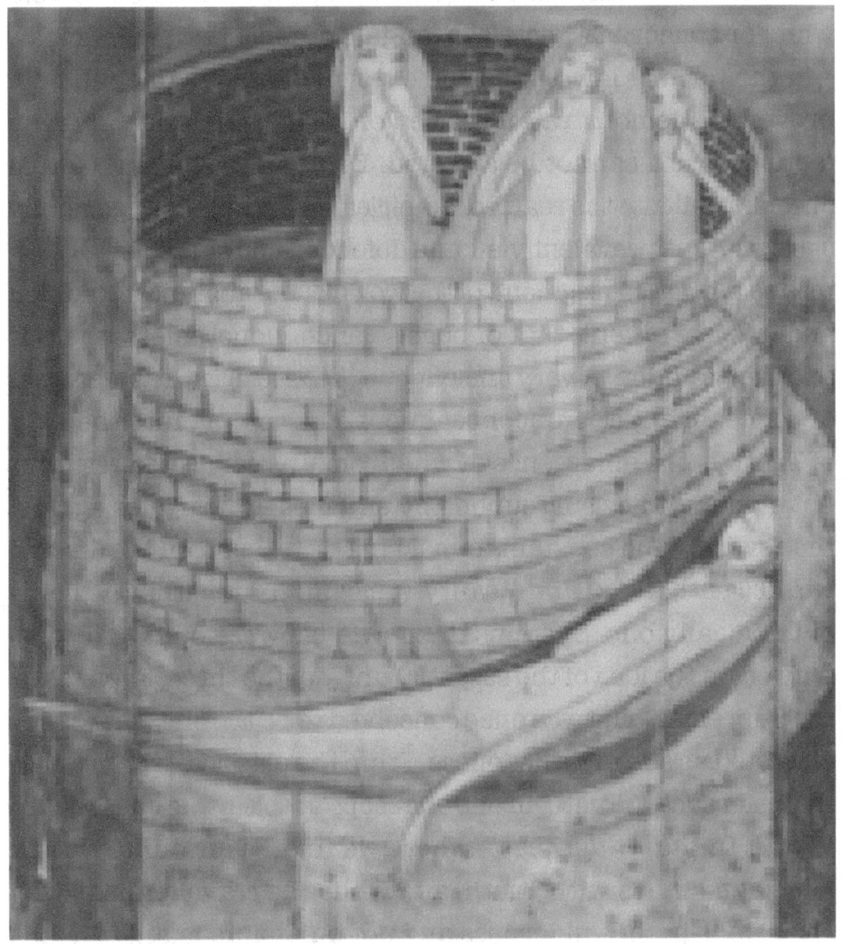

Truth lies at the bottom of the well by Frances Macdonald MacNair, circa 1912-1915

The search for truth is one of Philosophy's most important tasks. On this never-ending quest, both disciplines, Philosophy and Theology, were intertwined in pursuing the meaning of truth. For centuries the idea of truth as adaequatio intellectus ad rem or veritas is adaequatio intellectus et rei, using Aquinas's famous formula, headed and grounded Metaphysics, Ontology, and Theory of Knowledge. But the idea that Truth is such as for an empirical reference that can be established with an object and a link or concordatio between language, concepts, or principals —in the form of laws— and the external world is undoubtedly proven via demonstration, either/or logical, analytical, or even factual, Truth cannot be attested. Demonstration and factual checking fall into the realm of empirical science. This is, generally speaking, one prevalent view and defended and shared by a large, maybe the largest segment, of the world of the analytical tradition and to some extent, that of pure science. Nonetheless, there is another tradition. A very ancient one that sees Truth as a process of concealment and unconcealment, the coming into the light of Truth is the emergence of what remains concealed. Truth is not evident it lies surrounded by enemies. It struggles against the covering and constant unmasking of its Being. In the ancient world Truth, Good and Beauty were taught together as being ontologically one. Systems of knowledge were built and constructed on the idea of the essential unity of the three. Even more, the Supreme Being was once conceived to be the one where they all rested as one in its deepness. From the classical world comes this reference to Truth, in one of Aesops's fables, this one is called *"Truth in the Wilderness"*, where we find an encounter that a journeyman has with Truth, and while the traveller asks why she dwells in the wilderness and not on an important city, the reply is remarkable: because nowadays lies inhabit almost all of humanity as opposed to yesteryears when *"among old people, few lies could be found"*.

Ετεή δε ουδέν ίδμεν. Εν βυθώ γαρ η αλήθεια. This is the famous quotation from Democritus, or at least attributed to him by Diogenes Laertius, render as the version *"…for truth is in a well."* (Hicks, 1925). But the idea or tendency of translating aletheia as Truth is and has been contested and put in doubt, αλήθεια is a very peculiar Greek word, the alpha at the beginning carries a negative connotation and from there we go to the notion of Lethe, Λήθη, which we all know is one the five rivers of the Underworld, the ones that drank from his waters, will forget all previous knowledge and experiences. It also carries the meaning of concealment and forgetfulness. Forgetting that which is most fundamental, what is forgotten becomes hidden not simply disappears. And Truth lies at the bottom of a well. It comes out from the depth of the well. There is a long road to the idea of the Nude Veritas but emerges from the original experience of truth as being absent, secluded, or even precluded in the deepness of concealment and forgetfulness. Now the idea of knowledge as remembrance becomes even clearer. What we see isn't only false but set upon us with the clear intent of deceiving. Deliberately creating the conditions that Truth won't emerge from the well. The notion of a Naked Truth was very carefully crafted, discussed, and brought before the Light, in many ways and forms and impregnated all the humanistic disciplines, the arts, and even emerging science, during the times of Italian Humanism. We can find many examples and representations of the Nude Veritas the same idea is pregnant to this period of history where the demand for Truth as pure as only she can be, becomes a general trend in many disciplines and no exceptions made, the arts take center stage on this dearest demand.

There is a long and illustrious series of extraordinary works of art that have depicted the Naked Truth for centuries. It would be almost impossible to quote them and even a selection, regardless of how small or carefully picked might be, would undoubtedly leave out many or most of them. Let us refer to some of them in order, simply and modestly, to illustrate the arisen subject. Probably one that has become an icon in the post-truth culture, namely

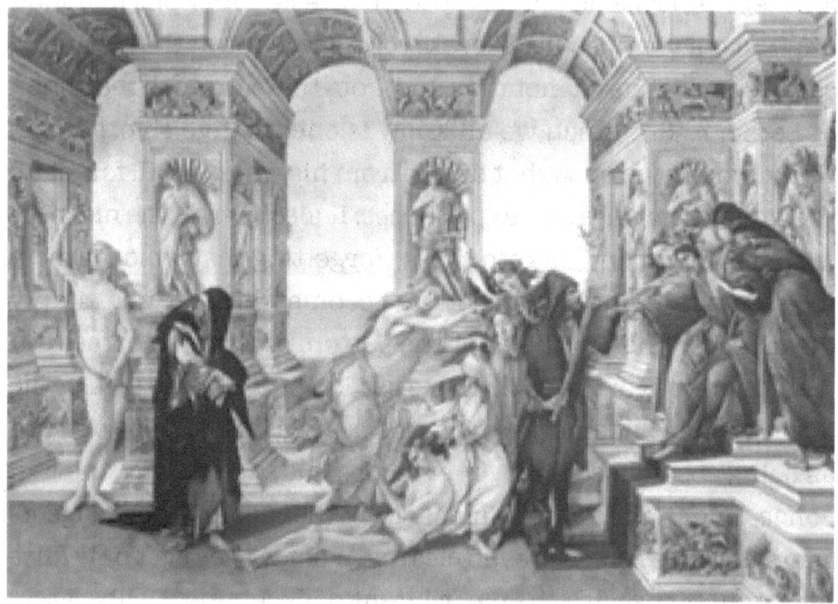

La Calunnia by Sandro Botticelli, which is safely guarded at the extraordinary Galleria Degli Uffizi on that marvellous Italian city-museum in itself, Firenze, as we said, this outstanding work of art has turned in the nowadays iconic painting of fake news, certainly am not sure whether this is something that such extraordinary work of art deserves but it is a work of art, a remarkable one must be underlined, dated from the period the Italians named as Quattrocento, history has it that the hidden narrative calls on the fact, that Botticelli came to know an antique Greek painter, Apelles from 4 BC, found the description on a book by Lucian of Samostata, where the story is told, the book's name is De Pictura di Leon Battista Alberti, where the Apelles painting is described and allegedly served as inspiration for the Italian master.

In the painting a story is being told, for our purpose what matters is that here we find a clear depiction of Nuda Veritas, alone by itself, standing in a semi-distancing pose from the rest of the main characters of the story, they all seem to be quarrelling about a young man, who is been dragged from the hair to face King Midas. Other characters in the painting namely, are Ignorance, Suspicion, Envy or Rancor, Slander or Calumny, Conspiracy, and Fraud. The character dressed in black, Repetence stares at Truth with a certain shyness or even guilt. While Calumny dressed with great elegance drags from the hair the young man in the opposite direction where Truth is standing. The imaging is so powerful that few words are needed to address the emergence of Truth from concealment and the dangers or enormous threats surrounding it coming into the Light. The experience of the unconcealment and concealment of Truth is present in this unique work of art. Truth speaks out loudly about the threats she faces constantly and her power to conquer and defeat lies and slander.

French artists from the late 19th Century to the beginning of the 20th Century left an interesting series of paintings —not only in the great French tradition but also in some other European countries as well— retelling the story of Nuda Veritas and the well. Sometimes it comes out of the well and others are laying at the bottom, awaiting, gazing, observing, watching, guarding even and protecting themselves from slander and lies, falsehood and envy, like the rococo painter Lemoyne (1737) presented Truth being saved by Time. Gerome (1986) depicted Truth as *"shaming mankind"* showing herself in its total nudity meaning in the full light of its truth. Debat-Ponsan (1858) gave us Truth fighting to come out of the well, Nec Mergitur, half-dressed and struggling with two males dressed figures, one wearing a mask and the other with a hat, to hold her down, on the process they seem to be tearing away the robe that barely covers her. *"Truth still awaits to be seen.*", is the final line of the famous Amir Fable, which tells us about the encounter of Truth and Lie and how they exchange dresses Lie tricks Truth into exchanging clothes and since then Lie wears Truth's clothes and has been walking rampantly among mankind while Truth *"awaits to be seen"*. Come out of concealment.

The concealment/unconcealment of Truth happens on the Earth and in the World. Mankind has been fighting this never-ending showing and disappearing of Truth without stopping. In today's world, it has taken other forms and can be typically illustrated in the different alternatives that facts and politics are presented or given on a constant everydayness that takes all sorts of shapes and presence. *"Democracy dies in darkness"* is a very powerful motor that is attached to one of the leading newspapers in the country. News is presented as a "show", like a carrousel of smiles. The idea of the old journalists as truth seekers —one of the main characters of the recent sitcom, *"The Morning Show"* remains her co-anchor: *"journalism is about the truth"*— has been substituted by modern anchors, millionaires work for billionaires news chains. And they bring us their version of the Truth every day. Rating rules this cruel and intense business, in the post-truth reality of business and success. Ratings become thus, the new metrics for Truth. A successful anchor is also a businessperson surrounded by entrepreneurs and mega billionaires that from someplace in the whole wide world, watch and follow their interest and signal instantly what can be said and how it can be said and of course, what must be suppressed or silenced. And the categories for this new subverted reality, none other than ratings and profits, circulation, and advertising, or even better, sales, the almighty sales, rulers of profits. But is not that simple. Global business is political at the same time. Cannot be otherwise. The ancient mantra of the universal Truth

—one that is always valid despite any given circumstances—sedes silently to the new metrics. The global rules, corporate management, as the only model, has defeated the pursuit of Truth a long time ago, like in academia or even in diplomacy as well as other dominions, in the past considered sacred and whose missions were essentially linked to wisdom and peace. Truth is more hidden nowadays and the simple eye is incapable to see through the enormous complexity that post-modernity has left us. Two illustrate this summary presented ideas, let us address two recent shows running or not, on the streaming alternative of the visual and optical presentations by two very intriguing and even opposing options. *"The Morning Show"*, which is about to complete its first season and Press a British —and we are very thankful for the British shows or sitcoms as well as their extraordinary actors— a very welcome option. They both deal with similar elements and objects. But their complexities vary. Nonetheless, Truth is the matter in both cases. Journalism and Truth. There was a time when they were synonymous. Not anymore.

While this currently open process unfolds and spreads in its complexities and many manifolds, the educated and observant seeker remains truthful to the old ways. But can tradition overcome such colossal obstacles? Can the culture of image continue to subjugate reality and present it as a new recipe ready-made and easily absorbable, consumed even without the slightest hesitation? The more we move away from the carefully crafted and sturdy built Weltanschauung that established the pursuit of Truth as being linked with Wisdom, Good, and Beauty, we'll be left with shambles and confusion inherited by the prevalent and dominant *"theory of chaos"* that rooms tyrannically in our current pseudo-realities. The ability to differentiate between Truth and Lie turned so blurry and the borders and limits of a hidden reality are so overwhelming, that even the mere skill to raise the question for Truth is almost immediately cast away as useless and insubstantial. Bears have no relevance. That is why forgetfulness must be overcome and the search for aletheia carries also this pregnant meaning, remembrance, the restoration of the question of Truth implies the recovery of memory or to use the Ancient Greek, Attic to be precise, word: ἀνάμνησις anamnesis, reminiscence or deliberate recollection. Our indispensable task and mission are none other than the recollection and bringing into the light, that which is the worthiest of all our goals, namely the remembrance of Truth and bringing out of the deep of the well, that which lays dormant, forgotten, and we can only achieve this by not forgetting and remembering that which is the ground of all that is Truth.

THE EPISTEMIC OF HATE, FAKE NEWS AND "THE MEN OF THE TONGUE"

Ysrael Meir Kagan. Hofetz Hayyim. Mishna Berurah. Circa 1873, Radun

רְבָד הֶסַכְכמ_חור-וָמֶאְנוּ ;דֹוס-הֶלַגְמ ,ליכָרְ דְלוה גי.

Although the term *"epistemic violence"* (Foucault-Spivak) has been used extensively our intentions and the reasons for our preference to employ the concept of *"epistemic hate"*, should become gradually clearer as the argumentation is further developed. Hate precedes violence. Might not seem an apodictic construct but in its essence, violence is the outcome of a deeper and more pervasive and darker disturbance. A malady of the soul. Sometimes incurable if we could address it within psycho-pathological conceptions. Much is written about and on violence, suffice it to say that the inner or fundamental relationship between both alluded forces cannot be only viewed as casual conditioning or determination of one over the other but rather as an enormous complex ontological configuration or mapping of the individual's existence. Whether culture or society generates hate and violence remains to be seen, because at the core hides an obscurer trigger that could be rooted on deeper levels and forms of the human tragedy and it is a lamentable condition. Violence and hate emerge from the lacking-off that is essential to the human condition and its finitude.

The ancient Greek verb, ἐπιστήμη, if we can still recreate the Greek experience of language, refers to systematic knowledge, the one that comes from study and discovery, as opposed traditionally to dóxa, δόξα, but what is fundamental is that epistemic is related to the truth. That is the reason why I choose not to use the term *"epistemic violence"* but *"epistemic hate"* is what we constantly come across and reveals itself as a pre-condition for the other to take place. But how can we relate violence and hate with true knowledge remains an elusive and open question. In general, we see a lot of pseudo-epistemic hate expressed constantly through many means. Social media curren-tly occupies the epicentre where hate in all its forms takes place. Under the form of attacks and slander, disqualification, insult, degradation, and also and to no lesser degree, journalism is infested with this malady, not to mention the *"comments"* the amount of hate spilled is extraordinary, language becomes an instrument of the purest manifestation of hate, hidden on anonymous trolls, new words emerge and unthinkable ways of insulting erupt like volcanic explosions of magmatic violence eroding, reaching out without exception at politicians, so-called celebrities, whatever that might mean, Hollywood people and even artists, no-one is exempt to be labelled under the epistemic hate. Sometimes when we follow the public debates not only on political issues but on other matters as well, we sense that the truth doesn't matter anymore what counts is the ability to impose a certain view on the other, force the opposing party to submit to labyrinthine argumentation and especially, create chaos and confusion on the audience and followers. *"Embrace debate"* —this comes from the world of sports *"reporting"* or the dialogical exchanges between individuals attempting to introduce Shakespearean language into the world of professional sports even abroad when soccer commentators explain the *"art of soccer"* as a superior spiritual endeavour and the ball manoeuvring of a certain star in artistic terminology— is the motto regardless of the validity of the argumentation. Most of the time these so-called debates are presented with many forms of personal attacks, shouting and naming names is permitted and even encouraged, quasi-information filtered as facts and at the end, the idea that the world is a theatre of struggling *"enemies"* prevails over factuality and truth. Hate replaces knowledge and the establishment of truth becomes meaningless.

In Judaism, there is a very interesting concept that acts as a rule of ethical behavior and also embodies a certain cultural ethos that characterizes Jewish culture. Lahson Ha-Ra, ולשן ערה, *"that means the evil tongue"*. In The Talmud, Sanhedrin 31a, Rav Ammin relates the story of a particular student that was removed from a study hall for disclosing a certain secret that was agreed to be kept as such, and the secret was made public many years after —the time quoted on the text is twenty-two years after the revelation was made known— what is fascinating is that he is named the *"reliever of secrets and cannot be trusted"*. This brings us to the problem of the concealment and unconcealment of truth. We are not going to go into the deepness of the discussion and construction of the Lashon Ha-Ra which stems from the Torah itself, Tehillim 73.9, and other references such as Proverbs XI, 13 or Leviticus, 19, 16 that lead to ideas or principle of the parameters of the Law that rule these interpretations. What we find fundamental is that dedication and commitment to truth remains the highest ethical standard. Compliance is also dedication and devotion to the Law. The original hermeneutics of the *"evil tongue"* and its presence in mankind is simply fascinating. This goes back to Eve and the Serpent and how using the *"evil tongue"* the serpent confuses Eve and leads her to eat from The Tree of Knowledge, Kabbalistic versions do elaborate even in more detail on the process of introducing through speech and tongue, evil in the mouth and how humanity became *"men of the tongue"*. Evil speakers started to walk the Earth. This the-cultural introduction and usage of Jewish tradition or Jewish wisdom are immensely important. Jewish wisdom is constantly shared with the rest of humanity. It is even mandatory; we may dare to state. Here we find an example to be followed regarding the recurrence of the words hate.

And then came fake news. The debate is probably just starting. The matter is as old as slander and libelling where words were spread and used for different and sometimes very dark motives. There are well-known legal consequences for such actions. But there is also a universal system of protection in the western world and the civilized nations. Freedom of speech or freedom of the press. Also, much has been written on this subject. Movies that not only come from Hollywood culture but from Europe and other regions as well. The UN has a body to protect this *"basic human right"*. As with the second Amendment, constitutional hermeneutics by the Supreme Court created and generated tools and means to correctly read and interpret these very fundamental cornerstones of the American way of life. As a country where the Rule of Law is widely respected, a debate or controversy, for better understanding, is continuous and remains open. A wonderful collective experience, unique to the extraordinary Judiciary System that governs America. The wider a constitution is debated, studied, and analysed freely and openly the more it becomes a leaving entity that permeates the life of the individuals and persons, constituting and shaping the persona of the citizens. The two clauses contained in the Second Amendment are now being debated in the light of the horrendous and tragic events that have taken place throughout the country and more recently in Parkland not to forget this has happened abroad too, remember Beslan, 2004; Blacksburg, 2007; Ma'alot in Israel, 1974; Sandy Hook, 2012; Dunblane, in the UK, 1966; Columbine, 1999, Rio de Janeiro, 2011 and even in Finland, Kauchajoki, 2008 and the list is longer and darker.

We know for a fact that words have played an immense role in these terrible tragedies. Reading texts that were drafted almost two hundred years ago and under other contextual and historical conditions is very challenging, however as the firmness on the defense of individual liberties is deeply rooted in American culture the need to regulate certain factual realities occurring before our eyes, claim for responses and answers. This is not religious dogma but man-made constructions and therefore will always remain open to interpretations and discussions. They affect human lives, the well-being of others, and the protection and safeguarding of our youth. There can be no hesitations on the necessity to promptly reply to this essential's demands. The presence of the evil tongue seems to run rampant surrounding these enormous tragedies. Hate in the form of epistemic hate precedes violence and seems to be the obscure layer or motivation that engenders these atrocities. The need for a new cultural éthos cries out from underneath these unexplainable events. The language of generosity, acceptance, and care most at once speak louder and louder to silence the epistemic hate in all its forms.

ON IMMIGRATION AS INCORPORATION AND THE DISCOVERY OF THE "OTHERNESS"

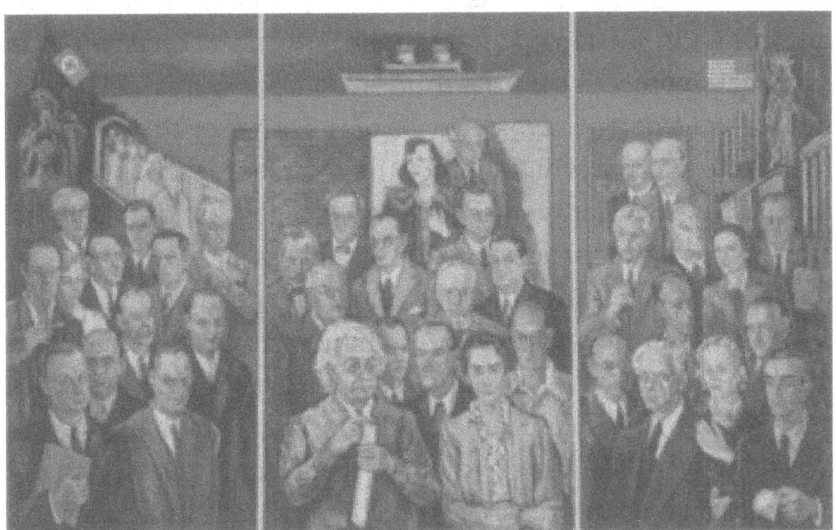

"Die geistige Emigration" by Arthur Kaufmann (1938-1964)

"This is a kind of communication between others that are different and yet care to talk and listen to each other because they know there is something worthwhile to learn from each other's thoughts and because due attention will be granted by them to our thoughts as well." Marcelo Dascal, Colonizing and decolonizing minds, TAU, 2009. The experience of *"the other"* is present on Marcelo Dascal's impressive body of work —his vast contributions is of central importance to actual philosophical thinking—, if we can think or see, since lógos is seeing, from the position of the other, then we begin to encounter otherness. Living into the otherness is the most essential experience of the migrant or should we say, the contemporary migrant as opposed

to previous forms of migration, either voluntary or forceful, and therefore immigration versus emigration. Leaving to become the other and thus facing that which is not our self, the language of existential ontology needs also the language of Pragmatics or to further employ descaling language, the metaphor of "the colonization of the mind" as a form of "epistemic violence" that must be addressed to understand the nature and essence of the *"migrating process that the human being endures"*. My focus here is the existential experience of the other or the necessity to become another while *"living"* the complexities of the migrating process. The individual not only becomes the other but also transforms his otherness into the otherness of the other. While on a recent post I called the Northern Triangle migrants, desert walkers (caminantes del desierto), the idea was to create a metaphor that would illustrate the changing of nature, the process that they go through, the immense suffering, and finally while arriving beyond the desert —many of them literally walk, actually do walk to cross the desert— to encounter "the otherness" and then begin to attempt to become another.

Attempting to start or establish a new life in a foreign country is hazardous and challenging. For unskilled individuals, not knowing the language of the country, lacking in education, and being condemned or lured to take on unwanted jobs and perform undesirable tasks can be an almost impossible fight. That is exactly what many or most of the migrants face and must endure. There are, of course, the highly sought after, the *"gifted ones"*, the already recognized intellectuals and scientists, in today's representation, the techies, and the computer savvy. The talented, the ones that can teach and bring not only wisdom but contribute to the expansion of knowledge, and, to a lesser extent, the political refugees, those who can successfully claim that status or are protected by groups of interest or governments fulfilling

—this is very uncommon— promises or simply pursuing private agendas or interests. In a certain way all must face the becoming another experience, Erlebniss, to use a German term extracted from Phenomenology that is seldom employed nowadays, nonetheless an interesting one and extremely useful to describe this existential "living through" process. Trying to become one in another culture and society, vastly different from where the individual comes from, requires not only an extraordinary effort but a lengthy and uncertain climbing battle of hurdles that can be very easily turned into a mere impossibility. Success as a form of incorporation is not guaranteed and sometimes only becomes plausible for the second generation, this is especially so amongst unskilled migrants and their families, having the second generation the important advantage of having access to an educational system that might prove to be the opening key to the unknown that awaits the newcomers. Education can be assimilating and an opening to the sought-after *"otherness"*.

During the times of my diplomatic tenure —had the privilege to serve in all regions of the world where my country has had resident embassies— one of the most relevant and difficult goals that career diplomats and political appointees also, should perform or are required to, ask even, namely, is a subtle incorporation into the society and culture where he or she has been posted. The diplomatic reading of the otherness. The ability to perform this reading contributes immensely to the success or failure of the envoy's mission. It is not an easy objective to reach. If a diplomat is sent to another country protected by an international system that regulates and safeguards diplomats and their families, imagine what an unprotected or worst, a nonlegal —I dislike and find cruel and offensive the term *"illegal aliens"* or any of its derivatives, it is nothing, but *"epistemic violence"* as quoted above— migrant can come to face. So, *"incorporation"* into the society and culture, power inner circles, public entities, and even into the government itself, as means and ways to conduct *"the diplomatic reading"* turns into a delicate process where boundaries and blurred lines come into contact.

Cases, where the so-called diplomatic agent is too involved in local affairs, are constantly documented, and recorded. Diplomacy is an activity where the scrutiny of the agent's actions is under constant surveillance and even investigation, from many different sources. Becoming one with the other. It happens quite frequently. On the migrant's side, the story although similar in the sense that *assimilation* runs rampant, the disadvantages are enormous. Generally speaking, the migrant faces unwelcome and unfavourable conditions. Remains constantly under fear, dwells on the limits of the legal system of the other, and relies on generosity and kindness, qualities that are scarce and not all the time will be granted or given. The hand that helps walks step by step with the migrants and if it isn't the ever-accompanying presence, danger and rage can strike as easily as morning light and not only in the form of *epistemic violence* but actual violence, real aggression.

Exile, migration, and ostracism as other forms of auto-imposed emigration, in this case, also must face the process of becoming another while remaining yourself. Although these are merely metaphors to describe an Erlebniss, the transformation or pseudo-assimilation occurs. It happens. And here we have to say, to close my brief remarks on immigration as an encounter with *otherness,* or worded better, address the issue of the so-called *"class of cultures or identitarian transformation,* recurring to more recent languages. If the Northern Triangle migrants or dessert walkers do share to some extent the western civilization vision, insofar as they are Christians or Catholics, nor are they enemies of the *"otherness"* if this is understood as the western world but on the contrary, want to become a member or a part of the dreams of the West, aspire to a better and more decent life for them and their loved ones, families and relatives, come out of the terrible indemnifying poverty rampantly present in all its cruelty on this countries, the walk towards the lost Arcadia is not a path of destruction of the other but a dream of at least become similar —as in being assimilated— to the otherness of the other. The long search for the utopia or the scape of hell and all its forms. They know very well about the presence of the *"hidden demons"* in the Mesoamerican tropical forest and its incredible exuberance and beauty. The Arcadia searcher is not enemies or forces of destruction they share the same values and hope for new skies, they walk the path of light not the one of darkness, on the contrary, they are running away from darkness as a lack of humanity and from the demon of poverty and its poisonous force. This is a different reality from the one that is threatening the European World which is reshaping and even substituting the original core of European culture and grounds for another Weltanschauung in the old Dilthey-Jasper's sense and use of the term, in the European case the complexities are colossal and far more disturbing.

8
ON JERUSALEM AND THE "ART OF THE DEAL"

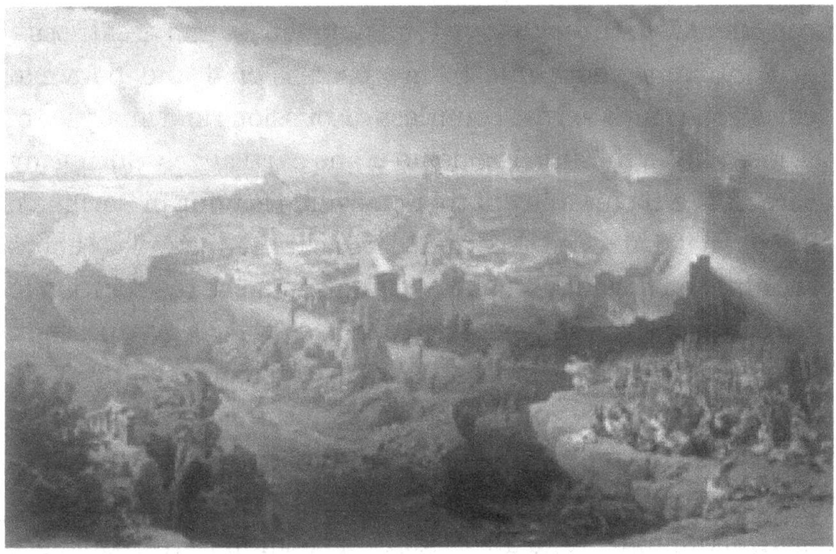

"The Siege and Destruction of Jerusalem by the Romans Under the Command of Titus, A.D. 70." David Roberts lost Painting.

The city is more than a city. It embodies many things, from miracles to destruction, from hope to despair. So much has been written about and over this extraordinary *"place of encounter and reunion"*, where holly men walked and died. Poets, journalists, thinkers not to mention theologians, and of course, even Prophets. Wisdom walks within the city walls and streets but also there is a sense of a divine presence that as soon as you not only enter the city but when you are approaching it, is there, everywhere, even the air and atmosphere surrounding the mystery that the city protects, begins to manifest itself and you feel engulfed by it and you cannot understand nor describe what is it about like you come in one of the sacred places of the world and you are overwhelmed by the sheer reality of its might. Jerusalem is there and you sense the weight not only of its history, terrible history of war and destruction but also and at the same time the coreness of everything that ultimately matters reveals itself silently to those that visit its uniqueness and greatness.

For many years due to my professional and personal dedication I came across countless discussions and analyses of the meaning of the city. I remember one particularly during my years in The Hague and another one while leaving in Berlin. To all of us that dedicated time and tears as well as countless hours of reading on how and what could and should be the solution to the reality of this wonderful place an idea was always present, if the so-called *"peace process"* had any kind of meaning at all, the Jerusalem *"solution"* would be left at the end of the negotiations, it was the most complex and difficult one to address. History has it that the Camp David meetings hosted by then-President Bill Clinton, broke up because Arafat and Barak could not agree on the *"final settlement"* and the told story probably is only a rumour, Arafat wasn't prepared to go back to Ramallah and tell the Palestinian people that an agreement with the Israelis had been reached and particularly on the future of Jerusalem. Conversations could not continue, and we know the rest of the story. This is one of several moments that illustrate how difficult it is to address the status of Jerusalem or even more to dare to come up with an answer that might solve the question. Many times, like so many of us, I feared that no solution was foreseeable. Personally, the thought that Jerusalem can be the subject of political negations that can be dealt, bargained on a trade, or be subject to the *"art of the deal"* and treated like it can be sold or bought, simply is unthinkable. Unacceptable. A horror. A sheer monstrosity. Maybe Jerusalem should not be touched because the touch of men brings sometimes darkness and injustice. Its uniqueness shines above the dealings of men.

In my quoting above about my meetings that were mentioned in the preceding paragraph, The Hague meeting was private, the central idea was over the challenges existing to divide the city and in my Berlin meetings, more than one, also of a private nature, dealt fundamentally with the safeguarding of the city and its religious significance to the Peoples of The Book. Israel carries the weight of not only safeguarding but at the same time protecting sacred places. It is the responsibility of the highest order. This is when Jerusalem unveils as much more than a city no ordinary capital, which is as well, the capital of the State of Israel, historically and de facto, as a political entity but as a sacred city that is essentially linked to the essence of the western and eastern world and beyond. Although am a man devoted to International General Consensual Law, the path that leads to the disputed issues and controversies, am sure my dear friend Marcelo Dascal is following from his Tel Aviv home, every small detail of this newly formed and constituted controversy. Is Jerusalem a subject of an international dispute or a deeper controversy, rooted in more fundamental and essential views of the world, man, religion, and ultimately the shaping or definition of a New Vision of the current world and its situation? It seems so nowadays. Sovereignty, borders, territorial dispute, statehood, and other matters about International Law are there to be faced and solved if they can be solved at all. Here is where the "art of the deal" comes into play. Both President Trump and Prime Minister Netanyahu are very aware of the newly installed reality and the introduction of a different set of variables. I do not use that language or that methodology, but it is there imposed on this very old controversy. It is indeed a controversy not only a dispute. It demands and requires other means and views to solve it and even less, to merely face it. That is why Jerusalem is much more than a political entity. Here is where its uniqueness shines and comes forth. Let us not forget that and do not fall prey to the narrative that Israel only needs the United States, and the rest of the world is irrelevant. Beware of such naiveté. Simplicity is the small brother of ignorance. The complexity here involved is enormous.

So much can be said and even more. Can politicians and deal makers break the deadlock and bring about a resolution? I do not know but remain very sceptical. History has it that the Templars discovered a hidden secret kept in Jerusalem. Such was the importance of the discovery that until our present times, we still search for that *secret* that could reshape the whole of the western and eastern worlds. If the Templars ever reached the Holy of Holies, מִישְׁדָּקָה שֶׁדֵק, Kodesh HaKadashim, as has been rumoured and written, we can't be certain. Probably we shall never know the truth about this unveiling. Mystery surrounds most of the deepest corners and streets, turns, and hidden alleys of that extraordinary city. My approach is different and is grounded on respect and never stopping awe. Jerusalem is much more than an ordinary city it carries the mysteries and answers to our more fundamental questions. We cannot bargain nor deal with what is and holds our foundations and destiny.

9
"KING CHARLES THE THIRD"
OR THE END OF POWER

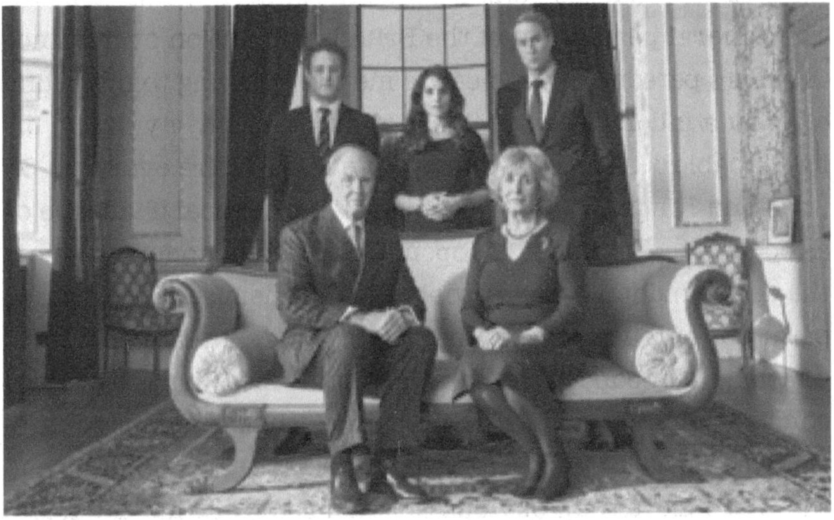

From left, Harry (Richard Goulding), King Charles III (Tim Pigott-Smith), Kate (Charlotte Riley), Camilla (Margot Leicester) and William (Oliver Chris).

Could not resist writing as soon as I finished watching the Masterpiece presentation of the play written by Mike Bartlett in blank verse that premiered at the Almeida Theatre, in London, in 2014. Even the drama surrounding the play as such, Tim Pigott-Smith passed away just a month ago, the Shakespearean tone and spirit of the whole work and the characters, alive persons, namely, of course, the British Royal Family, iambic verse, the presence of a Ghost —Princess Diana— and the terrible ending a la King Lear, when Charles is abandoned by his entire family and the political establishment, to nobody's surprise. Fate and Destiny are interwoven in prophetical language and narrative.

An ever-present sense of Moira webbing its trend to the impotence of the humans despite the earthly power that they are embodied with. Greek heroes are victims of the Moira, their own Moira. Prince Charles is portrayed by a known-looking alike Pigott-Smith who sought to capture this aura of royalty that covers the persona, the real persona, the human being, the suffering human being. The general perception of the British population over Prince Charles's persona is not clear to me but is daring to make him already a fallen Greek or Shakespearian castaway due to his inescapable destiny or arbitrary rule of the Moira over him. On Gods and Kings. What stroke me as a theoretical challenge or as controversy —this is an open controversy, nonetheless— is the not-so-hidden pseudo prophecy of his demise. The downfall of the out-of-touch royal with actual or current reality seems to be a very poor conception or argument. Prince Charles is a very complex character. Let us not forget that the education of European royalty is closer to what Germans called Bildung and there are more than obvious German roots around the Royal Family. They are unique individuals that must dwell —maybe here there is indeed a sort of Destiny— on a different reality. The nature of their call and the tasks they must face cannot be matched by traditional or formal education, regardless of the excellence and quality that it might carry. There cannot be Oxfordian royalty or Harvadian education. Although it has to be said that Prince Charles attended Trinity College and holds a degree like his son Prince William, Eaton, most royals have had extensive military gaining and/or been privately tutored. The late Francisco Franco claimed direct participation in the education of King Juan Carlos, so important the matter was considered and weighed. The building of royalty. Dwelling in another place demands another view of the world and primordially of themselves. Elitism, naturally Britain is being ruled by elites and grounded on the experience and struggles of its elites.

The presence of the Ghost of Princess Diana, dressed in white and uttering prophetic words of wisdom about the future to come, expressed in cryptic language that carries a message of almost religious merit a prophecy hidden in her advice about how a King must act. No doubt that the life of the late Princess inhabits that of the Royal Family and her sons are intimately linked to her mother. The Mother. Like the solemn and silent funeral in honour of the late Queen that her passing triggers this tragedy. It is not only her death that opens the controversy of the character and preparedness of Prince Charles to Rule but most importantly her life and legacy that covers the whole Kingdom and that of its citizens. How can anyone rule after the Queen? The nature of the evolution of the society demands a modernization of the Building of Royalty and this is not a matter of education but of being able to read and be closer to their subjects, the population as Charles claims throughout the drama. But the population is painfully divided and speaks in the language of violence and aggression. Leaders must unite not divide, and never cause disagreements. The Crown represents unity not dividers. The King cannot and never be a divider. Charles is unable to read this language or hear this voice caught by his loyalty and devotion to principles he sees as sacred. Is very striking that the topic of choice for the controversy is none other than *the freedom of free speech* or *freedom of the press*. Proven so controversial in the current situation almost everywhere in the world where it is followed or protected. The King takes a strong stance and forces the collapse of his entire life before his own eyes incapable of understanding what is unravelling around him. And the call on the use of force is the symbol of his downfall. Then they are forced to intervene and put an end to his brief and tragic reign. Unfit to rule, out of touch with *modernity,* and unable to speak or read the language of his people who are screaming for justice and equality. Isolation versus merging or alloy, blending the two elements to forge a stronger one. Reunion in one. A Kingdom. The United Kingdom.

Power. King Charles comes to face *the end of power.* The limits of power. Like, most Greek heroes and tragedies, the heroes or the individual comes to the limits of power. But Shakespeare and the great Greek Tragic, confront us with the metaphysics of power. Facing our limits. Loving our borders. Knowing when to halt and go forward is the fundamental acceptance that the mystery of power unseals only on the understanding that leaders rule by constructing agreements once it was called *a process of building consensus.* Can only be achieved by listening and exchanging views with others? Real power emerges from accepting others as equals. Talking to them and taking into consideration their views and conceptions. And on this intricate subject, everybody fails in the tragedy and the characters face harsh criticism. Nobody listens. The Prime Minster refuses to listen, the King wants to listen, and the young Royals want to reign because they claim they are the only ones that listen. The drama is served, and the metaphysics of power takes center stage.

10

THE WORD SEARCHERS: LEONARD COHEN, JOAN MANUEL SERRAT AND BOB DYLAN

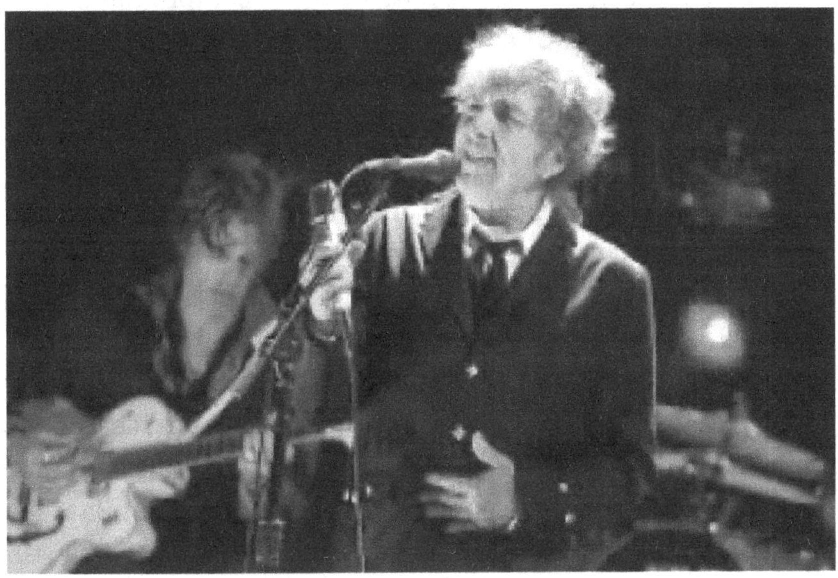

Music and poetry do have an old relationship. It is older than what we call the western world. Greek tragedy was represented with music —a lost scale like the real pronunciation of ancient Greek we can only guess, also the music but it was there. And remains so. Even nowadays. Schiller's poem An die Freude became an icon and intimately linked to that symphony. Operas, others like Liszt, his famous Faust symphony and choir lyrics from Goethe's ending of the first part of Faust, Liszt called it *"chorus mystical"* or Shostakovich's Baby Yar constructed on Dyetuchenkho's poems. And let us not forget the world of Opera where another kind of blending and spiritual homecoming takes place. The human voice is the ultimate musical instrument, music as such, and words. Blending into this magical creation of mankind. But popular music is a foggy term to refer to other music, not the industrial one or the technologically induced but the one that comes from the soul of the people. There is where the searchers of words look for the most fertile ground to emerge with the expression of voices that we try to comprehend.

When I was growing up in my country during the sixties, my friend Luis Carlos, nowadays one of the most important sculptors in Latin America and himself a great artist with an extraordinary ability to create beauty and at the same time, challenge us with his masterful creations. His work deserves to be known worldwide and the recognition is slowly coming out. We were young students and we used to meet at his family's house I'll always remember those wonderful trees that witnessed his growing up and the marvellous love story of his youth. Music was a great part as well as reading and the constant search for everything that could generate amazement. And it happens. That was the first time I came across Dylan and Joan Baez, as well as Janis Joplin. Luis sang very well I don't know if he still does it but is sure the guitars should have a place in his home and life. Luis sang Dylan's "Blowing in the wind" with a special guitar that to me, had a curious shape. That's how I learned that the question was open, ...*how many roads must a man walk down/before you call him a man?* As is well-known nowadays the questions remain unanswered, and they are "*still blowing in the wind*". Since those early days, Dylan has been a companion and creator of questions that have walked with me as with many others. When recently the awarding of the Literature Nobel Prize was announced, I have to say that I was very pleasantly surprised, still myself and many others keep awaiting when Amos Oz will receive the Prize, "*the answer keeps blowing in the wind*". And recently Dylan's statement on not attending the ceremony in

Stockholm came as little surprise and to some extent, it was expected.

There are so many stories that can be recalled surrounding Dylan's elusive ways. Mysterious ways, sometimes. But the poetry is there. Ever-present. Real and challenging. One can seat in the dark with a glass of the best bourbon and read out loud, any of his lyrics and the fluency of the internal music will light the room. Sometimes those lyrics do not need music. The music is within. But sometimes they beg to be sung. *I got lost in the river, but I got found / I got lost in the river, but I didn't drown.* Like so many other lyrics and songs, essentially, from the famous *Basement tapes* lost and found, by the way, reinvented and performed safeguarding Dylan's magic and touch. There are around twenty versions of the song. Twenty. And when the beggar is asked, again questioning, *Is it a mystery to live or is it a mystery to die?*. The buffoon, the fool, and the fairy in Kingston Town asked for the love of Spanish Mary, the reply is that no word will be given.

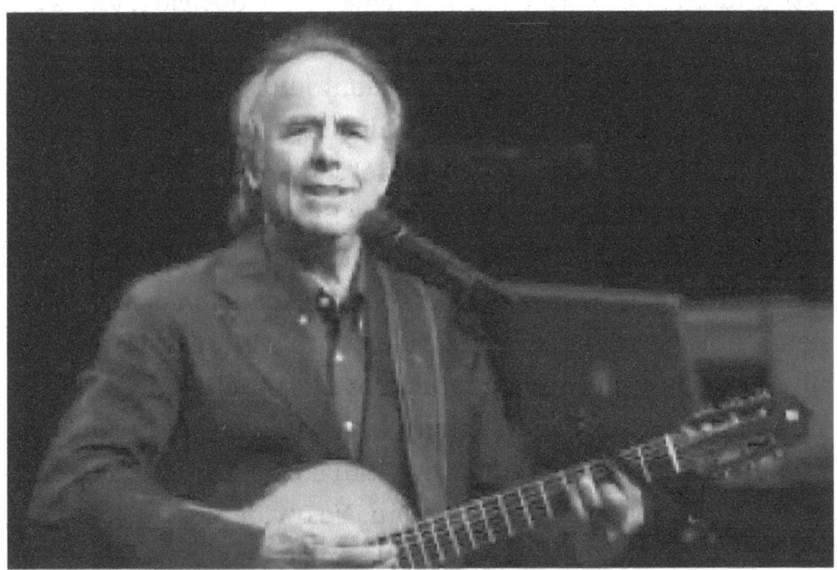

Joan Manuel Serrat. La primera vez que lo pude escuchar cantar en vivo fue en Guatemala, en el antiguo Hotel Ritz —su historia pasa por la de la Guatemala reciente, hoy día no existe más y el edifico, si permanece, es ocupado para oficinas del Organismo legislativo, ¿paradójico, no es cierto?—, en el penthouse donde operaba un restaurante y allí lo escuchamos cantar. Corría el principio de los setenta. Serrat cantaba la poseía de los grandes poetas españoles. Primero fue Antonio Machado y luego fue Miguel Hernández. Y por supuesto, sus propios poemas-canciones. Hoy seguimos maravillados por la magia del mediterráneo; *de Algeciras a Estambul*, un catalán universal enseñó al mundo a caminar caminos, a hacer caminos de nuevo, a perderse y reencontrar el camino, y ese largo e interminable caminar nos llevó por muchos lados, ya fuera siguiéndolo o sencillamente caminando con él. Desde aquel *poco antes de que den las diez* a las sombras de la China, pasando por el Sur, ese Sur de Mario Benedetti, que nos dejó para siempre aquella *compañera, que puede contar conmigo* o la mágica *mujer desnuda y en lo oscuro, que es una claridad que nos alumbra*, al afirmarnos y decirle a todos los que podían y querían saber, *que el sur también existe*. Hay un Serrat militante y uno profundamente intimista, lleno de un lirismo saliniano, o cargado de un albertismo potente. Un Serrat que también se acercó a la poesía del tango y cantó más de uno, en esa mágica ciudad, donde María de Buenos Aires deambulaba de la mano de Piazzola y las palabras de Ferrer. También la lista de las canciones es enorme y los poemas canciones reflejarán siempre el enorme talento de Serrat y su magia creativa; también su influencia y sus amistades maravillosas, cómplices tal vez diría él, porque Serrat abrió mundos nuevos. Muchos lo siguieron y algunos, tal vez no seguidores y tan solo admiradores, están y son muy cercanos al gran catalán. No olvidamos que parte de su gran obra está escrita y cantada en su lengua materna. No sé qué tanto se llega de Serrat al Caribe, al cual sí llegó nuestro Ricardo Arjona, con una Galería Caribe excepcional, donde un confesor recibió una muy tropical y rítmica confesión de amor y donde el Mesías llega a Nueva York o la anterior y legendaria *para qué quiere la libertad, la luna un tigre*. Y no podemos dejar de pensar tanto en Silvio como en Pablo, como "buscador de arcoiris", que dejó atrás a "una mujer con sombrero", que a lo mejor se llamaba Yolanda.

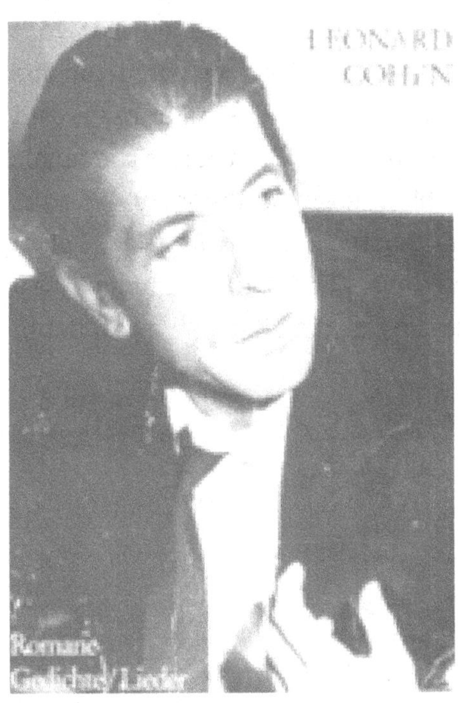

And then Leonard Cohen, who very recently passed away. A very special deep bass voice charged with tenderness and sweetness and countless cigarettes, and the clouds of smoke probably added a touch of that old mystery, that some singers that smoke learned to master in the ways Sinatra did, and maybe that is why they seemed to *talk through the song*, almost invisibly and creating that atmosphere that we are in the presence of the sacred. Leonard Cohen achieved this to the highest levels especially when he came back and generated that old magic once again. Remember the tour in London. Thankfully it was recorded and somehow, we can grasp some of that greatness. *The poet gave me back my spirit/which I have lost in a prayer*. Claims Cohen that Vallejo revealed some secrets to him, while ... *because*

I was the next one/to explain the weakness of love. (The Next One, from Death of a Lady's Man or to remain us those things *are better in Milan.* It's well-known of his constant wondering between religion and the world until he goes into the eternity of love. But his poetry deserves careful reading, the journey of love and pain. The dark lyrics of Flowers for Hitler refer like none other to this incomprehensible pain inflicted and suffer by the silent millions of victims. This very obscure silence, which calls out as *Silence and deeper silence/when the crickets/hesitate.* (Summer Haiku), is the-human silence, the silence that goes beyond. When The Genius speaks and utters words, from the Dachau Jew, that come from another dimension of pain: *and bloated pain/no mind can understand.*". But there's the music too. Again, poetry and music blended magnificently. *We take Manhattan and then we take Berlin...,* ...*lift me like an olive branch and be my homeward dove...* and the list is very, very long. We listen in silence because only in silence we can listen to the music and the words.

11
ON THE POLITICS OF THE IMAGE

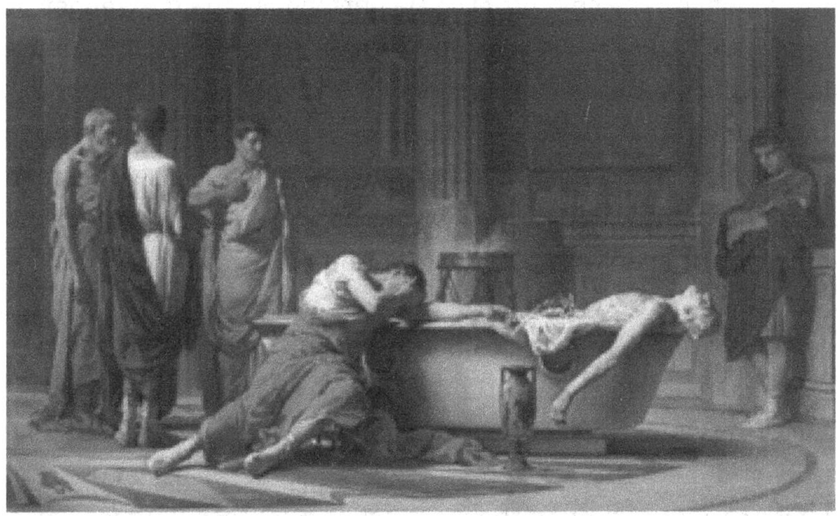

El Suicidio de Séneca. Manuel Domínguez Sánchez (1871) Museo del Prado.

While following the recent debates, that means not only and exclusively the political debates, although they are at the center of the current state of affairs but debating takes place everywhere and in all sorts of communications means, radio, streaming, social media, of course, television and the *paper/internet* newspapers, some of which print extremely lavish and artistically presented weekend magazines or even the serious ones, where the image is at the core of its publications. A well knows reality. Image supplants words. Creates and establishes a new language or another language. Codes are there for everything one cannot imagine a red-dressed Hilary Clinton in the first presidential debate being called "the devil" if she would have chosen the colour for the second presidential debate, as Donald Trump called Secretary Clinton dressed in blue and white. Like many of us watching and following felt that the colour of choice was not an adequate one. Red has its problems, especially at specific moments. There is a reason why men use blue or dark blue suits an almost neutral signal letting the colour of the tie perform as the messenger. A light blue tie carries a different message than a red tie. Madelaine Albright described some years ago in a famous interview, *Diplomacy as a world of men dresses on grey suites* and she introduced the now very famous pins, undoubtedly her message was heard out but essentially was seen all over the world. The pins can be seen as a symbol of uniqueness and individuality introduced in a world where uniformity prevails.

But the image is limited. As powerful as the visual impact might be, it is essentially limited in space and time. Has a brief historicity and must evolve and transform in order not to lose impact or actuality? The image contained in the essence of the image cannot survive without a tangible reference. *Image is everything* the popular iconic motto of a generation ceased to appeal to a more complex audience. The current audience who is so impregnated with images that became as such, a creator of images, won't be impacted by the old images, they rapidly evaporate in their own evanescent. To continue impacting the consciousness of a wide audience must transform itself into a metaphor or simply disappear. This transformation of the image into a metaphor is a process that can be understood in lakkofian terms, for example, in his Theory of the event structure metaphor which Lakoff characterized in terms of space, motion, and force. This translates into object and location.

When Marcelo Dascal discusses the idea of the metaphor as a trope in Aristoteles he emphasizes the analogical aspect of the metaphor. If we follow the arguments we shall have that an image to be metaphorical must have some educational function, object, and location. Political images —if there is anything that can be named as such— emerge from a conception of analogical thinking, thus they are impregnated with metaphorical inferences, *we are going to make America great again*, that is an image transformed into a metaphor. It has an object, a location, a space, and an analogical educational inference. There is a rather unambiguous necessity to map these metaphors and on the above-mentioned one, this is what we might call the metaphorical mapping of *political images* knowing and understanding that they function more as metaphors than images.

There is a western/Latin American tendency to mark and note the words of the politicians not only their promises. From this, the natural tendency to not comply seems to be overwhelming and sometimes taken for granted. They will not fulfil their programs and a large baggage of empty words remains at the end. But the nowadays trend to map their words is new and challenging. Aside from the old ways or evading manoeuvring or the use of common topics and the employ and recurrence of obscure and imprecise meanings, to confuse or safeguard from being forced to address controversial issues or take a stance before difficult and delicate matters, let us not forget that words relate to cognitive acts. The choice of one over another sends an open message for interpretation. Read and be wrong. Dare to interpret. Risky business. Peter Sloterdyk used the wonderful metaphor when referring to man as *a watcher or observer of horizons* when man became erected he could watch from a distance different horizons thus creating a sense of anticipation. Heidegger called this Vorgriff and Sloterdyk deepens its meaning. The origin of the word is well-known. Continental philosophy sees it present in different traditions even Karl Rahner used it in its pregnant sense of answering the call because there is a predisposition or a Vorgriff to listen to the content of the call. But from an observer of horizons man must turn into a reader of horizons and an interpreter of what was read.

Image as a character. Lacking or possessing character is not only a value judgment or even more a pre-judgment a prejudice even, although both expressions are not interchangeable nor synonyms. Accusing or recurring to harsh language is part of the image sought to establish. There is a conscious renunciation of substantive debate and the reasons for this are many and complex. Open political technical debate is senseless serves no purpose and lacks any analogy except the self-depiction of the self as being a *wise man*, *highly educated*, and *specialized*. Immediately labeled as pure arrogance. Just imagine a political public discussion on micro economical models employed by the FED to measure currency fluctuations and how the value of the dollar is affected or influenced by such movements worldwide. This also applies to taxation and that is the reason why there is very little discussion on taxes aside from the general remarks. It is either/or rise or lower. Arguments must the time be emotional and deliberately avoid the technicalities of taxation. It is also valid for other fields. The presentation of ideas has little value vis a vis for the image of the contenders, the way they dress, the way they look, and crucial, how they react to the attacks raised by the adversary. The scrutiny becomes even more physical. Looks matter and matter immensely.

In the *Age of the celebrity*, in which we are leaving, the image has gone to the extremest. The so-called *reality* superimposed on real life, penetrates and permeates everydayness and presents itself as being *natural and yet polished*. Reality starts —if there is anything like it and the names align in all directions and congregate large audiences, their influence is more real than their lives. Image monetized as a phantasy. The image becomes imaginary. There is an array of complexities involved in this transformation, quasi-hallucinatory representations emerging from a world in which all extremes seem to reign rampantly. However how this relates to the image of politics deserves careful and in-depth analysis, some *celebrities* even endorse candidates, and if you considered their *"lists of followers"*, counting on the millions, professional politicians and political consultants-the ultimate manipulators of the image-crave for this kind of support. An endorsement from a 19— or 20-years young celebrity might trigger enormous figures. It would be interesting to know if these followers vote. That is an entirely open question. We are about to witness that, here in the United States. Maybe this time there will be better answers or more studies on this elusive subject.

Controversies gain in-depth and tend to expand themselves, as Marcelo Dascal has shown us. But the road from image to the metaphor, to the controversy we are just beginning to travel and grasp. The establishment of controversies is governed by other rules, and they entail bodies of conceptualizations. We lack that. The trend moves between the image and the metaphor. We do miss the substantive debate or controversy. Politicians tend to avoid it and the few ones that look to ground their campaigns on conceptual principles find themselves on the minority side. The current campaign but not only here in the United States is indeed a world trend and is a strong example of how an array of harsh language, insulting, name-calling, pundits, and disqualification, prevails over substantive or concep- tual argumentation or contra-argumentation. And the extensive use of black humor, opportunistic responses, and honour of the old saying, attributed to Shakespeare without having strong supportive evidence has not been found in any of his texts, none- theless suffice here to conclude this alternative proposal to understand and interpret the "image of politics" introducing new tools and horizons of interpretation: "*I would challenge you to a battle of wits, but I see you are unarmed.*".

12
PHOENIX, THE MOVIE:
ON THE ICONOGRAPHY OF THE HOLOCAUST, SYMBOLS AND TRAGEDY

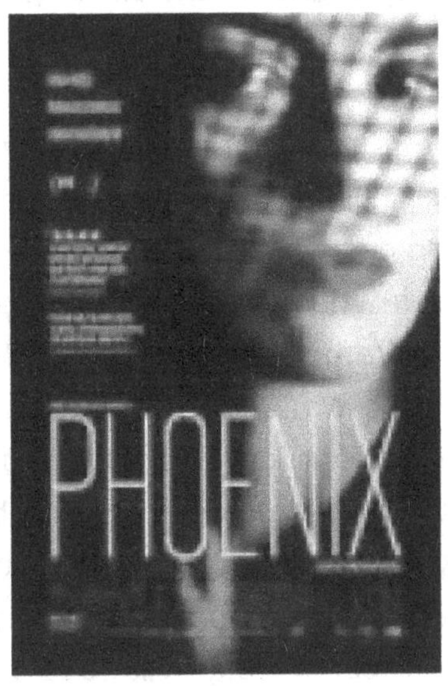

When speaking or writing about the Holocaust I pursue the utmost care and respect. Watching the German movie, Phoenix (2015) directed by Christian Petzold with a superb Nina Hoss as Nelly Lenz –you can watch her also on the latest Homeland that also takes place in Berlin—, the name of a dark cabaret that carries the same name of the old western symbol of the coming back from the ashes, which is the English title for the black and white British version from the early sixties with Maximilian Schell, Ingrid Thulin, and a young Samantha Eagar.

This one is also freely based on the French book by Hubert Monteilhet, Le Retour des cendres, described in French as *"roman policier"*, published in 1961, there is also a French version from 1982, Le Retour d'Elisabeth Wolff. Having taken all that into consideration and the other description of this wonderfully symbolical movie as a Hitchcockian biopic, I would like to focus exclusively on two elements of the iconography of the movie, namely the Kurt Weill song and the intimate betrayal that is at the core of the story.

Speak low, the famous song by Weill, who happens to be Jewish and who fled Berlin to escape the Nazi persecution also, was used in other movies, who can ignore or dare not to remember Ava Gardner (Eileen Wilson) singing it on the black and white movie One touch of Venus, the line *"speak low of love"* really comes from Don Pedro, Much Ado About Nothing, Act 2, Scene 1, *"Speak low if you speak love"* on the original text. The song is played throughout the movie from the beginning till the anticlimactic end when Nelly sings it with the betraying husband playing the piano and when he sees the number tattooed on Nelly's arm confirms something that he had suspected before, Nelly is her outcast wife.

The movie ends with Nelly simply walking slowly towards the door and leaving the room behind filled with the presence of her past and the non-concealment of the double betrayal that his German husband inflicted on her. A remarkable movie to be seen and watched many times, the intimacy of the horrendous human tragedy is portrayed on the aspect of the intimacy and pains that the human soul can bare and how deep betrayal, without any kind of justification, occurs and darkness even the more sacred of places of human nature. *"Speak low, darling speak low"*.

13
ON MARCO RUBIO'S "WELDERS AND PHILOSOPHERS"

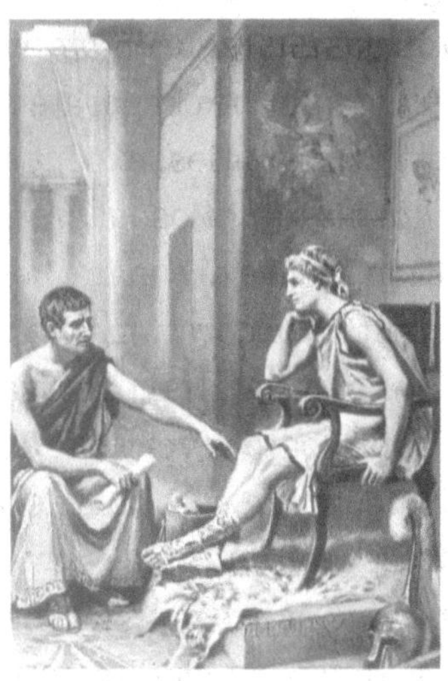

Aristotle and Alexander the Great while discussing Philosophy. (Image by Stock Montage/Getty Images)

The quoted saying from Protagoras has been analysed and commented on extensively and is not my wish to do it again nor when discussing an expression taken randomly from a leading Republican candidate and a very impressive one, may we add. But the comparison between *"welders and philosophers"* goes beyond the political debate. It poses a fundamental question. One that needs to be addressed and is particularly interesting. Protagoras talks about *"methron"*, liberally translated as a measure, broadly accepted, the idea is that man is *"the measure of all that is"*. If man is the measure for all that is and is not, then how do we measure man, we are not completely sure what Mr. Rubio means by "philosopher" because there have always been very few. Worldwide even. Welders on the contrary there are quite a lot of them. So it seems that he is favouring a *"republic of welders"* not a *"philosophers' republic"*. Those who generate wealth, to avoid using the word *"money"*, are the ones that carry the measure. Man must be measured by his ability to create wealth, once again, *"money"*. The corporate model is nowadays the paradigm for most Universities, except of course for those who still value *"thinking and philosophers"*. But this might be a dangerous proposition. There are many corporate leaders or at the top of some gigantic corporations who fancy philosophy degrees, even more, we can find top politicians that also have philosophy degrees. The debate is very old. Tekhne or thinking. As such there is nothing wrong with this debate.

But the classic idea is that *"man"* is the measure of all things, being or not being, that are or are not, in general, all that comes to be. To some the Protagoras saying could be the birth of *"humanism"*, classical or old humanism, to others merely a sophist principle, *"man catches men"*, on the form, a political concept, linked to the actual *"catching of men"*, fishing with a hook, which is none other than language according to the Socratic-platonic debate, the use of language to hook men, but not any language, the one that lacks *"virtue"* and *"true"*. Meaning that this hooking is deceiving and ill-intended. For some, politics is essentially attached to this type of hooking. Once again, a deliberate use of language to confuse and lead men away from virtue and truth. When in the postmodern world, the classic humanistic conception is substituted by the *"I"* or the ego, in the sense of the grounding of reality on the sole's ipse or the emergence of everything that is, from the activity of the *"I"*, we face a new type of political post-humanism.

While following two political campaigns, the recent one in Guatemala, my beloved country of birth, and the one taking place here, in the United States, my mother's country of birth, where I nowadays reside, is very interesting to see that the Guatemalan newly elected President, Dr. Jimmy Morales, campaigned using the *"we"* instead of the *"I"*. The extensive use of the *"we"* tells us a different narrative —to use a term that is very popular today and widely employed, the latter one, speaks of a world where power and representation come from the collective will and commands of the many, it is indeed tempting to accept the consequence that when the *"we"* is used primarily over the *"I"*, the used language addresses a non-mentioned or publicly articulated reference, *"am here to serve you"*, ultimately if am elected, I stand before you and will act and guide my political behaviour, weighing permanently what you need and what you instruct me to follow. This is the language of the *"we"*.

The reason why to use as a title the Greek quotation of Protagoras is very clear but if we touch on the language of the *"I"* while seeing the Republican debate, where Senator Rubio used the expression, *"welders over philosopher"*, before thinking, human action over thought, the priority of achieving, man is therefore measured by what he does and more importantly, his skills on creating or producing an outcome that is called success. The *"I"* is rationally articulated under different expressions, but on the clash of the *"I"* that we name debating, many examples can be brought to illustrate the extensive use of such language. *"I am the only candidate in this group that ...."*; *"I am the only candidate in this group that has..."*; *"I am the only candidate in this group..."* that is using, pursuing the art of hooking men to *"me"* because by doing so all of you will be making the wisest choice which is none other than to put me in the White House because *"I am the only one"* that will solve these incredible problems that flood us and *"I"* have the secret to restoring thing as they were or should be, to ease away your pain and frustration. Hooking men became in the post-modern world, the art of selling. The selling of the *"I"*.

This of course is not a rule. It is not the description of a dialectic between the *"I"* or the *"We"*. But its use of political language or the preference of one over the other illustrates a type of choice. A position. A language without virtue or truth, to follow the Socratic argument freely, which seeks only to hook to the *"I"* can and am the best amongst my peers, as narcissistic as it may seem, can be extremely effective, especially within a world that tends to follow *"winners"* and *"success stories"* with almost an irrational passion. The *"We"*, more elegant, presented as a more humanitarian and sensitive telling of the pain and suffering of others, can be labeled as non-political, about a religious or communitarian view, prone to idealism, and the return of classical humanism. The old debate is served. With a new narrative.

14
ALEXANDER'S TREBUCHET: FROM GREECE TO GUATEMALA. ON THE ECONOMY OF DEBT

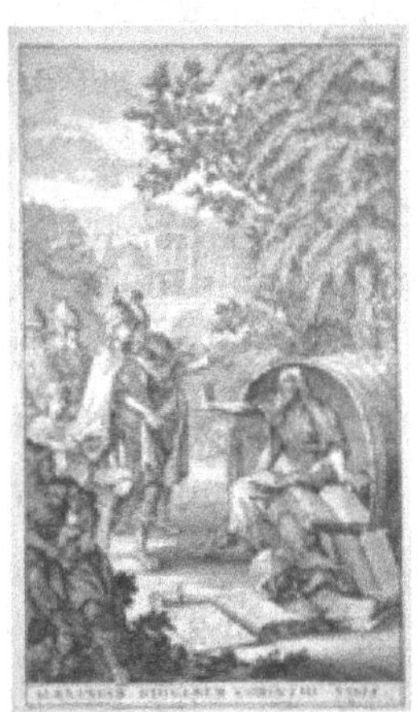

The Latin historian Quintus Cursius Rufus recounts the story of Alexander's siege of Tyre (Historiarum Aleandri Magni Libri Qui Supersunt, L. IV) that comes on his intent to visit and present his prayers and respect to Hercules, at the city known during the period as Tyru Neptunium. The trebuchet was the war instrument used to overtake the walled city and conquer the fierce resistance. To some Alexander is the first *"globalizer"* and Hellenism that came after his death moreover, his most important heritage is not the building of a vast Empire but the expansion of a culture that blended and created a new and genuinely Weltanschauung that expanded and safeguarded at the same time vast knowledge and influence through the Mediterranean basin, Asia and of course, the Middle East, as we called them today. Ancient Greek in all its forms was the lingua franca and as well the language of choice to erudite and philosophers before the absolute empowerment of Latin as the dominant language. Greek is not only the language of the philosophers and early Alexandrian theologians, but it is also the language of the New Testament and the course, of the Septuagint. The use of the "trebuchet" served as a powerful means of conquest. Walled cities were almost impenetrable, immense suffering accompany those everlasting sieges with all the tremendous consequences coming from these enormous mobilizations of means of war and human beings upon which indescribable suffering was inflected on both sides. The use of *instruments of war* and its creation and manufacturing continues throughout human history and the current significance and capacity to generate pain and death remain rampant and widely extended. Science and engineering are backing the production and expansion of the *"instruments of war"*. But the sophistication of this means has expanded in such a way that in the current situation, the *"instruments of war"* are not only built, made creations, there are even some unseen and abstract forms that can defeat a walled city and overcome its defenses. The Greeks succumbed and fell to these new *"instruments of war"*, they fought a war against an invisible trebuchet, namely the abstract numbers and new paradigms established by the economy of debt. Loan to grow and loan to be doomed. Poor administration and insatiable corruption. Irresponsible politicians and unscrupulous bankers. Cheap lending and the conundrum of taking loans to be paid with blood. The diabolical circle of the economy of debt.

The *"walled cities"* were built, kept, and designed under the spirit of the sphere, Sloterdyk described with immense detail in excellent plus delicate language, how this phenomenon originated and what the sense of *"being walled means"*. There nowadays invisible walls and even more *"walled regions"* exist all over the world, the walls fight against globalization in a certain way, self-defense or self-preservation or identity protection and even cultural safeguarding and not to forget, languages, dying languages, these invisible walls carry the heavy burden of solitude, there is an invisible road that leads to all the places and loci where this struggle is taking place. That is why we must see the road that goes from Greece to Guatemala, my country of birth. The economy of debt that has installed the mighty grasp on Greece, presents itself in the form of pure power, not to say that it is an entirely foreign event, by no means, past Greek leaders, both businessmen, and politicians brought upon themselves and the people of Greece, this pain and aggravation. While following the debate and the multiple intents to explain why and how this happened, one element is notoriously absent, namely who are the ones that must be held responsible for all this madness? The blaming games are confusing and pointing fingers serves only to worsen the relationship among Europeans. This is not only a greek invention but a two folded creation within the European Union, Germans, French, and others, even outside the European Continent, the United States is involved as well, Greeks politicians took the loans and spend them irresponsibly, built a false sense of welfare and betrayed the nation and the Greek people. Inside Greece, this is an open debate. Outside Greece we all read and see the language of power: *"you must pay what you owe"* the international architecture of treaties and agreements, is deeply grounded on full respect and compliance with treaties and agreements, and here lays the limit of the economic and financial debate, the legal debate takes over the scene.

In Guatemala a colossal struggle is taking place, unravelling a corrupt and putrefied system. A dying one goes through the well-known seven stages of decomposition. And for similar reasons. The economy of debt has finally been established in a country that ten years ago, barely had any foreign debt. In the past five years or so, it has escalated enormously and for the worst reasons. Debt is beginning to rule a country that for decades has not been able to deal with issues of inequality and injustice. A two-world country, where both coexist deeply embedded and webbed within each other. The people of Guatemala and many of the independent leaders, from academia, social sectors, and even some politicians fighting to dignify and recover the lost prestige that politics currently enjoyed in the country, are altogether looking to stop the other ones, the so-called *"same and old politicians"* that viewed and used power and politics to profit and access rapid wealth. Manipulation of law and an absurd reality of *"money presence"* in a country described as *"medium income"* while is a confusing blend of extreme wealth with extreme poverty and misery. Guatemala has been a walled country since its founding and creation. As such preserved itself from the economy of debt, when it faced isolation while going through what has been named, *"the internal armed conflict"*, or some simply call it *"civil war"*, the leaders of the country got together and redefined the whole system. The Peace Agreements were to shape a new society and new rules to move away from a past of violence and corruption. Slowly the old foes and demons crawled back and recover the lost power and thus bringing "the old ways" with them and the country began to sink into darkness and chaos. But the people stood up this time. The walled country is fighting once again for justice and self-preservation against the predatory forces of the economy of debt. In Guatemala, because the macro-economic indicators have shown a continuum of stability, lending was easy. And so, the decline began very rapidly. Far apart both countries are showing signs of the same sickness, that in the past has infected other countries in both regions and everywhere else. Prometheus has visited the House of Xibalba.

Although a deal has been reached to address the current Greek situation it simply doesn't seem to be enough. The coldness of the figures and facts asks for the hated reality of Greece's inability to pay back its debt under the present situation. Cannot grow enough to fulfil its obligation, can barely service its debt and the future looks gloomy and dark. Prometheus remains enchained. As for my beloved country of birth, Guatemala, the path not to walk through is before the eyes, crystal clear, refuse the walk the economy of debt, wall yourself from corruption and decay and build a bright new way for the younger generations of Guatemalans, that deserve much more than we have experienced. Sent the demons back into Xibalba.

Both countries should recur to Alexander's trebuchet to fight the economy of debt and the invisibility of the aggressors, the demonic internal ones, and the devilish foreign ones. Oppose the lenders and stop the lending. Restore dignity and pride to old countries that emerged and come from old cultures grounded on strong values.

15
WOMEN IN GOLD

Sometimes is better to write while the emotions are still strong and vivid. Watching this remarkable movie brought back a series of fundamental events that took place during my tenure in Vienna. One of the most beautiful cities in the world. And not only from the architectural viewpoint but the treasures, those sometimes hidden erupt and hit your eyes with dazzling power. My stay dates during the middle of the eighties, when the past century entered its final stages. Ronald Lauer was appointed American Ambassador to Vienna, Kurt Waldheim was voted as Federal President –the Austrian presidents are elected by direct and popular vote unlike some other European republics–, on a second round, replacing the two times elected Rudolf Kirchslaeger, a distinguish Austrian diplomat and jurist widely respected and loved in his country. Waldheim –a former United Nations Secretary-General– was forced to face his past military service and his legacy was tinted although the whole history was very dark, the dubiousness of the affair and doubts were never totally clarified. Nobody was happy. Austria as a nation was forced again to come face to face with the ugly consequences of the Anschluss. The film brings us back to what some of us like to call, Wittgenstein's Vienna, where an array of great artists, thinkers, writers, poets, and musicians, contribute to this extraordinary period of Austrian and European history. The lives of the main characters in this story come indeed from these notorious Viennese families, Schoenberg and Altmann, which intertwine in many mysterious and obvious ways. Almost paradoxically.

The narrative or the language of the film is constructed and rests on the two times and travels back and forth with the utmost care and presents the tragedy to its fullest extent. The city is ideal to tell and recount the events. Vienna has been conserved as a leaving museum. It touches not only on individual tragedies but on collective ones as well. We still saw Adele Bloch-Bauer on display at the Belvedere. There was also a wonderful near-terrace restaurant, where I tasted for the first time, a bottle of Chateau Kirwan, which during all my years as a diplomat, has been one of my must-cherished Bourdeaux's. Andrea, Momo, was supposed to be borne in Vienna. All the plans were made for that, the Rudolphinner Haus, was the place selected. But something unexpected changed our plans dramatically and we were forced to completely drop our dreamt project. The Chernobyl accident took place. My period in Vienna was marked by my dedication to the Atomic Energy Agency and managing to get my country elected to a seat on the Board, was not an easy task in those years. Due to my close work on the Board, while dealing with these issues, we were forced to face a horrendous reality, namely the magnitude of the event and the incredible dangers posed by the madness unravel with the disaster. My wife left Vienna –and that was one of the saddest moments of my life– and went to Guatemala to safeguard her health and well-being and of course, that of the coming baby, Andrea. Watching the movie and seeing how the city remains the same brought back to me all the memories arousing from our experience in Austria.

The movie by retelling the known facts surrounding this notorious case emphasizes the legal components of the case. They were very well presented. The conflict between the so-called doctrine of absolute immunity or the principle of immunity of jurisdiction and on the other side, the individual fighting a state and its powerful machinery. The ruling of the Supreme Court on this matter and Chief Justice Rehnquist's well-documented position, favouring the individual over the government, is marvellously and wittingly recreated by Jonathan Pryce in his short but powerful portrait of the late Justice. This ruling opens the case that is finally submitted to an arbitration panel in Vienna that emits a laud granting and restoring the property of the painting to Altmann, amongst others. The enormous importance of the legal proceedings is treated in the movie with accuracy and precision. As for Mirren and Reynold's treatment of Altman and Schoenberg what should be said is that the tension and internal conflict as well as the pain of the Jewish families disposed of their dignities and properties, the humiliation and ultimately the destruction of the Jewish presence in Vienna during the times of the Anschluss and the horrific manifestation of the brutality of anti-Semitism and its barbarism, occupy the central thematic of the movie. In the end, justice was made. The government faces the limits of its power, and the individual is protected by a legal system that is deeply grounded on the rights of the human person, regardless of their race or religion, the colour of their skin, preferences, and origins. Beauty and justice triumph over abuse and horror.

One last reflection to close this brief note on a very special movie and an astonishing story. Since Aristotelian thinking has influenced philosophical thought, the idea that beauty, truth, and goodness are unique attributes of the supreme Being, maybe in a time where money rules tyrannically all levels of human existence —it is becoming almost impossible to think when we face the figures and statistics of the enormous amounts of money being made and lost constantly or, worst, wasted or thrown away in political campaigns throughout the world— that in an incredible twist of events, the return to the origins, repossession of a magnificent work of art that speaks in a language that transcends that of money or merchandise, so, therefore, the conclusion of this story can maybe be summarized, on the at least three times repeated phrase, that Altmann uses on the movie: *"I just want a new dishwasher"*. There was, of course, restitution and retribution, even moral reckoning, but essentially, this extraordinary work of art established a world and grounded earth, where the hope on the values of the spirit and the creation of beauty prevails over barbarity and evil. Once again, maybe Aristotelian thinking is correct and the Superior Being speaks back at us from the depth of beauty, truth, goodness, and justice.

16
THE ABUSE OF THE AUTHORITY

While watching The Hunger Games, the most striking part is its profound and almost religious idea of the conflict of the individual against the authority. The State or the Superior Force incarnated on a collective entity that overwhelms and falls on top of the human person making her or him the subject and object of its pure power expressed in cruel and barbaric ways. Ruling in the sense of taking away from the individual the possibility to choose, condemning existential individuality, and depriving the human being of their nature. Fooling him through the image or representation of the extraordinary as unachievable. Passive spectators of the prowess and beauty that it's ultimately denied as being attainable. Taking away the dreaming for the visual. But missing that the uniqueness that emerges from them brings out redemption and hope. Beauty and courage are the most powerful forces of liberation. Seeing the world through the eyes of my daughter –who nowadays is attending Bangor University's Graduate School for her Neuropsychology Degree– allows me to see a different reality that my vision does not captures. But the old idea of rebellion against authority when this one oppresses and nullifies the essence of freedom and with it negates the fundamental meaning of mankind is neither original nor new and has been humanity's most important struggle.

When Adorno and his group of distinguished scholars and friends, in the safety of Los Angeles without the threat of persecution by the obscure dark apparatus of an authoritarian regime, crafted the so-called F-Scale during the 1950s, the basis of their remarkable work was grounded on the Horkheimer and Adorno extraordinary book "Dialektik der Aufklaerung" originally published in 1947 by the Querido Verlag in Amsterdam. This is a story by itself that demands to be retold and the world needs to remember the names of these extraordinary human beings that made it possible for us to have the luxury of reading and having this remarkable body of work. The Nazi Germans took Emanuel Querido and his wife to the Concentration Camp in Sobibor, Poland, and they died executed on the 23rd of July 1943. Querido a descendant of Portuguese Jews was denounced by Nazi collaborators in The Netherlands where they headed an editorial firm, that also published German authors that were banned in Nazi Germany and in 1947 printed and published the first edition of Adorno and Horkheimer Dialektik der Aufklaerung under the collaboration of Fritz Landshowhohom manage to survive because he was in London by the time when the Queridos were denounced to the Gestapo. During the nineteen eighties while lecturing on the Frankfurt Schule and specifically on Adorno and Horkheimer in my country of birth, Guatemala, at the Jesuits University –Rafael Landivar– to a group of young Guatemalan intellectuals who today hold important posts in Government, the center of the debate was precisely how the individual can overcome the forces and power of authoritarianism which is at the core of their work: the crucial question was how is it possible the transit from the mythos to the logos and therefore how to explain authoritarianism and the barbaric exploiting from it. An illustrated world that collapses into such barbaric atrocities to a scale that creates the most horrendous of human experiences, namely the deliberate extermination of human beings for totally irrational reasons, mythological thinking founded on barbarity that establish itself as the extremist form of the authoritarian leading to what humanity knows as probably its darkest hours. The extermination of the other just for being different and equal at the same time.

In my country of birth nowadays there's an ongoing struggle with authority. The abuse of power sets up the country to face its must-challenging quest. The true foundation of a civilized state lies in the full respect and proper enforcement of justice and the rule of law, without hesitation and doubt, until the nation as a whole and the State don't fulfil its fundamental duties to respect and execute, act accordingly to the complete and total commitment to the sacred mission of holding and abiding with no exceptions, to the implementation and respect of the rule of law, we will continue to be cast away from the civilized nations of the world. But this is the nature of the struggle against authority. The abuse of authority and the lack of justice generate the condition for deep satisfaction and even rebellion. Almost like a positive regression on the movie, the return to the idea that beauty, goodness, and truth are essentially the same, a thomist conception, where true, good, and beauty constitute the primary attributes of being, displays its magical visual phantasy in an array of stimulating and even intoxicating series of wonderfully crafted images. Opposed to the ugliness of the dark side. But this can also be deceiving. In my country, the abuse of authority has been increasing its darker presence. But is facing the struggle of many. The judiciary is sending a clear message that it is not going to bend to the power of the abuse and the barbaric oppression of the few. Historical cases are facing justice in these moments and even here, at the South District Federal Court in New York City a case of enormous importance not only for my country but the whole region, is about to be tried. If all these cases are solved according to the fullest respect to justice and law, and there are many reasons to believe this will be so, then the future for the individual hope would have won a crucial battle and the abuse of authority will be confronted to its limits and succumb to the light of the pure enforcement of the law as the grounds for the civilized behaviour of the countries that live under a constitutional state of law. There are meaningful signs that this can be achieved and there is hope for the struggle of the individual in their quest to limit the abuse of power.

17
EL SILENCIO DE LOS POETAS

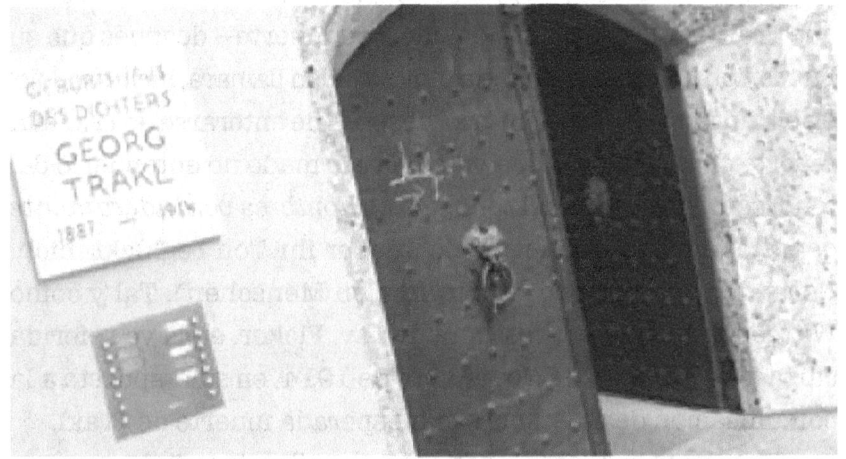

La casa de Nacimiento de Georg Trak, in Salzburg.

Cuando los poetas dejan de hablar y el silencio se impone, la gravedad y la angustia del mundo se hacen más fuertes, sensibles. El oscuro espacio instalado, que emerge después del silencio o de esos grandes silencios, es sumamente profundo. En la oscuridad del silencio se hacen más patentes la ausencia, carencias y faltas. Lo que perdimos o aún no tenemos. Lo que se ha marchado o lo que tal vez aún no ha llegado. Son los "tiempos de penuria", de los que nos hablaban Rilke, y Heidegger nos hace ver, como los pensadores en constante diálogo con los poetas conservan, guardan, protegen y aquella tarea de guardianía, nos mantiene cerca de lo humano. Trakl hablaba de aquel *animal humano*, que *deambula por la tierra de la noche*, el gran destructor, el aniquilador de mundos, y es una historia terrible, para quien logra ver la profundidad del abismo del silencio y al asombrarse, se espanta y enmudece. Se calla. Camus nos decía, en esa obra extraordinaria L' Homme Revolté, que los *poetas le agregan al mundo lo que le hace falta*. Recordamos la historia narrada por el propio Wittgenstein, quien buscara conocerlo personalmente —cuyo texto se conserva a través de una carta, que Trakl nunca recibiera debido a su muerte— después que su Fundación le otorgara un estipendio, a quien llamara, incluyéndole, en el famoso breve comentario, después de enterarse de la súbita muerte de Trakl, de quien ya había afirmado no entenderlo del todo, como poseeder del *tono*, de los *hombres verdaderamente geniales*. (Ich verstehe sie nicht, aber ihr Ton beglückt mich. Es ist der Ton des wahrhaft genialen Menschen). Tal y como Wittgenstein se lo expresa a Ludwig v. Ficker, en la ya referida carta fechada el 28 de Noviembre de 1914, en su respuesta a la comunicación de éste, sobre la inesperada muerte de Trakl.

Es sumamente largo el camino de los silencios y de los encuentros, entre los pensadores y los poetas. Viene a cuenta acá porque nos hallamos en esos tiempos de graves silencios. El último poema que Trakl escribiera, previo a su muerte —la cual no ha sido nunca del todo aclarada—, titulado "Gródek", que en los tiempos de la Primera Gran Guerra, en lo que entonces era el Reino de Galitzia y Lodomeria, fuera teatro de una terrible y devastadora batalla, entre los ejércitos imperiales rusos y los austro-húngaros, estos últimos sufrieron una de las más terribles derrotas, con una enorme cantidad de muertos, mutilados, heridos. Mientras, Trakl, que participaba en el frente como *Apotheker*, víctima de un colapso nervioso, tuvo que ser remitido a un hospital militar, específicamente a un pabellón neuro-psiquiátrico, en Cracovia, donde falleciera a los veintisiete años, en condiciones complicadas, lo cual generó dudas sobre un suicido o una muerte accidental, debida a una sobredosis de cocaína. En ese poema, el Gran Poeta del Silencio, Trakl, emplea dos expresiones alemanas, referidas a los silencios,

...stille sammelt im Weidengrund... y más adelante, en una de las últimas estanzas del poema, se lee el misterioso verso, "*...es schwank der Schewster Schatten durch den schweigenden Hain, ...*".

El vocablo alemán Hain tiene una serie de connotaciones muy particulares. Encontramos sus orígenes en el alemán medieval y en el antiguo sajón, hagan, dornstauch, y también en el denominado mittelhochdeutsch, hägen. Aparentemente entre las dos formas Hain y Hag se derivaría la forma contraída Hain, la cual se vincularía a formas más recientes, como Orten y que hacen referencia a lugar o villa. Aunque el camino de las variantes dialectales del habla popular y antigua del alemán es riquísimo y muy complejo, podemos tal vez inferir que la referencia mantenida y buscada, es la de lugar, locación de alguna manera; de tal vez una antigua y pequeña villa o pueblo. De allí que las *sombras hermanas o las hermanas de las sombras*, a través del silencio del lugar, se muestran, en medio de un breve relato, presentado en un teatro completamente absurdo. Es el Relato de la Guerra puesto en escena. Lo interesante es como la alusión al silencio y su poder son capaces de contarnos una historia terrible: la más despiadada destrucción de las atrocidades de las guerras. Es este pues el silencio, que ha dejado su lugar, en el lugar de la destrucción, para que las sombras lo ocupen, en su relato de la caída completa, ante el horror abismal de la muerte y la destrucción. Trakl presenció y comprendió este horrendo misterio, el de la más absoluta destrucción.

Los teatros de las grandes guerras cambiaron el mundo. Después de los enormes niveles de mortalidad y destrucción sufridos, la probabilidad de la extinción total planetaria, la duda prohibida, en el porvenir de una humanidad llena del optimismo de la Ilustración, tanto en el centro de la naturaleza como en la expansión de un saber ilimitado, se quebraron. Una post-modernidad y visión de fin de la historia empezaron lentamente a tomar el centro del debate. Los graves silencios se ausentaron. Se construyeron los laberintos del *nuevo orden mundial* y la pseudo cultura de la post-verdad, especialmente dentro de una política global expansiva. No es la primera vez, que pasamos por períodos sombríos y obscuros, donde las expectativas apocalípticas desplazan las esperanzas. Sin embargo, cuando la renuncia a los criterios de verdad se profundizan y establecen, como tendencias dominantes, los silencios son cada vez más inaudibles. Menos presentes. Los poetas empiezan a callarse y ese es un riesgo de una enorme gravedad. Si el principio de razón suficiente es casi irreconocible hoy día, la experiencia de la verdad, en su permanente ocultamiento y desocultamiento, ausencia y presencia, que habría en cierta forma prefigurado la era del final de la Metafísica —sobre esto último aún guardo fuertes reservas—, en favor de un auge total de la ciencia y las verdades comprobadas y demostradas. El Fisicalismo, del que se hablaba en los años del Círculo de Viena y los debates posteriores alrededor del pensamiento analítico, guardan aún la memoria presente del célebre dictum del Tractatus y su célebre proposición séptima: *Wovon man nicht sprechen kann, darüber muss man schweigen..* Muchísimo se ha escrito y debatido alrededor no solamente del texto y su significado, sino de sus interpretaciones. Algunos sostienen, que el Tractatus es un texto con un arquitectura musical. Esto no es nada extraño, el elemento vienés es obvio y la relación matemática, de las teorías de la armonía y composición musical, tienen clarísimos tonos matemáticos, medidas, tiempos y mucho más. Y el cierre sería una referencia al silencio final, que deviene al concluir la ejecución de una obra. Aquí me interesa sobre todo su relación con Trakl, la cual no es ni puede ser considerada casual. Los une la preocupación máxima por el lenguaje y sus significados, su sentido y posibles interpretaciones, tal vez más importante aún, sus usos. El límite del lenguaje, de lo que se puede decir, después de una experiencia absoluta de destrucción, del completo absurdo de la guerra, los silencios que emergen no exclusivamente de la muerte, sino de las más atroces muestras de barbarie. El silencio se impone ante lo inexplicable. Así pues *…de aquello que no se puede hablar….se debe callar.*

Los políticos actuales –y aquí tal vez caben muchos más, no solamente los buscadores del poder, sino todos aquellos que viven y pululan alrededor de éste– bien podrían aprender de la experiencia del silencio y de los límites del lenguaje. Esto inevitablemente lleva a la pregunta por el sentido la verdad y, sobre todo, la relación fundamental con la misma. Aunque pareciera casi impensable que en la era de la imagen, donde lo más relevante son las cuestiones ópticas y pseudo-estéticas, no es que surgen por cuestiones de apreciaciones *de belleza profunda*, sino más bien manufacturadas, producidas por una ingeniería genética o meramente técnica, las cuales nos han situado, o instalado, en el lenguaje de la analítica existenciaria, en un medio plenamente controlable, predecible y por si eso no fuera suficiente, calculadamente creado, artificialmente producido, cuyas reacciones son esperadas. Decir o hablar sobre algo en público es una actividad plenamente medible, se ponderan las frases y su eficacia, desde su manera y forma de articulación, las expresiones cálidas o frías, distantes o cercanas; ese enorme conjunto de formas anticipadas, prefiguradas y por supuesto, efectivas. Su efectividad es medible como resultado. Los efectos generados son los esperados e incluso buscados deliberadamente. No importa, y, para nada importa, el contenido de lo dicho, sino el efecto de lo transmitido. La verdad no solamente está ausente, sino que ha sido brutalmente expulsada, excluida, se ha tornado en meramente irrelevante. Nada ejemplifica este mundo de la post-verdad –no estoy del todo satisfecho con el empleo y recurso de ese término, post-truth; no obstante, su amplia difusión y discusión facilitan recurrir a él, para posibilitar el debate– como la *acción política* y su práctica. Debates que no lo son. Discusiones sobre cómo imponer un criterio o visión sobre los demás o de una disidencia antagónica; el fenómeno de las fake-news, es uno más de los muchos efectos de la renuncia a la comprobación y facticidad de lo real. Y en esto la economía y la política siguen germinando, dentro de la misma tierra de interpretaciones parciales, limitadas y obedientes a horizontes deliberadamente enmascarados. Se ha renunciado a la profundidad del silencio y se abandona la búsqueda de la verdad y del saber. El poder y su procura son absolutamente dominantes. Mantenerlo, conservarlo, aumentarlo a cualquier costo y sin límites, es la más obscura de las realidades del mundo actual, de lo no-evidente, de la imagen y su interminable confusión. Nuestra capacidad de comprensión e interpretación de lo real se ha tornado elusiva y hermética. Nuestras circunstancias desafían nuestros límites de aprehensión de realidad, para usar la expresión de Xavier Zubiri al referirse a la inteligencia sentiente. Aunque no solamente se trata de nuestros propios y evidentes límites, estamos sumidos en confusiones y deliberados procesos de aislamientos de lo real. El ser real y su dureza quedan ensombrecido y cubiertos por ese extraño y gris manto tendido, sobre cualquier forma de facticidad. La imposición del desorden y la confusión dominan por todas partes. Somos habitantes de laberintos.

18

AN OLD PATH TO THE DEUS ABSCONDITUS: THE SEARCH FOR THE HIDDEN DIVINITY

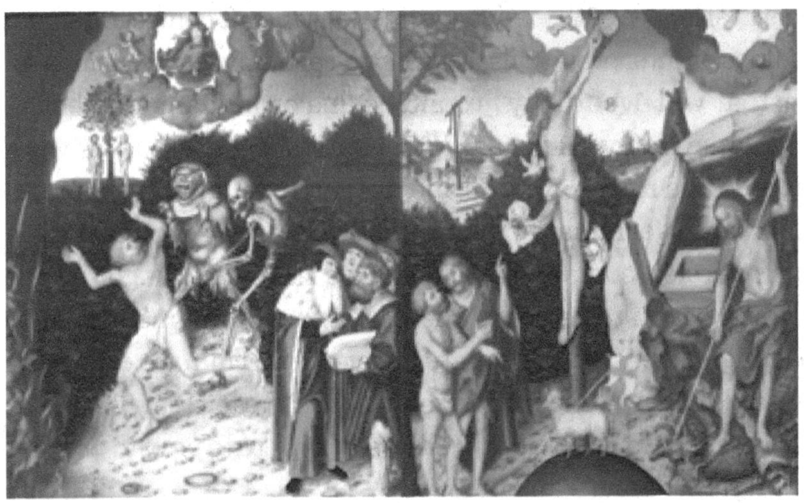

Lucas Cranach, der Ältere: "Allegorie auf Gesetz und Gnäde", circa 1529. Germanisches National Museum

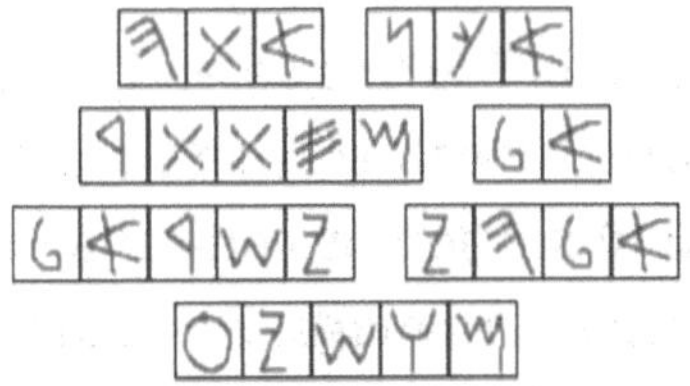

The above-quoted text of Isaiah Chapter 45:15 on its *original version*, circa 485 BC, where the expression regarding the Deus Absconditus is employed, and most likely not for the very first time, in the Latin Vulgate, ...*vere tu es Deus absconditus Deus Israhel salvator...* that has sadly been translated in so many different ways, however, the two dominant versions generally accepted, refer to *the hidden* or *hidest thyself* in the sense of the capacity or faculty of the Divine Presence either to show or manifest Himself or not to do so and therefore to retrieve Himself into his being. Sacred texts can be deceiving and extremely difficult to read and translations are most of the time inaccurate or the chosen words cannot reproduce the original meanings and experiences of the language as such when it comes to certain readings or interpretations, better said certainly given hermeneutics, that will eventually ground dogma or fundamental belief, failure inevitably takes place, let us not forget that wars were waged in the name of words and of course, religious beliefs and continuo to germinate never-ending disputes and unsolvable controversies, some wars of today are still being fought on the grounds of religious ideas and so-called, divine mandates or heavenly orders, to annihilate or even exterminate others, in the name of very obscure commands from a raging divinity that demands the extinction of the others, that dare to pray to another divinity. So obscure and dark.

Martin Luther introduced, from the famous Isaiah quotation, regarding a God that is hidden or if the third person is chosen, a theological dictum distinguishes a God that chooses not to manifest, which is very difficult to defend or to sustain, and the same God that reveals Himself through his Son, Christ, Jesus and through His manifestation or self-revelation shines in his light, using the Reformers language which in reality stems from the Greek Fathers and the combination of an old tradition, Neoplatonism, the Stoa, Plotinus and other greek thinkers that constituted an important and core tradition of early Christianity influencing greatly on the ancient Patristic thinking and nascent Tradition. Luther knew this world very well and has been known since the beginning of the Reform Movement, Luther wasn't an

expert on ancient languages, ancient Hebrew, Aramaic nonetheless bases most of his translations on the Vulgate and was
helped by Erasmus and Melanchthon amongst others, that were
indeed great scholars and well versed on ancient languages,
however since the work was so demanding it required a long
time and endless consultations to be completed.

Morphosyntactically ancient or paleo Hebrew had no punc-
tuation marks so miss-translations and errors were very
common and still are, The Talmud —that extraordinary work
of collective Jewish wisdom— gives us a very lengthy and fruitful
array of different examples of all sorts of disputes, many never
resolved, others illustrate the intricate hermeneutical tools employed by the Ancient Rabbis to interpret a text and come up with
an answer or even established or create Rabbinical Law, regulations or norms and rules on a distinctive matter. We can find
throughout the different Tractates, disputes on the correct
interpretation of a word, even on its accurate and precise writing, the finding of the common root of a word that might even
carry different meanings despite being the same one. In our
present case, the keyword is an Ancient Greek verb, namely,
ἤδειμεν , if we could dare to read the original meaning of the
verb that speaks or names the retrieval of the Divine Presence
into His Owners we are in the face of a very profound mystery
—not an appropriate term to refer or designate an actual withdrawal
of G'd— that tells us that sometimes for unknown causes the
Divine Presence simply isn't any more present in the world.

According to the Book of Names (Exodus) the Divine Presence
dwelt with the Israelites on its way to the Promise Land (Erestz
Israel) and later on when the Temple was finally constructed,
the Divine Presence had a special place of dwelling in the Temple,
Holly of Holiest is the name given were the High Priest came
into the presence of the dwelling G'd, like in the times of the

dessert and the original Tabernacle after he revealed or manifested His Presence to Mosses in Sinai and the Cloud. When the Temple has been destroyed the mystery of the absence or retrieval of the Divine Presence raises the question of the Deus Absconditus. Sometimes the Gods abandon their places of worship or they choose to leave the world when humanity walks a path of self-destruction or distances from their Gods. Temples remain empty. Nowadays we can see many empty Churches, Temples, and places of worship, and after the times of the Death of God were proclaimed —is curious once again how an expression can be so poorly interpreted: Nietzsche's real meaning of the Death of God is completely the opposite to what has been attributed to his thinking, anew the wrong readings and misinterpretation of a word or in the Nietzsche's case a phrase— the search for their return or the path to look after the hidden place where the Divine Presence decides to withdraw. During medieval times, Meister Eckart used a wonderful description when referring to the being of the Divinity: *the being that is and dwells on his light* probably here we find the source —on a pre-metaphorical language— of the absence of light and the intruding presence of the darkness when the Gods or the Light of the Divine Presence ceases to be present in the World, stops dwelling in the world, then the darkness takes over and pain and suffering prevail. The absence of light is the presence of suffering. From the Deus Absconditus to the Deus Incognito we travel into different paths. From the so-called Self-Concealing G'd to the Self-Unconcealing G'd to the Unknown divinity that chooses to retrieve into his absence two opposite conceptions emerge and this is crucial because it deals with the all to a well-established tradition that the Divinity —however, the thinking or representation we choose to follow— is a living God that dwells with Humanity in this world. Somehow. The ancient Israelites walked the desert and through the desert accompanied by the Divine Presence, either protecting them and even more, forgiving them for their wrong actions —trying to avoid the language of guilt, transgression, or even sins, deliberately— and same can be affirmed from Christianity regardless of their divisions, through Jesus comes salvation and the rituality and liturgical elements both explicitly called for the presence of the living Christ celebrated in the eucharist no matter what pattern you follow: the blood of the Christ redeems and saves and is present permanently in the people or assembly, and especially in the hearts of the persons-believers, singling out a special and unique direct relation to the living G'd, once again regardless of the liturgical conception that was to be accepted or one chooses to celebrate. To some this is nothing other than revelation, the Deus Absconditus chooses to reveal himself to his people and the sinners to save them from darkness and fall, no matter the preference you are into, either by birth or by a personal election, the revelation of the divinity is the center and core of the unconcealment by which the bond is grounded: the living G'd now address the world and the assembly, people, community and the individual can recognize his presence and reply to his voice or his call and like the great catholic theologian, Karl Rahner, used to say, the hearer of the word emerges.

The idea of describing G'd with human qualities or constructing a vision of the divinity to which we will ascribe all the attributes that humanity can possess or even more, achieve. During medieval times, more specifically during the period when scholasticism dominated not only philosophical and theological thinking, grounded on Aristotelian metaphysics, the idea of a Supreme Being that is necessarily Good, Beautiful and Truth, can be exclusively predicated on G'd, however, this Supreme Being cannot remain hidden in its eternal perfection —even whilst employing this type of language remains within the limits of human attributes— because an isolated in Himself Perfect Being who maintains a distance from his creation, generates a serious difficulty addressing the special bond originally established with the product of his enormous task as a Life-Giver. Creation is essentially a given act and what is given as the most perfect gift of all, none other than the gift of life and although Man is also given the ultimate gift is also the receiver of the ultimate grant, the mystery of freedom. Freedom to choose. Libero arbitrio, otherwise human life and his relation to the Divinity is completely senseless even more, human life as such becomes absurd if the possibility to choose is taken away from life. Almost all aspects of what some call *"human action"* are deeply rooted in freedom, man's central engine and all his most important faculties and creative impulses come and stem from this extraordinary capacity to choose, human creation surges from the unconditional exercise of freedom. Enslaved human beings are dehumanized and their nature is sunken into the darkness and the abyss of the lacking, or the incompleteness that negates the essential drives of humanity and more specifically, separates mankind from his true being, mission, and even destiny to use a more metaphorical language and this inevitably leads us to the other crucial problem, that of evil.

The ever-present problem of evil and the terrible injustice reigning worldwide, the atrocities committed constantly against other human beings,s and even more, against our natural habitat, our dwelling-in-the-world being, have become more than dramatic. Words won't supply answers to what we witness regularly and have turned into some sort of new everydayness. Never-ending wars fought for the obscurest of reason or causes, madness spreads and dominates in all corners of the world. Darkness seems to be winning the sacred war against the children of the light. Hope recluses and retrieves from the aspirations of our daily activities —and now sinks even deeper while humanity struggles to comprehend and combat the current malady that has brought the world at large, into an abyss of fear and discontent: the fear of imminent death—, we find extenuating to pursue dreams and maintain minimum stability, if those words still have a certainly given meaning. A powerful chaos rules and the old sense and sensibility balance wither away into a greater degree of inaccessibility, meaningless pervades the calmness of what once was hopeful and ascertainable.

The famous painting by Cranach and the reference and use Luther introduced into art as a means to communicate and convey the message of salvation for humanity, emerging from the cross worlds of the reform movement and later on the so-called contra-reform, established the widespread view of the crucial question individuals face when it comes to understanding and more importantly, living accordingly not only a certain ethos but a Kerygma that leads directly to the ultimate and most radical of all questions: can I be saved by my deeds or only the chosen ones are saved by the almighty. This fundamental and core question lies at the mere core of our sense of meaning and sense, individual lives will have meaning from a certain commitment to govern everyday actions by abiding by rules, given to mankind, or, on the other alternative, little can be done if we'll be granted the grace of being saved as a gift, done into humanity by the ruling and decision taken by the Almighty Deus absconditus. Kierkegaard and some other Lutheran and protestant theologians, display an incredibly attractive conception that was in those days, named the "Scandal". Kierkegaard specifically signals the scandalous nature of "being called to be saved" which, come to me, means nothing other than a calling. I shall save you if you answer my call. Come to me because you are invited and here lies the notion of the "scandal": not only all humanity is invited into salvation and joy but not everybody listens nor replies to the call. How much profound deafness can be so widely spread and the lack of response points perhaps to the mystery of evil. Silence turns not into this modern notion of going inside our being and penetrating our most profound sense of truthiness but on the contrary, the lack of answers or proper replies even furthers the nature of the "scandal".

A powerful and deafening silence dominates a very loud and transformed world where madness and the loss of deepness and ability to hear that is the fundamental calling. This and none other is the experience of the retrieving gods and the empty temples, churches, and places of worship. Whilst some considered denying individuals their right to pray publicly —even to children— as a form of respect to otherness and difference in the name of openness and tolerance, waging the weaponizing idea that as a respect to the different all forms of praying in public spaces, might hurt all that don't share the same beliefs and faiths, namely preferences. Total deafness reigns. The allegory and the need to display the contents of a given disputation serve the crucial purpose of setting up a very important controversy. The Deus absconditus, the grace and law, the salvation as such, the dwelling divine presence, and the fight to stop the gods from fleeing these horrendous conditions that are creeping up incessantly all over the world, calls for a renovation of the old Kierkegaardian notion of the scandal. The ancient Israelites quarrel and established a conversation —to recur to a modern expression or the so-called metaphorical speech— that keeps itself alive and ongoing. Praying publicly in the Kottel carries the powerful meaning of the ever-present mandates and fulfillment of Torah Law. We pray in the Kottel because we choose to continue this never-ending conversation with the Divine Presence that once dwelt in the Temple. Wars, destruction, persecution, condemnations, denials, and even,

state-sponsored policies, the Nazis and others even, to annihilate
that very strong sense of commitment, failed and were unsuc-
cessful, still, nowadays people travel from all corners of the world
to seek that invisible Holiest of Hollies were they say a dwelling
G'd once spoke directly to his people and now speaks to all
humanity. None other than the oldest "scandal". We must listen
and hear and more importantly, reply and answer.

19
AN OLD PATH TO
THE DEUS ABSCONDITUS:
THE SEARCH FOR THE HIDDEN DIVINITY II.

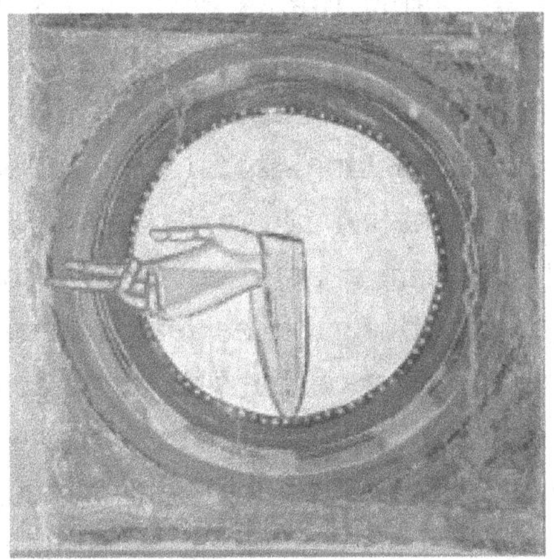

The Hand of God of Sant Climent de Taüll, Anon, 1123. Mà de Déu de Sant Climent de Taüll, Museu Nacional d'Art de Catalunya, Barcelona.

As we close the current year, the Second Year of the Pandemic, elusive hope lingers tentatively from some corners of the vast world, that wide and unconnected world, as the great Peruvian novelist, Ciro Alegría, once called it in the middle of the last century. Calling upon G'd was the normal trend for previous maladies running rampantly and devouring countless human lives. There are many stories told by different sources, historical ones or sacred literature, recounting the events of plagues, droughts, or the great pestilence that under the darkest of times the call for divine intervention became an urgent matter. There's one in the Talmud (Taanit, IV, 19.), that shares the tale of Honi HaMe'aggel, the Circle Drawer, who had the extraordinary gift of being listened to by G'd or to use current terminology, had G'd's ear.

So, in a time of a great draught asked for divine intervention and the rains came and they poured down and the situation went from extreme drought to extreme flooding. In another chapter of Tractate Taanit, Taanis, Fast, IV, 25, the story of Rabi Akiva and the origins of the famous and extraordinary Jewish prayer Avinu Malkeinu, Our Father, our King, is narrated, and how it came to be whilst asking also for divine intervention during times of dire need. Somehow many of this and other stories not only kept and told in the Talmud but many other sources and different sacred texts, describe the desperate seek for answers from the absent divinity or perhaps the more accurate —if there are any when addressing these conversations— is the dialogue with and the praying for help under the most desperate circumstances. The hidden or concealed or maybe simply absent divinity answers in ways such that the extraordinary emerges simply happens.

The rains came down. The pestilence ended. Remarkable events recorded in humanity's memories, enormous tragedies overcame by an intervention so difficult to explain and taken as an answer to a sincere and very deep prayer. The unconcealment of the *hand of G'd emerged from a circle, being the circle the image of perfection*, as in the fresco from Saint Clement. The hand emerges from the sphere as if the divinity dwells on the innerness of the sphere and as a reply, response, to the prayer's invocation reaches out to humanity's desperation to bring about consolation and healing. Suffering ends. The narrative of the never-ending and always continuing dialogue, and conversation, between the Creator and the whole of creation, specifically with mankind, is restored, in the humbling of the prayer, the answer is healing.

The Deus absconditus is unconcealed through the mystery of the praying. There's an inexhaustible history of this complex dialogue as none other than the search for the hidden divinity which we attempt to describe as the Deus absconditus or the old and long aspirations of man's desperate attempts to find the source of all and the ultimate concern, after all the ancient idea that the word religion, comes from the ancient Latin verb, ligare, whose meaning is to tie and in religion the construct signals at to join again what was split or probably thorn apart, separated, through the never ceasing dialog or conversation someone might dare to call it nowadays.

The ultimate concern becomes that experience of the bringing back that originated on the tie and somehow became disjoined, grew apart from the essential origin. Sometimes we call the experience of the silence of God which refers to empty temples of prayer or abandoned places of worship, where the lack of answers leads to the wondering of the seekers, the never-ending sought responses from the silent Deus Absconditus.

Sacred texts have suffered the ordeal of translations, transliterations, rendering through a third language, and sometimes, probably the most difficult task faced and undertaken by interpreters, come across languages that aren't spoken or written any more. The outcome of these mischievous versions is grounded on mistakes, either purposely or naively committed but have nonetheless enormous consequences for mankind and the correct hermeneutics of ancient manuscripts or fundamental passages from different books. The story is too vast and complex to be addressed here but let us look briefly at one of these extraordinary examples, the translation of the Greek word for brother as found in Mark 6:3 in the original version, αδελφός, the countless disputes around the mention that Jesus had brothers and sisters and therefore the Virgin Mary somehow also had other children, gave birth to other children, established an essential break amongst Christians since the times of the Reformation although the knowledge of the issue dates even to the Patristical times, there are abundant texts dealing with the matter, too many to address here, just to recall some of them, the Protoevangelium of James, circa 120 A. D., some explanations deal with the quasi argument that adelphos, plural adeplphi, also means brethren or simply is used to refer to fellow members of a certain group. More serious arguments called for the fact that Greek wasn't the lingua franca amongst Jews but Aramaic and most of the evangelists communicate with each other on what might have been called Imperial Aramaic, achai —a cognate from ancient Hebrew ach which means simply brother but has a multi semantic use also meaning, kinsman or even friend, loosely— is most likely that word and it has even on nowadays Syrian-Aramaic a language still spoken, a definitive and restrictive meaning of brother, however the original and employed on the Greek version of the sacred texts, adelphos, comes from the alpha prefix and here is probably the crucial difficulty, deplhus means womb, so Adelphi would be those who share the womb, to make matters even more difficult. The complications can go even further, deeper, and extremely sensitive to address.

Calling for kindness and humbleness is an essential manner to continue the humane dialogue with a not-so-evident divinity. Concealment in the form of non-answering or the lack of a clear and open response generates a strange paradox or is better worded as a form of perplexity. We've seen through history in all the different credos, claims of being the Messiah or the reincarnation of some divinity that chooses to come back into the world either to bring an array of hope and peace —one that should last thousands of years— or even more, judgment and condemnation to evildoers or sinners that abandoned their brethren or simply turned their backs to the faith of their respective forefathers in which they were once raised. The reply of fire and rage has scared mankind for thousands of years, the eternal fear of condemnation and damnation even, the construction of physical places of never-ending suffering and pain, the eternal fire awaiting those who left lives of wrongdoing and sin, committed evil acts against their fellow humans, waged a war of destruction and annihilation, deserved to be condemned to the deepest abyss of misery and suffering. The Dalai Lama, one of the world's most respected spiritual leaders, calls for kindness and humbleness in our everyday actions and relations with others, our fellow humans, calls for a world of respect and non-violence, the building of a place where words will not be waged for the sake of domination, narcissistic fantasies of ruling and imposing will and power over populations and nations.

The idea of repetition becomes central to praying. Kierkegaard addressed this very issue rooted in the coming-to-be within praying. Praying is an art in itself. Learning how to pray, the pronunciation of the words, the understanding of the deep meaning contained in the prayer uttered, not to mention its origins, and especially complying and fulfilling the exact and precise timing and whole liturgical and rituals aspects of the way prayers should be said and/or singed. Prayers are forms of anticipation and replies to what is happening they address not only the past but what is further away. Prayers are drawn from the past but refer to the future and that is the reason for the strictness of their utterance and the rituality accompanying the way they are said. The linkage of singing and praying is present in all forms of liturgies and even the oldest ones, where praying is signaled in other contexts, the in-depth learning of the correct way to pray and sing or the correct manner to say a prayer and pronounce each word either by memory or by reading, here again, the notion of the repetition is present, leads the individual or the congregation, into the realm of the never-ending dialog/conversation with the Divinity by simply chasing or fulfilling the obligation or commandment, mitzvah, of when and how to utter the prayer. Here is where the fundamental question of the answer to the praying comes into the center of the meditation/act of dialoguing with the Divinity in the form of praying to the Deus Absconditus and asking/begging to come out of concealment.

One last word on the notion/image of the Hand of God coming out of the Sphere of Perfection. Since Sloterdik's Sheherology we have a very sound idea of how the metaphor of the circle became the Sphere of Perfection since ancient times the circle represents that which is enclosed within the absolute closure. If the Divinity thought in a manner that ranges from lyrical and poetical representation to sublime works of art even coded by rules and regulations on the imagery and style in which it can be depicted, to the general and absolute rule that no imagery is aloud and even more, should and must be met with the harshest of responses or ways of punishment if the sacred rule is violated, but the sphere has no beginning nor an end, its circular shape encompasses all that is included within its realm or domain, Leibniz and the late Husserl's view of a monological phenomenology hinted at this conception that probably all start with the sphere or that which is spherical contains perfections in itself so at the end or maybe at the beginning, it seems all to adequate that the Hand of God emerges from the concealment of its spherical own perfection, perhaps the mere dwelling in perfection itself. Probably that is the not-so-evident reason why Isaiah, 25:11, calls for the Hand of G'd to ...*descend on this Mount....and will be spread on their Homeland.*

CHAPTER II
ON FOREIGN POLICY

1
ON THE END OF DIPLOMACY

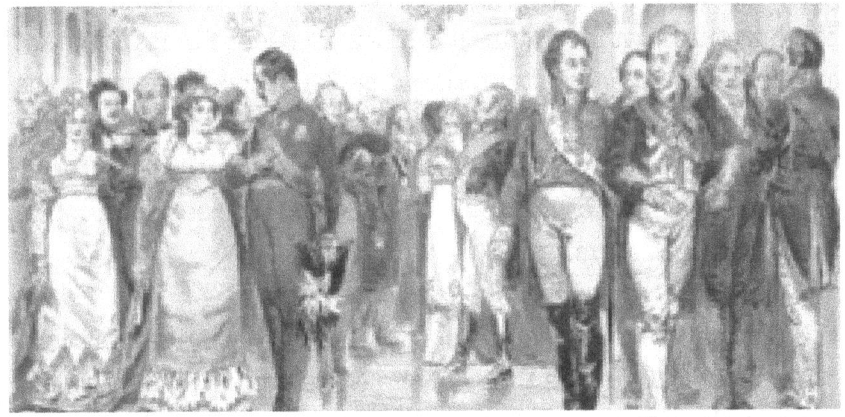

Fest-bei-Metternich-Weiser. Wiener Kongress.

After the turbulent period of the Napoleonic Wars, it is a well-known fact that the times of the so-called Modern Diplomacy began. Peace to end wars. But more wars followed and probably the Twenties' Century witnessed the worst wars fought almost everywhere in the world. Horror and destruction walked the cities of major countries regardless of their geographical location. Wars are a recurrent spectre of mankind. And the struggle to put an end to or stop them walks closely with the never-ending human Trieb to use Freudian language, which eludes translation as so many other terms coming either from Freud or in a wider sense, from German philosophy or even in general, from other languages. Trieb is not only and is not a drive or an impulse or the Lacanian version of pulsion/dérive. And let us avoid the temptation of using it as the instinct to which many have fallen victim Heidegger leads us to go through the path of authenticity by confronting the fundamental meaning of Dasein in Angst or Cura using the Latin term which he employs in Sein un Zeit and the Sein-Zum-Tode (Being-towards-death) as an existential come-into-face-with-death in a non-biological meaning but in a more pregnant and deeper sense. Diplomacy and war in their constant rendezvous must face human´s natural essence in its poignant and more grasping existential reality. The subject demands the utmost seriousness and dedication and cannot and should never be addressed within a framework of superficiality and lightness, or with ease of gaiety of style or manner. We see too much of the latter nowadays.

Gravity follows deepness. Diplomacy presents itself very differently than in the times of the Napoleonic Wars but there is a certain seriousness that still is present and dominant. The hundred years of transformation are enormous. Codification, to begin with, the Conventions, The Law of the Treaties, Multilateralism —although this form of diplomacy is experiencing radical transformations— and of course, the expansion of International General Consensual Law in all its forms. Even Criminal International Law has been rendering admirable outcomes. Criminals are facing international justice; Tribunals are rendering sentences and we have blossoming means to execute and fulfil judgments. The principle of complementarity seems to be generating the results so long-awaited. But war seems to be lagging, and the incorporation of the *human person,* as an eventual subject of International General Consensual Law, looms in the distance. It shouldn´t be only States but individuals, and persons, this is the next challenging step. In the end, they are the victims and the perpetrators. The fallen ones and the responsible ones. And as in the past, some have faced justice so many have not. The practice of current Diplomacy is intimately connected with the network of Conventions, Treaties, Agreements, and a long list of instruments that have established a system of international cooperation and assistance in almost every field possible. Bilateralism has become a very limited way of action and relationships are carried out within blocks of nations and countries. And the actual war against corruption, since the original OECD Convention on Combating Bribery of Foreign Public Officials in International Business Transaction of 1997; the Palermo Convention of 2000, UNTOC and its three supplementary Protocols to the Rome Statute of 1998 that enter into force in 2002 and all the Special Tribunals and Hybrid Criminal Courts, established to bring to justice the perpetrators of crimes against humanity, the path to international criminal justice have been paved and the rewards are beginning to be seen and all this is possible because of the multilateral approach even in the administration of justice. Only a few follow the exclusivity of bilateral relationships which seems very limited and inadequate due to the lack of success by practicing this seemly outdated approach.

The current diplomatic tendency rests on what is being called named Trade Diplomacy in which the main focus falls on trade and commerce, relationship or interests are mainly measured on the levels of trade and commercial exchanges and the ability to build *trade agreements* largely grounded first on the agreements that later formed the WTO or the NAFTA model and on the more complex and encompassing ones —which include clauses on Human Rights and or Democracy and the building of institutions— that the European Union has signed with some countries or group of countries like the one in place with all the Central American nations. If development can be achieved through trading as a means to grow economies and generate wealth inside the less developed economies thus many other political and security —this particular one requires and demand other ways and different, unique alternatives to effectively generate success, so elusive on this extremely delicate matter— issues can be tackled as well, namely and principally that of illegal immigration. Both the United States and Europe face a daunting challenge to contain the influx of persons, being smuggled through borders by criminal organizations and drug traffickers using their corridors to introduce and bring *cheap labour* or foster a secret war, like the case of the silent invasion taking place in Western Europe. Traditional diplomacy isn´t properly equipped to face these issues. Nor were diplomats formed or educated to assess and interpret these new faces or the changing reality of the current situation. The road from International Law to Commerce and Trade can easily be bridged because the legal frameworks remain there, and the construction and expansion of the vast network follow certain patterns and is ruled and governed by principles common to International Trade practices and regulations of those rooted on International Public and Private Law its scopes and general principles.

The World of UNCITRAL and the WTO are not that different than the world of organizations dealing with Disarmament, Labour, or Health issues. They are bonded and grounded on a vision coming out of the development of the United Nations-following the mandate of its third preambular paragraph contained in the Charter— a construct that created and crafted a unique system that can function in a very diverse world, that of the Member States. Regional models are constructed under similar visions and models. But this is not a merry world by no means. There are outstanding issues that are in desperate need to be addressed. Maybe we have come to the moment to redress the great Conventions that rule International Relations. There are loopholes and the evolution of the legal systems of Member States and the practices followed by some major States are breaching some of the principles on which the general practices of the nowadays ways in which countries conduct their affairs vis-a-vis some International Organizations and even amongst themselves, call for a more in-depth re-definition of certain concepts and terms that we deem unequivocal and in the general practice face a lack of universal acceptance or a main and inclusive meaning that prevails over different interpretations. Terms such as *diplomatic agent, consular agent,* and others, fall constantly into controversies. This is just a mere example taken randomly, others face deeper and more complex questioning. Some of these concepts are of absolute and central importance to conducting international relations amongst the different States and the international community and their use in Covenants, Conventions, and Treaties needs to be uniform and their interpretation is one and not manifold, multifarious, or subject to confusion and false interpretations. Clarity is an absolute necessity.

A vast and open area and field of uncharted waters lie ahead. Calling on a Review Conference of a certain international instrument may seem a very far-fetched idea. But in the practice and implementation controversies arise from its applications that question the capacity and ability to comply with some of its clauses or even, objectives that become conflicting with the Private Laws of countries and in some cases, breed constitutional questions on the legality of its implementation. Most of these instruments have the so-called clauses that are generally and broadly referred to as *settlement of controversies or disputes* which are very difficult to apply and invoke, mechanisms that border on the limits where internal and international practice come into crossroads, and spatial-temporal conflicts between systems and laws. Controversies spring. These cases have been documented and even presented on International Tribunals to solve a dispute or controversy as the only jurisdictions recognized to come up with the proper solution. This can be very lengthy and costly, and many countries find severe difficulties to take on litigation that represent a huge investment of time and public resources that are scarce and can face public scrutiny on the legal grounds of such expenses. Administration limiting diplomacy is a very general trend worldwide in the present times.

We began with a reference to war and death and the profoundness that it implies for Diplomacy and the modern negotiator or so-called *agent* a term fully inadequate and outdated but used extensively, which cries out laud for redressing. Insufficient means fulfilment. And there are several examples of such terms or concepts that generate profound discord. Once Diplomacy was described as an art, in the renaissance sense of the word. Required specific skills and was practiced by an exclusive élite of individuals. We have witnessed the mutation of such ideas into the modern world of the public servant and the emergence of the *professional diplomat* a term that is beginning to lose its grasp and pregnant meaning. Maybe is time to retake the old notion of Diplomacy as an Art that deals with war and death, peace and life, the most essential aspects of human nature, and not any individual is prepared and formed to face such mounting tasks.

2
ON FOREIGN POLICY:
THROUGH THE EYES OF THE MARKETS?

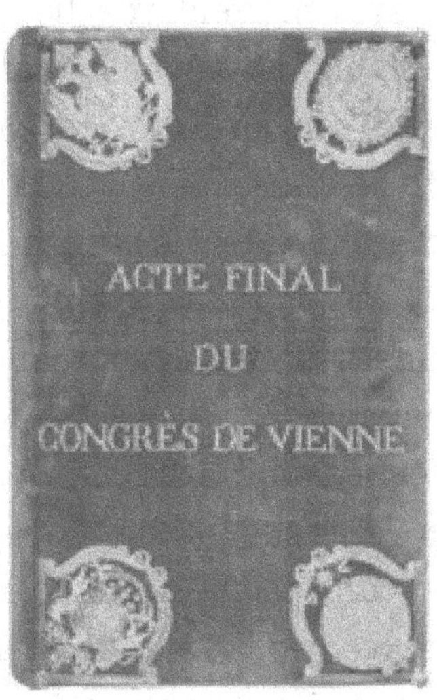

Foreign Policy nowadays is viewed by most major powers to achieve peace, universal justice, respect for human rights, and establish free trade worldwide. This cannot be disputed openly. But this is not the case. Achieving peace remains an elusive and perhaps unreachable dream, there are so many open conflicts that realistically and bluntly stated, lack the essential and fundamental will to be solved, exemplified in the fact that not always peace is the main objective to be reached. Quite the opposite. Diplomacy has had more to do with wars and the struggles to end them rather than establishing a durable and friendly peace. Although these aspirations remain very high on almost every foreign policy narrative there is another one that has been luring the backstage of the international main theatres namely, trade and commerce. After the Vienna Congress, conveyed to end the period of the Napoleonic wars, as is well-known, last-century diplomacy had to deal mainly with preventing and ending wars. The long list of failures is factually easy to establish. Foreign policy was constructed on the framework of General International Consensual Law —to follow the language of the ICJ— and sought to create a worldwide system to enforce the rule of law and create the institutions to fulfil this extraordinary conception. All nations of the world must behave according to the general principles of International Law to be a member of the "civilized nations of the world". This humanistic ideal is perhaps rooted in the practices of the so-called *renaissance diplomacy,* which pursue not only trade and commerce but also was conducted and carried out by enlightened individuals, the cases of the Vatican diplomacy and the Republic of Venice, whose diplomacy, as well as the other States on the Italian Peninsula of the times, the persona of the envoy, was as important as the messages or the objectives. Diplomacy saw the tragedy of human miseries and the worst of the human condition as well as the struggles to avoid the terrible wars and events since the times of *humanist diplomacy.*

If there would be a universal mantra for diplomacy that could be engulfed or encompassed in a word or concept, it must be *the defense of national interests.* It seems to be the general principle that rules state and individual behaviours in the realm of diplomacy. When an ambassador represented the Prince or the Ruler that had absolute power spoke on other terms and horizons. After the end of despotism and the emergence of democracy, envoys must take a whole new role and behave under a new set of realities. It is important to remember the practices of diplomacy amongst the nations on the Italian Peninsula. It was a sophisticated world run by elites that were not only aristocrats or politicians even bankers, speaking a language of enormous complexities, intricate and sometimes obscure twisted relationships, both on the personal level and *the name of the king* and needless to say that the Holy Seed was at the core and center of all this handling. The Vatican created and originated a special kind of diplomacy, which even in our actual world, is one of the leading diplomacies among the nations of the world. If one can read the Diaries of Johann Burchard, Liber Notarum, Pontificial Master of Ceremonies to Alexander VI, Rodrigo Borgia, and other Pontifices, the enormous level of importance attached to ceremonies, rituals, detailed accounts of the public meetings, reflect on the fact that diplomacy was beginning to come to light and the codification and registry of all the facts as well as the importance attached to detailed description and recompilation of what was said, achieved and ultimately agreed upon or not. Although trade, commerce, and banking were the main issues to be disputed, power and its struggles to rule, was without any kind of hesitation or doubt, the driving force either/or openly or by other ways and dark means.

We cannot describe here in detail the transit from nuncio, ambaxador, legato, oratore to the current and so-called resident diplomacy carried out by the modern Ambassador —or to be labeled as 'our-man in'— suffice to say that the nature of the message that originally, in the majority of the cases, was to convey to the other King, Prince or Ruler, became the intricate affair of state representation and execution of policies, public policies to use the language of the actual narrative. Nonetheless, the content of the messages, although the means and ways have changed dramatically, has not changed that much. From Banking, trade, and commerce to the construction of deals, current diplomacy is executed in a far more sophisticated fashion. If peace expresses itself cannot be in any other form than that of the construction of a more human, just, and free-of-opportunities culture for the Peoples of the world. And this is of course an ideal that is very far from being conquest. Poverty and lack of opportunities infest humanity and maintain a permanent state were maladies and diseases of the soul, walk rampantly in all corners of the world and we are not here, touching on the evils of war. They are deeper and must be addressed under a different scenario.

Here lies the reason why current diplomacy has to deal with and face the issues of trade and commerce to fulfil its internal meaning, the language of the *fight against poverty* and the *democratization of the civilized world*, and its duty to establish the rule of law and the respect for human rights, are not and cannot be empty language. To raise the conditions and standards of life in all nations is not merely an utopic speech it has to be achieved for humanity to come out of the maladies of poverty and malnutrition. This is the ultimate goal of dignified *trade and commerce or economical diplomacy*. To contribute to bringing about an end to the horrors of lack of opportunities and inhumane conditions in which most of the world population currently lags. Economic diplomacy cannot be an enterprise grounded on particular or corporative interests. Corporations are more powerful than the majority of medium to smaller economies which is the case in most countries and even internally in the larger industrialized world, corporations do not always behave with friendly intent toward the People where they operate. On the contrary. That is the obvious reason that current trade and commerce diplomacy must work together with corporations and the private sector but within the scope and guidance of public policies and a state grounded on the rule of law. Constitutional frameworks must provide the necessary horizon from which economical diplomacy operates and should be defined.

And now to the markets. Can Foreign Policy be seen, constructed, and formulated through the eyes of the markets or the scope provided by markets? If the *art of the deal* is going to transform current diplomacy into an efficient tool or an instrument for achieving economic success then something is deeply wrong, disturbed, and convoluted. Not everything is about making deals. There is the human rights agenda, the fight against poverty, bringing poorer nations out of their struggles with diseases and maladies. Markets are dangerous places. Build on the ability to predict the unpredictable behaviour of investors and their investments. Models based on statistical values or algorithms that read the future are grounded and based on probability. Statistical analysis is a probabilistic method. However accurate calculative thinking can become still carries embedded the mark of the risk. Is after all a gamble, essentially a game of fortunes and misfortunes. And the well-being and future of entire populations cannot be put at risk in a world of chance, mere chance, where probability rules. Is true that life is a dangerous place, we know that too well. But risks taken with the lives and expectations of innocent people have no place in the real *"art of the deal"*. Rationality prevails over risk. And Foreign Policy should never be rooted in chance and risks. Markets are for individuals or private corporations, built by individuals at the end. Nations speak to each other in the language of protection, protecting their interests has the meaning of protecting and safeguarding the lives and well-being of their citizens. Responsible states would never gamble with the future of their populations.

3
TUTELAJE O LIBERTAD EN LA POLÍTICA EXTERIOR

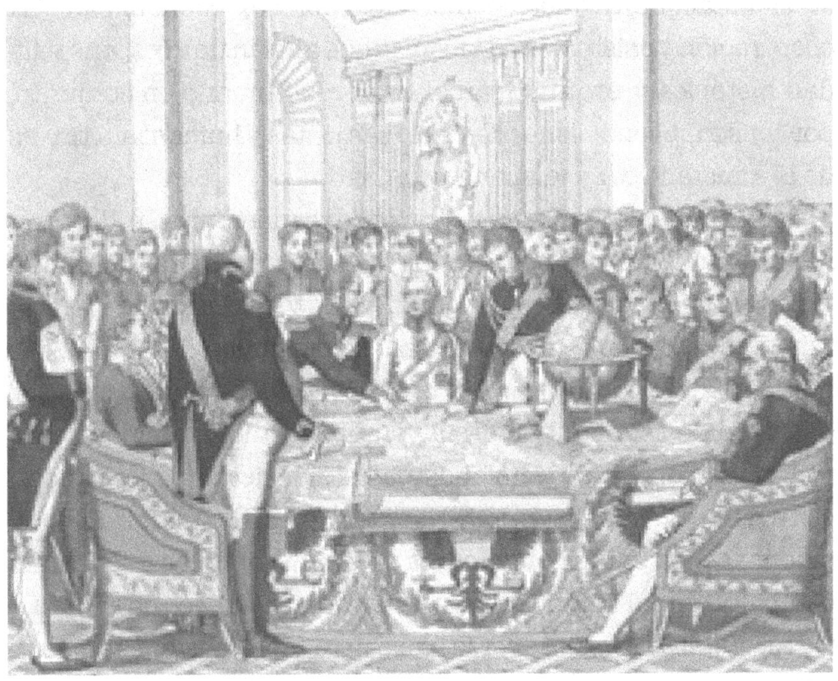

Como un viejo existencialista, siempre he creído y defendido el más radical y absoluto compromiso con la defensa de la libertad. Lo más fascinante del actual debate sobre el tutelaje y la defensa de la soberanía en la política exterior no es otra cosa que las condiciones bajo las cuales se ha generado y expandido, condición fundamental y originaria de cualquier controversia. Como un viejo diplomático, siempre he creído y defendido el más radical y absoluto respeto, como condición de cualquier práctica y relación, entre Estados y sobre todo, como hilo conductor, del comportamiento de los agentes diplomáticos, recurriendo aquí al lenguaje tradicional de la diplomacia. Las buenas formas no son solamente expresión de amistad, sino que el buen trato conlleva respeto y un expreso reconocimiento de la dignidad mutua, bajo la cual la amistad no solamente crece y se desarrolla, sino también se mantiene y conserva, a pesar de las asimetrías y diferencia, sean estas culturales, étnicas o incluso, económicas. La cooperación y asistencia son formas que alivian una responsabilidad histórica y profundizan el esfuerzo humano en conjunto, por construir condiciones de vida, más justas y humanas, a través de la amistad real y la buena vecindad.

Sabemos que las controversias se expanden, crecen, desarrollan profundidad y esta no ha sido la excepción, se da casi simultáneamente, con la tal vez originadora de todas las controversias vinculadas a la misma: la de las dimensiones del Estado, la metáfora del Estado *grande frente al reducido*, bien podría ser el origen de esta controversia ya que la cadena de metáforas utilizadas, sobre todo al defender la versión del "Estado grande", se revierte en la política exterior, aunque no de manera lineal, sino más bien estableciendo una contradicción, los defensores o impulsores del Estado grande, son también amigos de la tutelaridad, que si se avista de cerca, pareciera tener una línea congruente, o sea la *dependencia del afuera*, del otro, del mayor que nos llevaría de la mano, guiando y conduciendo, compañero del camino, acompañante indispensable, que *financia y tutela, apoya y coopera*, asiste y muestra su mano abierta de generosidad, aunque cierre el puño y apunte hacia cuál dirección caminaríamos. Los que se sitúan en la medida de la reducción, la menor presencia del Estado, *en favor de la acción humana y la libertad individual*, buscan pues libertad, independencia real, autonomía y respeto; demandan y no piden los derechos naturales, de los cuales emergerían todas las libertades y la justicia misma, el individuo como centro del *contrato social* y los acuerdos base de la convivencia, tanto hacia adentro como hacia afuera. Una amistad construida y cimentada en la igualdad y sobre todo, en una coexistencia respetuosa y abierta. Las metáforas, que se ocultan no muy bien, y las cuales subyacen en el centro de esta controversia, son muy antiguas y provienen de concepciones y disputas muy viejas y originarias.

Una de las características más notorias, cuando una controversia se hace pública, es el uso de lenguajes que recurren a metáforas de agresión, cargadas de códigos *ideologizados*, articulados desde posiciones irreductibles, cuasi trincheras, desde las que se lanzan una serie de conceptos-piedras, dardos, ataques e incluso hasta insultos y descalificaciones, en el mejor estilo troll de las redes sociales, portador de lenguajes absolutamente agresivos y claramente transformados en insultos. La cuestión es que en este caso hay una red de metáforas que están en pie desde hace mucho tiempo, fecha históricas —el 54 es el año del Apocalipsis guatemalteco, cuando todo se derrumbó, y la catástrofe total terminó con la pureza y la inocencia—, frases comunes, incluso una pseudo erudición económica, apela a términos como *cambio de modelo*, o el antiguo lenguaje de las ciencias sociales de los años setenta: subdesarrollo, colonialismo, dependencia, términos estos que tenían un origen formal en unas teorías sociales que defendían una posición y visión determinada. Claro, hoy día, ya se usan muy poco y han sido substituidos por otros: globalización, seguridad, que se ha vuelto una categoría extrema y en las relaciones internacionales ha incluso desplazado al lenguaje económico y comercial. Notablemente dentro de este complejo enjambre de terminología nada ha superado todavía a la cuestión más sensible, el tema que nos ocupa: podemos sostener relaciones de respeto y amistad, cuando evidentemente la presencia y ayuda no solamente son fundamentales, sino que implican invitaciones a conceder y permitir el acceso a espacios, que siempre fueron cerrados y propios, exclusivos, del país anfitrión, en este caso el nuestro. Si se ve el mundo desde afuera, esta controversia no solo es ficticia, sino plenamente innecesaria. Las condiciones actuales hablan de una constante e inevitable integración y cooperación. El mundo es cada vez más abierto y global. Esta es una realidad aplastante. La respuesta romántica: somos capaces por nosotros mismos, no vamos a aceptar intromisiones, debemos alejarnos de las formas nuevas de neocolonialismo o neoimperialismo. Esto pareciera perder su capacidad de respuesta, al convertirse en una forma de neonacionalismo. La cosa vuelve a ser de formas y buenas maneras. Lo que tal vez extrañamos es que la práctica de la diplomacia debería conservar su condición de *"ars"* y sobre todo, entre amigos, seguir una discreción y prudencia, que al abandonar las formas clásicas, cae en una muy desafortunada imposición y casi de agresión, la cual es leída como *intervención y amenaza*. Si sucede hay formas de conjurarla. Lo deseable es evitarla aunque también se la puede enfrentar. La realidad es que nadie la desea; no encontraremos ningún caso —salvo cuando las confrontaciones son abiertas y preventivas, incluso—, donde entre amigos auténticos, se desee deliberadamente dialogar a través del ataque y de la confrontación directa. Las buenas formas y la amistad superan las diferencias, si estas son reales y genuinas.

El mayor problema parece residir en el asunto del traslado de los lenguajes. La diplomacia tiene su propio lenguaje. El caso es que los temas vinculados a la misma, especialmente en nuestros países, donde las agendas de cooperación y asistencia tienen y toman formas vinculadas a otros lenguajes; o dicho de otra manera, las disciplinas que tienen principalmente por ocupación estas actividades, más ligadas a los lenguajes de las ciencias sociales o la economía, introducen, o han venido introduciendo, en el dominio histórico-tradicional, del quehacer diplomático, formas de expresión y conceptualización que son ajenas al lenguaje comúnmente empleado por los agentes diplomáticos. Hemos visto incluso emerger pseudo expertos en temas fiscales, intentando conducir la Política Exterior. Por supuesto que esto generará conflictos, ya que se instalan otras controversias existentes dentro del dominio de la diplomacia. Al estar la Política Exterior en proceso de transición y modificación, y los lenguajes del Derecho Internacional bajo todas sus formas, el Derecho Diplomático está siendo abandonado o puesto en un plano de menor relevancia, en favor de otros o tal vez adoptándolos e incorporándolos. Allí surgen y emanan las controversias.

La diplomacia y su lenguaje tienen un límite y no se le debe desbordar. Hay una condición única y especial en la conducción de los asuntos diplomáticos, por tratarse en su mayoría de cuestiones de Estado, que no deben estar ligadas a la inmediatez o al hic et nunc. La urgencia es dominio de la política. La cuestión fundamental gira en torno a todo aquello, ante lo cual hay que tomarse pausas y sobre todo, largos y complejos procesos de consulta, consultas reservadas. En algunos casos, esa es la naturaleza de la diplomacia. La enorme avalancha de comentaristas y analistas, aquí y afuera, que opinan y escriben de Política Exterior, es sana y deseable. Ellos opinan a través de los medios escritos, digitales, hablados, televisivos o incluso la radio, que en Guatemala han tomado una importancia particular y que muchos celebramos. Decía, pues, que todo ese interés es más que natural e incluso bienvenido, no es limitable y no se debe, bajo ninguna circunstancia, intentar limitarlo. Por supuesto que sobre todo hoy en día, en las llamadas *"redes sociales"* hay una explosión de agresión y furia, descalificación e incluso insulto y diatriba. Ese es un fenómeno que escapa al dominio, que nos ocupa, que es más bien típico de la internet y afecta otros dominios y realidades humanas. Poco puede hacerse y decirse; tal vez una invocación a la automoderación, al control y al respeto, ante un fenómeno universal, sencillamente. Aunque la resignación no es válida, oponérsele puede resultar una tarea casi imposible. En todo caso es una batalla a librarse, en otras latitudes y lugares.

La presente controversia se ha gestado a partir del choque de realidades y concepciones políticas enfrentadas, y es resultado de una mayor y que engloba a la misma. La discusión sobre si es oportuno o no invocar el artículo 41 de la CVRD no es nueva y sucede constantemente. La cuestión está en la manera cómo se hace y cómo se le llama a la discusión. No es correcto afirmar que Guatemala no tiene una tradición diplomática, eso sencillamente no es verdad. Sí la hay y larga. Tiene sus particularidades y su historia. La Cancillería actual es el resultado de una historicidad y de una práctica bastante larga. Sus detractores muchas veces están escondidos en agendas personales o sencillamente en posturas políticas, lo cual pude ser profundamente negativo, puesto que si en algo deberíamos mantener y sostener una sólida y congruente actitud y compromiso, es en esta materia, dado que los temas de la agenda son de interés nacional y no partidario. Guatemala, como un país pequeño, debería unificar una posición sostenida y a largo plazo, formulando una Política Exterior consensuada, y construir unos acuerdos estables y permanentes; defender principios y no individualidades, siendo la única manera con que podremos generar los beneficios necesarios y buscados. Es tiempo de elaborar un gran acuerdo en esta materia y poder mantenernos, dentro de la consecuencia y continuidad, lo que nos hará ser respetados y reconocidos y esto solo es factible a través de una unificación alrededor de principios universalmente aceptados.

El lenguaje unificador que jugó en el pasado el Derecho Internacional Consensuado, como el lenguaje de una Política Exterior, requiere de una complementación, con otros lenguajes, que han irrumpido, para quedarse, en este dominio. Las agendas de seguridad y comercio exterior pueden ser esos nuevos lenguajes unificadores. Tal vez la presente controversia, si depara algo además de la confrontación, sutil o no, directa o indirecta, sin considerar el alcance y el daño generado por la misma, puede servir para que nos planteemos la posibilidad de construir una Política Exterior consensuada. Claro que entiendo y veo el argumento constitucional sobre la responsabilidad exclusiva del Presidente y de la ejecución obligatoria de la Cancillería; sin embargo, eso no obsta para que después de un proceso amplio de consultas incluyentes; después de intentar la construcción de un gran acuerdo, un auténtico proceso de acción comunicativa, como diríamos siguiendo a Habermas, tal vez se pueda arribar a un consenso nacional y Guatemala se podría presentar, ante el mundo y la comunidad internacional, amigos y demás, con una Política Exterior emergida del más profundo consenso. Y como una sociedad tan herida como la nuestra, claramente necesita esto, que podría beneficiar a todos. ¿Será acaso, un reto o un desafío imposible?

4
ON THE NORTHERN TRIANGLE CONTROVERSY: A NON-ALGORITHMIC RESOLUTION

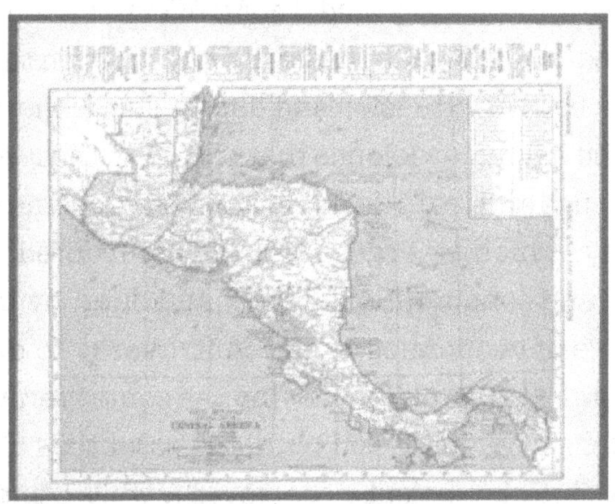

On the Northern Triangle Controversy: A non-algorithmic resolution

The Central American So-called Northern Triangle namely, Guatemala, El Salvador, and Honduras, has been depicted as one of the most dangerous and violent regions in the world. International organizations, human rights groups, politicians, and even churches and other religious entities and organizations, not to mention journalists or nowadays identified as *analysts* and some members of Academia from different universities local and abroad, contribute extensively to this narrative. From social scientists to politicians, everyone wants to provide an answer and a solution or resolution to this enormously complex controversy. If we could see through the eyes and horizon of the Theory of controversies and more precisely call on Marcelo Dascal's models to understand controversies, we should face it following certain principles which are widely used and are also attributable to Daskal's theories on this field. On his epistemic and Pragmatics, we can differentiate between strategical and tactical controversies, but this leads us to certain rules that can be applied to study and put forward an alternative to this cruel and ever-expanding problem.

According to Dascal's model controversies such as this one *doesn't remain confined to the initial question*, on the contrary, they spread both in extension and depth. This is the case for the origins of the extreme violence that occurs in the region, on the matter of drugs and trafficking we have an open and expanding controversy, which emerges from the confronted visions, on production and consumption, supply and offer, by introducing the language of economics in the controversy to explain it, a serious mistake takes place, viewing the controversy on purely economic terms confuses and blurs the essentials of its origins and expansion. This particular controversy while being addressed by a non-efficient language cause not only blurriness but contributes to hiding the other sides of this gigantic tragedy, that of the individual and the families of the consumers who fail or neglect to emphasize that which must be at the center of the debate: the human persona and the addiction to which falls victim and is preyed upon by all the individuals marketing or selling or simply targeting costumers. This is not an economic problem it is first a human tragedy.

The expansion of the controversy entails the questioning of the factual data, research methods, and the general framework or *conceptual presuppositions* surrounding the analytics of this *narrative*. Statistical data to support the general affirmation of the embedded violence, highly questionable figures that are extremely hard to collect and more importantly, to seriously trust; secondly, when we come to the methods, on a very harsh environment, data pertaining to drug trafficking actual seizure of drugs, consumption at the place of destiny is very hard to obtain, if it can be tracked or established how and where the trafficking ends, constitutes a fundamental element in order to fully comprehend the real construction of *the road of violence*, groups that deal with or are involved in this type of violence, act under extreme conditions, inner rules and the *culture* around so called *Maras* or gangs are almost impenetrable, very little do we know about their secretive organizations or ways, we mainly see what they want us to witness, their rage and cruelty exercised to the maximum limits, that is the essential reason it is so difficult to study and comprehend how they operate, we know about the origins but cannot grasp the internal construction; cold numbers won't give us the answers we need.

A hermeneutical circle is here created. Its interpretation, to borrow a not *"descaling"* term, deconstruction of the controversy requires an interpretation of all the elements that emerge from its expansion. But an empirical approach won't suffice to interpret a phenomenon inherent to human nature. By signalling out The Northern Triangle as the "most violent" region in the world, a value judgment is made, and a *"conceptual presupposition"* is created solely on the coldness of numbers and data. The interpretation of human violence is fundamentally and essentially linked to other factors of the human mystery that defy a quantitate model thus the interpretation becomes not only crucial but also must be –and here appealing to a Husserlian old conception– without pre-judgment or total lack of it. The political element attached to the controversy deviates from the proper interpretation, the hermeneutics is therefore tinted and falls under the prejudices coming from a certain position beforehand present. Here the caution on the use of language becomes even more central. Ideological horizons influence the dominant narrative creating a pre-conceptual malady that darkness the comprehension and correct hermeneutics of the causes of the controversy.

The openness of the controversy or its public condition, the constant expansion, and its permanent deepening demands responding at all levels. The urgency to find a solution involves actors from different areas and of course in the countries of the Triangle a legion of external influences from foreign governments to other parties, sometimes dark groups, are unequivocally involved in the origins, spread, and the possible solution or resolution of the controversy. There is not one cause for this violence, killings, and other gang-related acts of extreme rage and overpowering cruelty. Poverty does not provide the soil from where this type of irrationality blooms. In many cases, we witness rituality and revenge. Violence is exercised to create and impose fear, complete impotence, and pain. Suffering has become an everyday event amongst many humble and desperate people. So, they flee. Seek and travel to Utopia. The quest for lost hope forces desperate young people to initiate an impossible journey to the land of opportunities. And the contradiction settles in a region where immense wealth and the lack of hope and means walk side by side. And so far, the answer has been a corrupt political system that screams for change. All this takes place while the controversy presents itself in openness.

Closure or resolution, the solution of a discussion, a public discussion where everybody takes part. The events of last year that trigger the massive demonstrations in Guatemala that toppled or forced the resignation of the elected President and Vice-president due to extensive corruption and an investigation generated by a United Nations Commission established in Guatemala to investigate so-called impact cases, produced in collaboration with the office of the Attorney General (Fiscal

General) and other nations that contribute funding and other resources, led by the United State, generated the means to solve the controversy. Brought hopes inside the country and into the whole Triangle —however conflicting the use of this terminology might be and its usance probably should be substituted for a fresher and more neutral term— but these are only the first steps. A deeper investigation must follow, and special cases not only must fulfil and comply with due process but the judiciary and the correct enforcement of the Constitution are the only alternatives to find an elusive and evasive non-algorithmic resolution to this terrible controversy that has engulfed countries of the so-called Northern Triangle in this never-ending cycle and circle of ritual rage and violence. The language of weapons and death must be stopped to give way to conditions that might bring back hope to the suffering of millions of people in this extra-ordinary region of the world.

5
EL RETORNO A LAS CIUDADES AMURALLADAS Y LA TRAGEDIA DE LOS CAMINANTES DEL DESIERTO

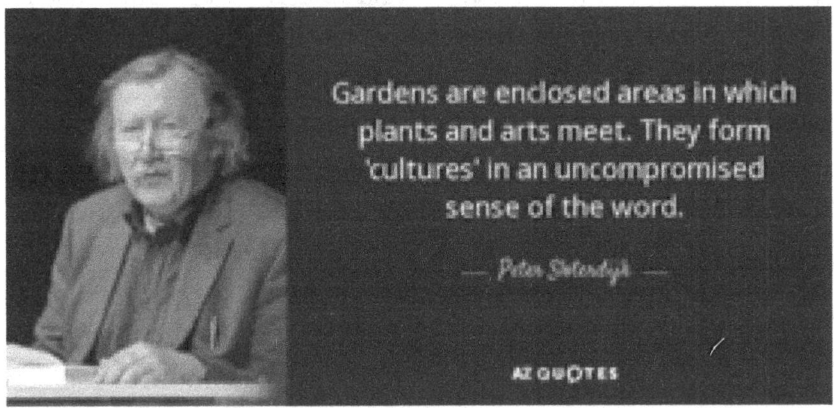

Cuando, en el segundo volumen de Sphären, Globos, Peter Sloterdyk desde la llamada Esferología, en su forma macroesferológica, nos describe las ciudades amuralladas, sus orígenes y posteriores mutaciones, una de las más evidentes causas de su establecimiento era la seguridad de sus habitantes; seguridad allí entendida como defensa. Ninguna ciudad del mundo antiguo o del más reciente pudo pensarse con la inmunidad o el derecho innato a la no agresión. No hace mucho vimos los ataques a Londres y la destrucción de Berlín, sin olvidar la ocupación de París y, más recientemente, hemos visto la destrucción de auténticas joyas de la historia humana: Aleppo, por citar una tragedia inmensa, que aún no termina del todo; y Bagdad, una de las más relevantes ciudades del mundo, aun está sumergida en una guerra interminable. Por no traer a cuenta Jerusalén, una ciudad totalmente única, por tantísimas razones, aquí imposibles de mencionar.

Las ciudades cruzadas del medioevo, amuralladas, cayeron una por una, sucumbieron a sitios de ejércitos inmensos y en condiciones innombrables. Jerusalén tampoco, con sus murallas, no pudo sobrevivir al cerco de Saladino. La misma Roma se desmoronó al final, aunque de manera lenta y agónica. Constantinopla no fue capaz de resistir a los otomanos. Y el mismo Vaticano —el más notable caso de una ciudad-estado amurallada— sufrió durante siglos un acoso constante e invasiones continuadas. Su sobrevivencia se vio amenazada durante varios momentos de su extraordinaria historia. Sin embargo, Washington, al contrario, es y ha sido siempre una ciudad sin murallas. Los que la han visitado, saben bien de su belleza visual, complejidad y misterio de su magnífica arquitectura, llena de símbolos y homenajes físicos a las grandes personalidades y guerreros de la libertad. De esa libertad abierta que la ha caracterizado. Washington es distinta, no fue una ciudad amurallada, no comparte eso con otras históricas ciudades, que sí lo han sido. En América Latina casi no hubo ni hay ciudades amuralladas, aunque un ejemplo de su presencia pudiera encontrarse en La Habana. Por eso siempre nos sumamos, con mucha facilidad, a las causas de la apertura y la fraternidad. Sabemos bien de los exilios y los retornos. Algunos han construido repeticiones de sí mismos y sus ciudades, en otras partes, siempre llevando con ellos, la alegría y la celebración de eso que Sloterdyk llama *vivir es crear esferas*.

Además del argumento de la seguridad, las ciudades amuralladas sufrieron procesos de higienización. La arqueología de las enfermedades, plagas, epidemias, es muy abundante, dada su condición monádica, su capacidad de intercomunicación era muy pequeña. La resistencia a lo ajeno, no propio, extraño, por ende al establecimiento del muro, dominaron el mundo de las ciudades amuralladas. Lo curioso es que el Imperio Romano no estaba amurallado. Claro que se conoce la versión del *muro de*

Adriano, para protegerse o defenderse de los ataques de los habitantes originarios, con los cuales no solamente se produjo un choque de religiones y culturas, sino una guerra de expulsión del ocupante-invasor. Los resultados son conocidos; sin embargo, los romanos actuaron como los primeros grandes globalizadores. Su expansionismo llevaba consigo una forma de civilización, y terminó en un complejísimo y muy largo proceso de incorporación y de hacerse-uno, los romanos instalaron un mundo y posteriormente lo habitaron todos aquellos que lo destruyeron. Se hicieron "uno", en ese mundo deparado y en esa tierra instalada. La arqueología de la intersubjetividad monádica se rompe, con la expansión globalizadora y la incorporación de lo ajeno como propio y que se transforma en lo ya no extraño. Las fuerzas de la globalización o universalización del Imperio terminan por fragmentarlo y al final, sucumbe ante esa inmensa ola, invasora y renovadora, introducida por todo aquello, contra lo que se defendió. Sloterdyk sostiene que son los griegos al reflexionar sobre la esfera quienes generan la globalización. La esfera es el símbolo clásico de la perfección. Allí empieza el camino de la esferología o teoría de las esferas.

Hoy en día se está instalando una controversia muy particular. Una controversia global que en realidad se ha originado hace algún tiempo, y está tomando características asombrosas. Desde su origen, transporta elementos bastante conocidos. Su globalidad obliga a abordarla tal vez no solamente desde su lenguaje, sino más bien desde su historia, porque como muchas controversias, oculta otras dentro de sí misma. Arriba anotábamos la cuestión de las ciudades amuralladas. Algunas de esas murallas aún subsisten, parcialmente o mimetizadas en fragmentos. Hay murallas o sus residuos de las antiguas, incluso geográficamente identificables, ubicables. Estados amurallados. Encerrados y cerrados es una forma del amurallamiento, producto de una reacción contundente ante la apertura. Las sociedades abiertas no subsisten, ni tampoco sobreviven, dentro de las ciudades amuralladas. Son esencialmente antagónicas. El problema subyace en la ilusión de una supuesta amenaza externa vista como agresión, ante la cual hay que defenderse. La amenaza se percibe como extrema y radical, organizada y deliberada, bajo formas demográficas e incluso culturales; y de allí que el fenómeno migratorio sea de una importancia global. La migración, en su complejidad, no es única y menos aún tiene una sola forma. No existe algo así como una migración unidimensional. Los fenómenos que vemos en Europa no son similares a los que vemos en el continente americano.

Los caminos de las migraciones son trágicos y llenos de profundos conflictos. Probablemente el regreso a las ciudades amuralladas es una reacción ante la incertidumbre y el miedo, generados desde perspectivas políticas contradictorias. Los imperios han sido multidimensionales siempre. Lo fue Roma y lo fue el Imperio Británico, la idea misma del "imperio", está ligada a la multidimensionalidad, es decir, a la apertura y expansión, así como la integración y asimilación de todo lo que es diverso. Son los encuentros, a veces, choques agresivos, inicialmente concebidos como conquistas militares, que no eran sostenibles ni perdurarían, sin la compañía de un fenómeno civilizador, cultural o de acercamiento. Microesferas y macroesferas. Para que los imperios perduraran se necesitaba del establecimiento, de comunidades monádicas. Solamente se explican así, ya que las resistencias internas siempre se mantuvieron. Amurallarse deliberadamente implica también autoaislarse. Las eclosiones imperiales son síntomas de temores atávicos antiguos, que retornan bajo nuevas formas. El occidente en general nunca se amuralló. Si la idea de la modernidad conserva algún sentido de origen, es todo lo contrario al amurallamiento. La modernidad puso fin a las ciudades amuralladas. El descubrimiento de los mundos nuevos, la expansión de la ciencia, del conocimiento, la salida interna hacia un exterior desconocido, ignoto y profundo, llevaron a la modernidad a una revolución y renovación asombrosa.

De la Taxonomía de von Linné a los viajes de Alexander von Humboldt a la América Latina, es verdad que hay un lado salvaje y barbárico de la modernidad y uno muy oscuro al desplegarse el comercio global, la esclavitud. Es una sombra que determinó los horrores de la modernidad, y las voces que se levantaron para detenerla y frenarla no fueron demasiado contundentes, hasta que libró su última guerra en los Estados Unidos. Su mutación, en formas de intolerancia y racismo, siguieron campeando en la Europa de las grandes guerras, así como en Asia, donde también se produjo una continuación de esas mismas formas de agresión y desprecio hacia lo diferente. En las guerras asiáticas se expandieron las murallas y fue con altísimo costo que se lograron frenar las murallas del odio y del desprecio.

Es absolutamente impensable que los caminantes del desierto busquen llevar el odio y la agresión hacia un mundo que ven como la única esperanza y el sueño de una Arcadia que nunca tuvieron, que les negaron. Nunca fueron o han sido partes de una prosperidad reservada, cerrada y generada de forma insuficiente. Tradicionalmente a los caminantes del desierto se les reconoce como aquellos que buscan refugio o santuario. Las prácticas humanas y éticas del Occidente, rico y civilizado, han sido extender la mano a los que buscan santuario, acogerlos y ayudarlos a ponerse en pie, a sanar las heridas del paso por el desierto. Es lo que nos ha hecho humanizadores y humanos.

6
CONTINUIDAD O EXCLUSIVISMO EN LA POLÍTICA EXTERIOR GUATEMALTECA: APERTURA O CLAUSURA

Al bajar de las montañas de Virginia al mar, no me imaginé ni esperé encontrarme con la inmediatez de un tema que me es tan cercano, ante lo cual no pude permanecer en silencio, al seguir de cerca y bajo la intimidad, el debate público sobre la continuidad o no de algunos miembros del gabinete del actual gobierno de transición y algunos que eran parte del gobierno Pérez Molina, por llamarlo de alguna de manera. Escuché, como suelo hacer, con bastante constancia, el programa "A Primera Hora", que me acerca a Guatemala, donde los presidentes Vinicio Cerezo, Álvaro Colom y el vicepresidente y también Canciller Eduardo Stein, opinaban sobre el tema del gabinete del presidente electo Jimmy Morales.

Me llamó mucho la atención la propuesta pública y abierta del presidente Cerezo sobre la continuidad y confirmación de miembros del actual gabinete del gobierno de transición y, en especial, del Canciller Carlos Raúl Morales. La memoria me acompaña en este complicado tema. El presidente Cerezo se enfrentó al mismo dilema: confirmar o no al Canciller de ese momento, Fernando Andrade Díaz-Duran, quien venía de realizar una de las gestiones más impresionantes y respetadas, en difícil y complejo momento: el diseño de la llamada "política de neutralidad activa", que no solo llevó a una exitosa transición democrática interna, sino que nos permitió participar nuevamente, como actores dentro de los países civilizados del mundo, para usar el lenguaje del Estatuto de la Corte Internacional de Justicia.

El presidente Cerezo hizo lo correcto. Optó por mantener el principio y la práctica. Nombró un nuevo Canciller, el ilustre jurista licenciado Mario Quiñónez Amézqueta, y nombró Embajador en el Exterior a Fernando Andrade Díaz-Duran, quien sirvió y continuó su notable carrera diplomática como Embajador ante la OEA y en Naciones Unidas, presidiendo en su momento el Consejo Permanente y también el Grupo de los 77. La política exterior es cuestión, entre otras cosas, no solo de un grupo de personas preparadas y calificadas, sino de unos principios y unas concepciones que Guatemala necesitaba, con gran urgencia, en este momento. Me tocó servir bajo el Canciller Andrade Díaz-Duran y posteriormente bajo el Canciller Quiñónez Amézquita. Recuerdo muy bien sentir y haber recibido; contribuir a los resultados de la aplicación de una política exterior basada en principios y concepciones rectoras. Por ejemplo, pude ganar elecciones en lo multilateral. Mientras servía en Viena, fui designado como uno de los vicepresidentes de la Conferencia de Naciones Unidas para la Segunda Convención del Derecho de los Tratados; gané una elección en la Asamblea General de la AIEA y nos sentamos en la Junta de Gobernadores de la Agencia. Esos beneficios se trasladaron inmediatamente a la administración del presidente Cerezo, para quien serví en Bolivia y posteriormente ante la Confederación Helvética.

Hubo pues continuidad de una concepción, ejecutada por unos agentes diplomáticos, que éramos parte de una generación que salió a defender a Guatemala, a narrar y relatar una historia distinta de la que se vendía en aquellos durísimos años. Logramos hacerlo. Los logros en Viena y en otras capitales así lo demostraron. Hubo pues continuidad con apertura bajo el presidente Cerezo. Hoy día la Cancillería actual es totalmente distinta a la de aquellos años. Serví bajo el presidente Álvaro Arzú y el Canciller Eduardo Stein, en Israel y en Barbados. Fueron años dorados para el servicio exterior también. Empezamos a movernos hacia una diplomacia comercial. Provengo de una generación que concebía y practicaba la diplomacia bajo el hilo conductor del Derecho Internacional, y como muchos de mis colegas y amigos, de esa y otras generaciones, nos movían ideas, ideales y grandes concepciones.

Hoy el peso es distinto. Nosotros recibimos con entusiasmo la noción de la promoción de inversiones, búsqueda y construcción de acuerdos comerciales, apertura de mercados, en fin, caminábamos hacia una *normalización*, palabra que se empezó a usar en esos y años y que no me gustaba nada, instalaba la dialéctica anormalidad/normalidad, lo hecho antes era pues "anormal", extraordinario, único e irrepetible. Había que *normalizar*, y así se hizo. La diplomacia comercial se fue introduciendo lentamente, y actualmente es irrenunciable, nuclea la política exterior por todas partes, y no podemos ser la excepción. Complementa y expande nuestra visión internacionalista, incorpora el elemento fundamental de las relaciones internacionales actuales. Bajo el vicepresidente Stein y el Canciller Gert Rosenthal, serví en Cancillería, diseñamos y llevamos adelante negociaciones con Belize, concluimos el Acuerdo Especial. Pocos saben que fui el jefe negociador de ese acuerdo y nuevamente, con un equipo de ilustres guatemaltecos, pues no es trabajo de una persona, aquí mis recuerdos, no sólo para el Canciller Rosenthal, sino para la Canciller Marithza Ruiz de Vielman, los embajadores Rolando Palomo, Efraín Aguilera, el ilustre jurista Rubén Contreras, quien nos acompaña desde otros mundos y cuyos conocimientos y talentos fueron esenciales e invaluables, y qué decir del Dr. Francisco Villagrán Kramer, alma de nuestra comisión y delegaciones negociadoras, cuyos aportes son francamente fundamentales; y, especialmente a Gustavo Orellana, quien caminó conmigo hasta el final en ese terrible andar que fue construir y concluir ese acuerdo con Belize.

Aquí nuevamente se optó por la continuidad de los principios, la idea rectora era someter el Diferendo histórico ante la jurisdicción de la Corte Internacional de Justicia, y el presidente Colom y el Canciller Haroldo Rodas así lo comprendieron. No solo concluimos la negociación, el Acuerdo se firmó en Washington, y el Secretario General de la OEA firmó como Testigo de Honor. Me dolió muchísimo no participar en la ceremonia de la firma del mismo, después de años de luchar y trabajar incansablemente en su diseño y su construcción. Siempre he preferido no hablar de ello, considero es un asunto de Estado y debemos respetar las reservas, que en su momento se recomendaran, para no complicar un proceso delicado y cuyas dimensiones históricas trascienden las de un individuo. Nuevamente prevaleció el gran principio, servir los siguientes cuatro años, en Países Bajos continuando la diplomacia jurídica ante la Corte como continuidad de ese horizonte guía. Prevalecieron las ideas y las concepciones. No participé en el Gobierno Pérez Molina; más bien, libré una compleja batalla judicial que me mantuvo alejado de una administración que le dio la espalda a los principios, por los que trabajamos y luchamos tantos años.

Mi refugio fueron las montañas de Virginia, donde volví a mis actividades intelectuales y académicas, seguí muy de cerca lo que pasaba y he sido crítico de lo que ha sucedido. El tránsito de los principios a la hegemonía de las personalidades, no lo comparto. Este relato pretende reflexionar sobre eso precisamente. No se trata de la prevalencia de la administración sobre la práctica diplomática real. Hemos caído en un abismo complejo. La obsesión por la administración correcta de los recursos públicos ha generado una fiscalización constante y profunda, lo cual es correcto incuestionablemente; sin embargo, debemos recuperar el horizonte de los grandes principios, perseguir ideales, y ese es trabajo de muchos. Lo que debe permanecer es eso: las visiones y las grandes concepciones. Guatemala necesita eso en este momento, basta con preguntar y obtendrán respuestas. El presidente Morales puede preguntar y abrirse a los ideales y recuperar las grandes concepciones más allá de las personas o de la hegemonía de unos pocos. Pregunte, Presidente, y se sorprenderá como si encontrara otras respuestas, que le van a asombrar.

CHAPTER III
BOOKS AND AUTHORS

1
JOHN BOLTON'S PRESENCE IN THE ROOM

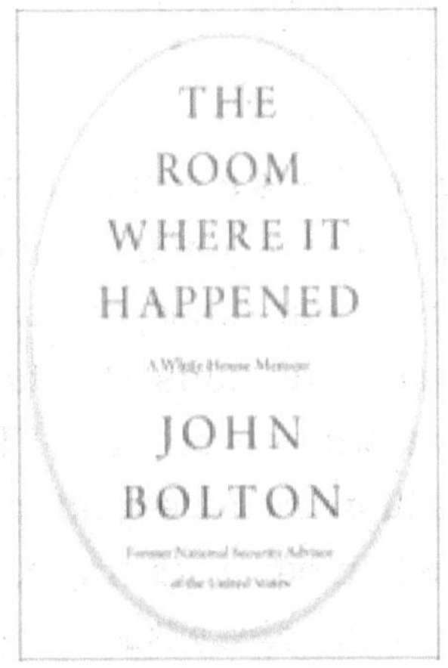

John Bolton's book "The Room where it Happened". A colossal clash of narcissism, minds and rude power. Just recently published by Simon & Schuster, New York, 2020

A controversy is installed. The book is very long. Detailed and carefully, very carefully crafted and built. Its internal and external architecture is of the finest and extremely well-designed and carry out, executed, and implemented. It is also very obvious from scratch, the mere beginning, that as soon or even before, Bolton entered the White House to assume his position as National Security Adviser, the book and the process of writing it down and structuring its content, came along and walked with him through every step, every meeting and consultation, mission abroad, traveling, phone calls and the rest, Bolton knew exactly and precisely that he was simultaneously writing a book, memoirs —although that is its subtitle— is not the correct term to refer to this book, although is widely and extensively employed when addressing this genre. Former Cabinet Secretaries and others have come up with examples of such genre, from Secretaries of State to others, paid handsomely to cultivate this literature trend or cynically worded, extract important figures to what was *a service to the country*. Not a beautiful image to be reckoned with. Questionable to say the least.

In essence, the book tells a story about how two forms of narcissism collide. On one side you have one of the most famous cases of narcissism in recent times, one that includes not only the classic trademarks but adds the forms, mutations, or additions, of the *billionaire's narcissism*. The debate about whether he is or is not a billionaire is redundant, he is an incredibly wealthy individual, when campaigning for the nomination of the Democratic Party, billionaire without any sort of doubt, Mike Bloomberg, began to draw the attention of many but one came from a fellow New Yorker who happens to live at Pennsylvania Avenue, of course nicknaming or branding another New Yorker was an irresistible temptation, so on came Mini Mike. Naming names or using a well-cultivated ability to predicate on degrading forms of colloquial language is a skill that he has mastered throughout the years and with remarkable outcomes. Nonetheless.

So came the reply. While the liberal media enjoyed the clash of the wealthy New Yorkers, someone casually mentioned in a poorly thought commentary, that an election between two billionaires might not be appealing or interesting to the American people, Bloomberg countered without hesitation whatsoever: *this will never be a contest between two billionaires because there's only one in the running*. He hit The President where it hurts the most and Bloomberg knew he was inflicting pain. Narcissistic egos have a fragile side and can be exploited. This current clash is of another type of narcissism displaying other aspects of the complexities involved here. The wealthy and successful one, in almost all levels of life, surrounded by beauty, elegance, and a combination of celebrity and politician, who succeeded where even he, thought wasn't possible. On the other side an Ivy Leaguer, reputed litigator, diplomat, and overall, a conservative very serious intellectual capable of understanding all the nuances of international relations, skilled negotiator, and with a vast knowledge not only of the majority of foreign leaders, with some of them even on a first name basis, not to say with —this is his horrible wording— *the sherpas* an analogy to Himalayan carriers that are the ones who know the roads and weather conditions and serve as *guides* and *helpers* of those who dare to take the adventure of the climb. So the world of foreign relations is not only inhabited by those who close de deals and take photos, there's an abundance of them at the end of the book, and of course, the lesser ones, those who carry the documents, draft them in a seemly never-ending bara rash of changes, re-drafting, additions, modifications, alterations, those who talk with their counterparts permanently and many times are sent, silently or even secretly, to discuss proposal, pre-proposal and last minute changes, *the Sherpas* that at the end put the final documents at the table for the final re-check and signature. Agreement and deals. This is so, another kind of narcissism, the one that stems from the mind and intellect. The arrogance of the superior and super-informed individual versus the adventurous politician/celebrity.

Probably after the Oedipus myth, the Narcissus one is the best-known and studied. It has created an incredible amount of literature and of course, influenced and even, gave birth, to one of the most important aspects of psychoanalysis and the different tendencies derived from the original, Freudian conformations. It's well documented that Paul Näcke (1899) was the first to introduce the term in its psychological or psychoanalytical shapes and forms. Nowadays the Lacanian interpretation of the myth is very prevalent. The so-called scheme L has replaced the old construct, one can argue that moving away from the biologist Freudian conceptions might lead to a structural interpretation of the myth and it'll be very useful to remember that the approach to the relation between the Other and the subject is *heard* through-out language, and this not only represents a novel conception but a transformation and important departure, from classical Freudian biologism. Let us invoke some general ideas in our present context to conclude how to read Bolton's book or more appropriately worded, the controversy —it is indeed a very large controversy— set up by the book, its publication, and the effort to prevent the book from becoming widely available, not to say that can be gotten online *illegally* too. If we remember the myth originally and if we were to be allowed to take Ovid's version of the myth —a crucially relevant version— we'll find his version of the myth —probably we should introduce here the notion of myth variation rather than version—, clearly presented in the form of a poem, as myth has it, Narcissus is born from a violent act, almost can be sensed as rape, Cephisus, a river violently *possess* the delicate Niad named Liriope and beautiful Narcissus is born from the encounter, described by the poet in terms of streams and taken by force by the waves of Cephisus. As is usual and very well studied in classical literature —remember Tiresias prophecies leading to the War of Troy or Cassandra's presages on the death of Agamemnon after their return from the war— a seer with prophetic vision is consulted and the poet leaves us this extraordinary line or prophecy, if we want to use the term freely: *si se non noverit* (Metamorphoses, Book III, 345). As difficult as it is to translate, let us dare an approximation *if he doesn't discover himself* or another more poetical one, used in a more poetic rendition *if e'er he knows himself he surely dies* (A.S. Kline). Effectively Narcissus dies trying to know himself, searching for himself, or not being able to recognize anything else but himself. In Freud's famous study on narcissism, the definition at the beginning of the text uses two German words that are crucial to understanding the phenomena —at least the theoretical and even methodological concept employed by Freud—, quoting Freud directly *...den Grösßenwahn und die Abwendung Ihres Interesses von Der Außenwelt (Personen und Dingen)*. Here we have the two leading terms that might help us to fully comprehend what the book and all the drama behind it unravels. The total lack of interest in the rest of the world unless is an extension of the image of the narcissist, generates what Freud describes as Größenwahn, probably translated as megalomaniac or a delusion of grandeur. Both main actors in the book have exchanged accusations following this line of argumentation. To conclude this brief commentary let us go back to the book and the controversy as such, to complete our remarks.

The extensive and even thorough details of Bolton's work as presented in his book show to what extent his mastery and knowledge of all the areas of his expertise are remarkable. Long years of experience plus an excellent academic background, provide a very solid and ideal profile to perform these duties. The President wasn't wrong when he decided to bring Bolton back to the White House as National Security Advisor. Qualifications for the task asked out of him, cannot be objectively questioned. So then, what fuels and stems the establishment of such a huge controversy? As Marcelo Dascal thought us while developing his now widely employed Theory, one of the first rules that govern controversies, is that once generated they tend to expand, and expand this one did. No end in sight yet. The liberal media has been also looking for ways and means to contribute to its expansion and growth, even more, it threatens to influence or might be used to influence the outcome of the November election. However, it is hard to see it lasting until the end of the year, nonetheless, both actors will remain very active during the whole process. Political Narcissism is a term or concept recently deployed and hasn't spilled out of academic circles or intellectual discussions. Probably it might be an exaggeration to bring to the domain of Social and Political Sciences, all the psychopathological and other emotional elements that characterize this type of disorder. Not all politicians or public servants as well as mega entrepreneurs or members of corporation's board and the like have a narcissistic personality disorder. To affirm such an audacity can only be grossly misleading but even very dangerous and irresponsible. When Freud introduced the term or concept of Abwendung to describe narcissistic behaviour he meant or singled out, one very complex pattern, and the appeal to the Narcissus myth provides tools to understand the structural elements of this *turning away*, *avoidance* of the real world and the understanding of the state of affairs, sometimes and maybe this is the depth of the tragedy, not even being aware of the averting of reality that is taking place, actually happening. The *I* or the *Subject* in Lacanian terminology becomes the only measure of reality. This is what Freud meant by Abwendung.

As a result of this particular and peculiar behaviour begins to rule politics the old motto of the blind seers comes into light: si se non noverit. Narcissus unable to distinguish or separate himself from all other things succumbs tragically to his destiny. And, how close to the abyss we walk not only by the ones that have to become the decision makers but probably worst, by those whose missions are none other than "the keepers of secrets". It seems that the so-called *Sherpas* in the end understand better their duty of being *keepers of secrets*. The nature of foreign affairs and international relations is grounded —and deeply and fundamentally— on the reservation and the ability to maintain discretion and silence. After all, Bolton quotes at least twice probably more, James Baker's —whose memoirs as Secretary of State fulfils unquestionably and abides by the Moto of the *keepers of secretes*— famous words, which I quote freely but emphatically, *after all, he is the one elected.*

2
ROBERTO ARDÓN: DE LOS TRIUNVIRATOS, LOS RECIOS TIEMPOS Y LOS VIENTOS NEGROS Y FUERTES

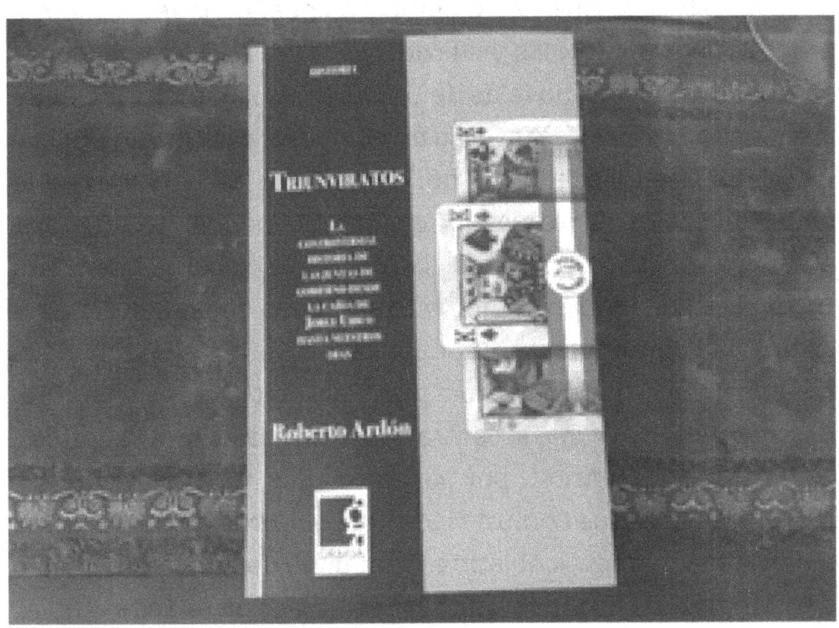

La lectura y estudio de la obra publicada recientemente, por Roberto Ardón Quiñónez, bajo el muy sugestivo título *Triunviratos*, contiene adicionalmente, un subtítulo aún más intrigante, *La controversial historia de las juntas de gobierno desde la caída de Jorge Ubico hasta nuestros días*. Cuando iniciaba la lectura de la misma, no pude evitar pensar en la reciente controversia generada por la publicación de la última novela de Mario Vargas Llosa, *Tiempos Fuertes*. Lo que pensaba al sumergirme en el estudio de la obra de Ardón Quiñónez, es lo lamentable que Vargas Llosa no hubiera leído este magnífico ensayo historiográfico y de análisis político. Hubiera evitado escribir y tener que defender tantos errores históricos y sobre todo, histórico-analíticos; habría conocido mejor la historia política de Guatemala, sobre todo la que reconstruye, bajo una imaginación muy fértil, no cabe duda, e incurre, en el hecho de la justificación, que se trata de una obra de ficción y no una novela histórica. Cuántos ejemplos se pueden traer a cuenta, sobre novelas históricas y sus derivaciones narrativas. Pienso en las maravillosas novelas de Umberto Eco, que contienen un rigor historiográfico, de un gran nivel, a pesar de utilizar personajes históricos alrededor, y de la creación de una narrativa francamente extraordinaria. Lamentablemente o tal vez, una auténtica bendición, Eco no recibió el Premio Nobel de Literatura y tampoco fue ungido como Marqués, pero quedan sus extraordinarias obras y el tratamiento respetuoso y ajustado de la historia, incluso la de su propio país. Pensemos en esa gran obra, *El cementerio de Praga*, al centro de la cual personajes históricos, de una gran relevancia, por pensar en dos, Garibaldi y Victor Hugo, son tratados con un rigor y de acuerdo a una realidad histórica sumamente objetiva. El manejo de la ficción, dentro del respeto a los hechos históricos, en el caso de Eco es ejemplar y por supuesto, hay otros más, los cuales no vamos a abordar acá, porque escapan los límites de este texto.

El desarrollo de los distintos Triunviratos, que básicamente se sucedieron a lo largo del Siglo XX –claro que hay otros ejemplos, especialmente durante los tiempos de las Provincias Unidas de Centroamérica, casos de las Presidencias, vale decir, José Cecilio Del Valle y Don Pedro Molina—, período en el que esta modalidad se empleó, en varias ocasiones y las cuales no son necesariamente idénticas o similares, algo pareciera ser común, fueron Juntas, para transferir el poder o establecer un nuevo poder, en los casos más relevantes, incluso abrieron procesos constituyentes, no siempre conducidos de la manera más correcta y menos apegados a los ordenamientos constitucionales y jurídicos o en respeto de los grandes principios de la ley y el orden. Más bien hay un caso notorio, donde se dieron una serie de anormalidades legales, subsanadas de formas muy tropicales, una notoria preeminencia de lo político sobre lo jurídico, para nada inspiradas en los modelos constitucionales o de respeto a las normas jerárquicas o lo que muchos siempre añoramos, la vinculación esencial entre el Derecho y el Estado.

Francamente no se trata de tomar posición, frente al debate clásico, monismo versus dualismo, sino simplemente recalcar que la historia política de Guatemala está dominada por la lucha, por mantener la Grundnorm, o sea, el constitucionalismo rector y conductor, base y sustentáculo, de nuestra arquitectura constitucional y por ende, de todo el sistema legal del país. Roberto Ardón nos señala a lo largo de sus análisis, de las acciones de los diferentes miembros de las Juntas, Triunviros, esta interminable y no resuelta tensión e incluso choque; lo hace, eso sí, de una manera sutil a veces y, en otras, directa y contundentemente. Un ejemplo tomado al azar, cuando se establece la Junta Revolucionaria, la vieja Constitución liberal, con sus remiendos y modificaciones, estaba parcialmente vigente y fue invocada, aunque ya hubiese sido derogada, para convocar elecciones presidenciales y luego se violentó también la sucesión presidencial, no obstante existir una normativa constitucional, que preveía un mecanismo de sucesión. Y a lo largo del estupendo texto —escrito y narrado en una prosa de un muy alto nivel y con una fluidez excepcional, que hace su lectura un placer— señala y apunta a varios casos similares.

De los capítulos que componen la obra, son siete en total, incluyendo en ellos apéndice y bibliografía, los referidos a las Juntas-Triunviratos, aunque no sean necesariamente sinónimos ya que hubo, o al menos hasta ahora, han habido juntas de más de tres miembros, unas que duraron un brevísimo lapso de tiempo y otras un tanto más. Decíamos pues, que los capítulos que tratan específicamente de las Juntas, son del segundo al sexto y tienen unos títulos muy acertadamente seleccionados, por ejemplo, "Los generales emisarios", el momento de la designación de un sucesor de Jorge Ubico; "Dos oficiales y un ciudadano"; "Sillas musicales"; "La hora de los coroneles"; y, por último "La junta y la juntita". La transición después de la sorpresiva renuncia de Jorge Ubico tomó a muchos de sorpresa, aunque en cierta forma era anticipada. Para otros muchos, generó un complejo proceso de sucesión, sin entrar en los detalles —se trata sobre todo, de motivar a la lectura de la obra de Ardón Quiñónez—. La descripción y análisis son francamente estupendos, incluso hoy en día a pesar de existir amplia literatura al respecto y obras de mucha importancia, la manera de presentar el drama de la salida de Ubico, es insuperable. Dejando de lado el relato, hay dos hechos que destacan muy oportunamente: el primero se refiere a la manera cómo se conforma la primera Junta o en este caso, efectivamente, el Triunvirato, por los generales Eduardo Villagrán, Buenaventura Pineda y el mismo Federico Ponce Vaides. Nos acota con toda corrección Ardón Quiñónez, que dicho procedimiento era espurio, violatorio de la remendada Constitución vigente, como lo hace e hizo ver, con firmeza y claridad contundente, el eminente jurisconsulto guatemalteco, a la sazón Secretario de Relaciones Exteriores, Carlos Salazar Argumendo. Estamos una vez más, ante un momento de tensiones jurídico-políticas, donde se actuó, a pesar de tener mecanismos constitucionales, para solventar la crisis, en base a razones políticas y personales, optándose por tomar el camino, de la ausencia de continuidad jurídica —tal y como sugería Salazar Argumendo—, en favor de los criterios políticos y de coyuntura. Y al final, la Junta quedaría disuelta al asumir Ponce Vaides, un sumamente frágil gobierno, el cual se desmoronaría ante el proceso casi inmediatamente desatado, al intentar imponerse autoritariamente un gobierno y, tal vez más importante aún, preludiando desde ya el final del período liberal, que se había agotado plenamente. A partir de esos cortos meses Guatemala vería surgir el fenómeno de la llamada *revolución de octubre*.

Antes de cerrar este párrafo quisiera referirme a la personalidad de Salazar Argumendo, un notable jurista guatemalteco quien tuviera un destacadísimo papel en el Diferendo Histórico con el Reino Unido; especialmente lo podemos apreciar, en la correspondencia sostenida, mientras se desempeñaba como Secretario de Relaciones Exteriores, en el año 1937, cuando propuso al Reino Unido someter la disputa a un Arbitraje y planteó que el Árbitro fuera el Presidente de los Estados Unidos, a la sazón, Franklin Delano Roosevelt, lo cual se puede leer en las notas de Salazar Argumendo, de fechas 24 de agosto y 22 de septiembre del 1937. Entre otros puntos notables, remarca e insiste, que la disputa es eminentemente jurídica, además de proponer el Arbitraje como mecanismo de solución de la misma y la importantísima carta del 24 de abril, del 1940, donde además de lamentarse de la falta de voluntad, por parte de La Corona Británica, de aceptar alguna forma de solución, reafirma los derechos guatemaltecos, al referirse a la Convención del 69 como un Tratado de Cesión Territorial y no de Límites. Jamás Guatemala ha aceptado este argumento. Además de señalar acertadamente otros elementos, que escapan a este análisis, opté hacer mención de la figura de Salazar Argumendo, por su extraordinaria contribución y coraje al sostener una posición digna y justa frente a las enormes presiones imperiales en ese momento y, resaltar así, el nivel excepcional de los actores de estos dramas históricos, en muchos de los casos, cuando defendieron la necesidad de conservar a toda costa la vinculación esencial entre el Estado y el Derecho; o sea, en defensa del constitucionalismo como la mejor vía para construir un sistema republicano de gobierno, añeja aspiración, de la mayoría de los guatemaltecos. Esta tensión se seguirá viendo al continuar comentando el surgimiento y disolución de las otras Juntas y Triunviratos en la historia reciente de Guatemala.

El proceso que siguió es ampliamente conocido, el derrocamiento del régimen de Ponce Vaides y el inicio de la revolución de Octubre. La creación de la denominada Junta Revolucionaria, constituida por el Mayor Francisco Javier Arana, el Capitán Jacobo Arbenz Guzmán y el ciudadano —como se lo denominó a partir de ese momento— Jorge Toriello Garrido. No vamos a entrar en los detalles sumamente conocidos, estudiados y sobre los cuales se han escrito obras así como innumerables otras formas, desde literarias, hasta una enorme cantidad de artículos de periódicos. Pocos períodos históricos han sido tan abordados, desde tantas modalidades y perspectivas, ideológicas, emocionales, líricas y un sin fin de expresiones más. Lo que más nos interesa destacar al tocar este tema, es que se trata de un complejo movimiento; sin embargo, quiero quedarme con la visión, que nuevamente resalta Roberto Ardón, de manera inequívoca: nuevamente estamos ante una ausencia de continuidad jurídica. La política y hasta el autoritarismo, siempre presente, provocan un desenlace forzado; la Junta misma, por sí y ante sí, obviando la ya vetusta Constitución liberal, sin contar con autoridad jurídica clara, decreta la disolución de la Asamblea y convoca a elecciones, bajo el amparo de normas derogadas y con unos vacíos constitucionales notables y evidentes. De cualquier forma se instala a su vez un nuevo proceso constituyente, que culminará con la Constitución de 1945, promulgada el 15 de marzo del año señalado. Lo que no cabe duda es que la Junta cumplió con los objetivos anunciados y el país entró en un proceso democrático republicano, que llevará a la presidencia al Doctor Juan José Arévalo Bermejo, quien regresará de la Argentina, donde incluso había adoptado esa nacionalidad, después de una muy exitosa y prestigiada carrera académica. Arévalo se constituyó así en el Presidente más popular que se ha elegido y su fama y reputación lo acompañó a lo largo de su vida. Los acontecimientos que llevan a la elección de Jacobo Arbenz Guzmán como su sucesor, así como el asesinato de Francisco Javier Arana arrojaron, sin duda alguna, una enorme sombra y duda, no sólo sobre esa elección, sino también sobre el futuro de una presidencia,que tuviera un final sumamente desafortunado. Eso lo veremos en la conformación de las Juntas, Pentarquía y Triunviratos, que sucederían después de la muy irregular renuncia de Arbenz.

Un muy importante punto, que el autor mantiene como *hilo conductor* de su narración y relatos, se palpa con mucha claridad, cuando describe la renuncia de Jacobo Arbenz, que se produjo un día 27 de Junio del 1954, renuncia pública, así como su posterior intento y, en alguna forma, aunque de manera efímera, intentara un traslado de poder al Coronel Carlos Enrique Díaz de León; pues bien, aquí nuevamente se incurrió en una evidente violación de la Constitución vigente, que se había aprobado el 11 de Marzo del 1945 y entró en vigor el 15 de mayo, del mismo año, allí, en el texto constitucional, la norma que regulaba la sucesión presidencial, en caso de ausencia definitiva o absoluta, del Presidente de la República debía seguirse, dejemos hablar al texto mismo:

Artículo 135. En caso de falta absoluta del Presidente de la República, tomará posesión inmediata del cargo el Presidente del Congreso y, en defecto de éste, o si no reuniere las calidades que esta Constitución exige, los Vicepresidentes del mismo, por su orden.

Si los Vicepresidentes del Congreso no llenaren las calidades o tuvieren los impedimentos constitucionales para el ejercicio de la Presidencia de la República, entrará a ejercer el cargo el Presidente del Organismo Judicial.

El sucesor deberá, dentro de los ocho días siguientes al de la falta absoluta, convocar a elecciones, las cuales se practicarán dentro de un plazo no menor de dos meses ni mayor de cuatro contados desde la fecha de la convocatoria. Efectuada la elección, el Congreso hará dentro de veinte días, la declaración a que se refiere el inciso 2o del articulo 115 y el ciudadano electo tomará inmediatamente posesión del cargo, computándose su periodo desde el quince de marzo siguiente.

No puede ser más claro y contundente el texto constitucional y la norma expresa totalmente lapidaria; más aún, se trataba de la Constitución misma, que la Junta Revolucionaria se comprometió, como garantía definitiva, de una transición de los autoritarismos anteriores, abundantes durante el período liberal, para concretar una democracia plena y republicana, y se cerraría así esa etapa autoritaria, que caracterizara a los distintos gobiernos liberales, hasta el final del fugaz gobierno de Ponce Vaides. Esa misma constante histórica, la cual Ardón Quiñónez destaca tan acertadamente en su obra, se repetía una vez más, como seguirá pasando, y el choque de las dos tendencias opuestas, se verán nuevamente confrontadas, en futuros momentos de la historia política del país. Lo veremos más adelante, con un resultado muy diferente, para asombro de muchos.

El período inmediato a la renuncia de Arbenz es uno de los más turbulentos, en materia de Juntas, Triunviratos e incluso una Pentarquía. El autor las describe magistralmente, una por una, con una precisión matemática, en cuanto a tiempos y lugares. Sólo para referirlas sumariamente, puesto que incluso algunas duraron horas y días, en algunos casos. No vamos a tocar la influencia del Embajador Americano en ese momento, John Peurifoy, sobre quien muchísimas páginas se han vertido, desde muchos ángulos y visiones. Lo cierto es que su intervención fue real y decisiva, así como la de su país lo ha sido en todas partes y momentos, y lo continúa y continuará siendo. Esto es innegable e ingenuo sería considerarlo de cualquier otra forma. Dejando esto de lado, lo interesante acá es el tema o materia del libro que nos ocupa, a saber, las Juntas y los Triunviratos. Después del fallido intento de literalmente *heredar* el poder o designar un sucesor —menuda práctica democrática aquella— el aludido Peurifoy intervino directamente, para aprobar y bendecir o sencillamente, tachar las juntas y sus maniobras autoritarias —es muy importante hacer ver esta tendencia ritualmente presente—, para conservar y trasladar el poder o sencillamente, para asumirlo o asaltarlo literalmente. Después de 17 horas el primer Triunvirato de la post revolución se derrumbó ante el empujón de los mismos oficiales y el propio embajador americano. Así pues Días de León, Monzón —quien jugará un papel central al participar en todas estas intentonas continuadas, hasta su exilio definitivo— y Sánchez, debieron ceder a un Triunvirato que se llegó a constituir y se semiconsolidó por unos días, integrándolo el ya mencionado Coronel Elfego Monzón y los coroneles José Luis Cruz Salazar —quien, hay que decirlo, tuvo una destacadísima carrera académica posterior e influyó decididamente, en los procesos democráticos recientes, después de una larga y productiva actividad política—, y Mauricio Dubois. A pesar de todo, el mayor escollo aún existía, el llamado "ejército de liberación" existía y esperaba ingresar al país. La confrontación había terminado, restaba que su líder y sus colaboradores entraran y consolidaran el poder real.

Faltaba un paso y ese se dio con el Pacto de San Salvador. A presiones de Washington fuera de manera directa o a través de Peurifoy, el frágil Triunvirato se reunió en San Salvador, donde el Presidente Oscar Osorio, un militar también, facilitó las consultas, a la cual el ilustre salvadoreño, con vinculaciones familiares y de otros tipos más, en Guatemala, Rafael Mesa, proveyeron las condiciones para que se efectuaran las negociaciones. No fueron nada sencillas y a eso del 2 de Julio se pudo lograr un acuerdo e integrar una Pentarquía, compuesta por los triunviros mencionados y además se unieron el Coronel Carlos Castillo Armas y el Teniente Coronel Enrique Trinidad Oliva —valga mencionar y aludir, que Oliva estaría señalado luego de haber directamente participado en el asesinato del Presidente Castillo Armas, en un siniestro y oscuro complot aún no del todo esclarecido, quien murió enfrente de su casa, no por un atentado de un coche bomba, delante de un Banco, que nunca existió, como lo hace morir Vargas Llosa en su polémica novela—, cuestión que habla de la cercanía de los dos e incluso, son ellos dos los que viajan constantemente al interior del país, visitando y coordinando, con los comandos militares, un posición común y una eventual disolución de la Pentarquía, como ocurriera posteriormente cuando Castillo Armas asumiera la Jefatura del Estado y luego la Presidencia, después de un plebiscito, que ganara con una mayoría abrumadora. Este tránsito de un Triunvirato a una Pentarquía y su disolución, vía renuncia de sus miembros, en favor de una Jefatura y ulterior Presidencia, duró unos 52 días de enorme inestabilidad, que lentamente se fue superando. El día 1 de septiembre el proceso había concluido. Lo que vendría después estremece todavía a los guatemaltecos. Afortunadamente los jóvenes, que no vivieron esos acontecimientos guardan distancia y calma, frente a uno de los momentos más oscuros de la historia política de Guatemala. La experiencia del llamado magnicidio, marcó a muchas generaciones de guatemaltecos, por diversas razones y no solamente políticas o ideológicas. Carlos Castillo Armas, el Presidente de la República fue asesinado en la Casa Presidencial. Su esposa y un vestido lleno de sangre fueron testigos mudos de ese dramático episodio.

Después del asesinato —el denominado Magnicidio— el mecanismo de sucesión constitucional fue activado, a pesar de los intentos de establecer una nueva Junta,. El Ministro de Defensa Juan Francisco Oliva, intentó en varias oportunidades asumir bajo la figura de un nuevo Triunvirato; sin embargo, prevaleció la voluntad férrea de varios civiles y notables juristas que eran parte del gobierno, como Ministros y otros altos cargos. Ardón Quiñónez cita en su obra la intervención crucial y decisiva del entonces Canciller de la República, el recordado jurista e intelectual guatemalteco, Jorge Skinner-Klee, quien espetó duramente a los militares, así como a los demás miembros del gobierno presentes, durante una reunión, para instalar una nueva Junta, en las propias palabras del autor y citando una conversación privada con el ex Presidente y uno de los más brillantes juristas y políticos, de la Guatemala democrática, Alejandro Maldonado Aguirre y recordando la obra de Mario Efraín Nájera Farfán, casi al final de una aciaga reunión, en la madrugada. Skinner-Klee les dijo frontalmente a los militares intentando constituir un Triunvirato, *...si ustedes salen anunciando la integración de esta junta, sepan que se estarán poniendo ante la opinión pública un cartel en el pecho que dice 'Yo mate a Castillo Armas...'.* El asunto quedó superado y la tentación por un nuevo Triunvirato se desvaneció. El mecanismo constitucional fue plenamente ejecutado, a pesar de la reserva, duda y profundo temor, del Primer Designado, quien casi se puede decir fue conducido de su residencia al Palacio Nacional para asumir la Presidencia. Es así que el licenciado Luis Arturo González López asumiría la Presidencia entre el 27 de junio al 24 de octubre del 1957. Después de una elección sumamente enredada, entre el licenciado Miguel Ortiz Passarelli, quien a la sazón era el Presidente del Organismo

Judicial, y el General Miguel Ydigoras Fuentes, resultó en una primera elección sumamente incidentada la cual tuvo que ser anulada y efectuarse una nueva, en la cual el General Ydigoras Fuentes resultara electo y ganador de los comicios, asumiendo la Presidencia un 2 de Marzo del 1958, aunque fuera derrocado por un golpe de estado directo, encabezado por el Coronel Enrique Peralta Azurdia, un 30 de Marzo de 1963, quien convocaría una Asamblea Constituyente, para redactar una nueva constitución y posteriormente convocar a una nueva elección, que ganaría el licenciado Julio César Méndez Montenegro, otro eminente jurista, quien asumiría la Presidencia, en una elección abierta y libre, en julio del 1966. Es oportuno mencionar aunque sea brevemente, que un último intento, que involucró a otro grupo de militares, durante el caótico momento de la elección de 1957, que se generó la tentación de sucumbir nuevamente a la fórmula de un Triunvirato, nuevamente encabezado por Oliva y que sería acompañado por dos militares más; empero, nuevamente se respetó el mecanismo constitucional y el Segundo Designado, el Coronel Guillermo Flores Avendaño concluyó la transición y posterior entrega del gobierno al General Ydigoras Fuentes.

La última Junta que conoció el país es probablemente la más reconocida de todas las que se integraran. Se trata de la resultante del movimiento que depusiera al Presidente Romeo Lucas García —un general sumamente impopular e incluso, al frente de un gobierno enormemente controversial y cues-tionadísimo— Pues bien, el 23 de marzo, luego de un movimiento militar, el General Efraín Ríos Montt encabezó un Triunvirato, que duraría 68 días hasta que fuera disuelto y Ríos Montt asumiera funciones de Jefe de Estado. Lo acompañaron durante la vigencia del Triunvirato, el General Horacio Maldonado Schaad y el Coronel Luis Gordillo, quienes fueron desplazados por Ríos Montt, hasta su derrocamiento por un nuevo golpe militar y el General Oscar

Mejía Víctores después de asumir el gobierno, convocara a una nueva Asamblea Constituyente —la cual redactara y aprobara la Constitución actual y vigente— y convocara a elecciones democráticas, las cuales resultaron en el presente proceso democrático, que desde 1986 ha visto continuar un transformador proceso democrático y una profunda transformación del país. La parte y descripción del proceso de consolidación del último Triunvirato y el movimiento que derrocara a Lucas García, están brillantemente descritos y narrados por Roberto Ardón, en la obra comentada, de la que recomendamos su estudio y lectura ya que las generaciones actuales son tocadas muy de cerca por estos acontecimientos que cambiaron dramáticamente la historia política de Guatemala. Nada puede substituir su lectura cuidadosa y meticuloso cuidado al presentar la sucesión de los hechos y los resultados finales, de lo que reconocemos como el último de los Triunviratos de la turbulenta historia política guatemalteca.

Roberto Ardón Quiñónez nos ha dejado una estupenda obra, para análisis y reflexión, de una figura sumamente controversial. Se trata de un texto de una gran seriedad y sobre todo, historiográficamente, muy bien documentado. La historia vista desde un análisis crítico y bajo una mirada analítica y valorativa, como es el caso presente, resulta esencial para la comprensión no solo de nuestra propia historicidad, en tanto que existencia, sino más aún, como nación y pueblo; es decir, bajo esos procesos transformativos que la política y la acción humana, sobre todo, desencadenan y precipitan. Es por eso que al pensar en los Triunviratos y Juntas, nuestra historia se muestra poblada por esos vientos negros y fuertes, de los que nos han hablado tantas veces, los cuales han soplado, con una contundencia abrumadora e incluso, en momentos, devastadora y destructiva. Hemos destacado como hilo conductor la interminable y constante lucha por encontrar a los juristas, jurisconsultos y *sus cajas de herra-*

mientas, para emplear la expresión misma del autor, que en determinados momentos de nuestra historia, tuvieron el coraje y la valentía, de enfrentar a las tendencias autoritarias —y tal vez, mejor dicho, ambiciones desproporcionadas y personales, en casos, siniestras y sórdidas—, siempre amenazantes y acechando la oportunidad de saltar y hacerse con el poder. La lucha por el límite del poder es esa constante, que el constitucionalismo republicano siempre debe sostener. Las tentaciones están siempre de por medio y por eso las amenazas de los vientos negros y fuertes no pueden ignorarse.

3
LA RECIEDUMBRE DE LOS TIEMPOS: VARGAS LLOSA O LA AUTONOMÍA DE LA OBRA DE ARTE

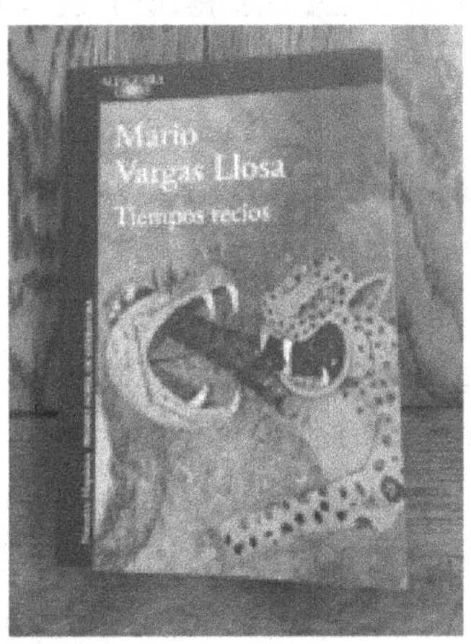

La lectura de la recientemente, muy recientemente, publicada obra de Mario Vargas Llosa, el último Premio Nobel de Literatura latinoamericano —en esta materia la Academia ha hecho selecciones un tanto polémicas—, dejando ignorados a muchos extraordinarios talentos, no solamente latinoamericanos, sino también de otras regiones del mundo. Personalmente, creo que Amos Oz es y será un gran ausente siempre, al igual que Carlos Fuentes, cuya obra es de una extraordinaria calidad y profundidad. Decíamos pues, Alfaguara acaba de lanzar la novela, en el mes de octubre del presente año, *Tiempos Recios*. Como casi todos los jóvenes, en la América Latina, en mi generación, tan cercana y próxima al *boom* latinoamericano, crecimos leyendo esas obras iniciales de Vargas Llosa, que encontrábamos fascinantes, — ¿quién no caminó las sendas de Pantaleón o se admiró con la historia de la Tía Julia, por no mencionar las Conversaciones y la Casa Verde y el que polemizara intensamente con García Márquez—?

Ese es el Vargas Llosa que conocía cuando una noche llegaba a Lima. Había sido trasladado de Berna, para volver a servir como Embajador de mi país, en una ciudad que me ha sido siempre sumamente entrañable. La habíamos visitado en más de una ocasión, mientras servíamos en La Paz. Tuve el honor de servir como Embajador en nueve países, de los cuales guardo extraordinarios recuerdos, y más de una vez he ponderado escribir unas Memorias de todos esos años y lo que nos tocara vivir; sin embargo, la diplomacia, en particular la nuestra, es un tremendo antídoto contra las formas de egocentrismo, narcisismo y otras maneras de autovaloración exaltadas, puesto que suelen impactar profundamente en la lectura del ser-sí-mismo y de nuestra particular situación en el mundo. Dicho eso, las dudas son demasiadas sobre la importancia de todos esos años, que al final dejan una profunda lección de humildad y conocimientos, con unos dolores y decepciones, nada dignos de recordarse.

Esa noche de mi arribo a Lima, y coincidía en la televisión peruana el debate entre Vargas Llosa y Alberto Fujimori de cara a las elecciones presidenciales. Era ya la segunda vuelta, y Vargas Llosa había ganado la primera, sin tener una gran mayoría. Por supuesto, me senté frente a la televisión a seguirlo. Eran los tiempos del Primer Gobierno de Alan García y la ciudad pasaba por limitaciones realmente importantes. Recuerdo me alojé en el Hotel César en Miraflores. La residencia no estaba en condiciones de ser habitada y mi familia esperaba las mejoras adecuadas, para llegar a Lima. Pues bien, era la primera vez que veía debatir y hablar en público al gran escritor, quien debatía con un profesor de matemáticas, ingeniero de profesión, japonés de origen, quien para mi asombro e incredulidad lograba mantenerse a la altura del debate —cosa casi impensable— e incluso las encuestas posteriores lo daban por ganador, como efectivamente lo fue después. Llamar constantemente a Vargas Llosa, *Doctor Vargas*, se quedó grabado en mi memoria, me daba cuenta que la posición de Vargas Llosa era precaria y su argumentación así como arrogancia y desprecio evidente del desconocido profesor de matemáticas, no iban a penetrar en el votante peruano; la retórica liberal o libertaria no eran suficientes; la defensa del libre mercado y el free choice, poco hicieron, para contrarrestar la mentalidad y visión pragmática y ejecutiva de Fujimori, quien se mostró incluso como un profundo conocedor de su país. Debate aparte es si Fujimori era o no peruano de origen o la posterior valoración de su larga gestión, plagada de corrupción y escándalos, aunque llena de éxitos en materias concretas, que logró terminar con el caos financiero que el gobierno del APRA dejó al Perú y logró reinsertar al país en el sistema financiero internacional en su primer gobierno. Lo que vino después y su lucha contra el Sendero Luminoso y la captura y prisión del Presidente Gonzalo, o sea Abimael Guzmán, es otro tema y escapa totalmente a este breve comentario. Al final de esa elección Vargas Llosa, por todos conocido, se marchó del Perú e incluso optó públicamente por la nacionalidad española, país donde reside actualmente. Y allí empezó una muy larga y fructífera etapa de creación literaria además de incursionar en otras actividades cercanas como el periodismo y la crónica, la buena crónica, no la de los escándalos y la publicidad negativa. Incluso se asomó, creo brevemente, en el análisis del balompié, para usar el término correcto, en nuestro maravilloso idioma.

No vamos a reproducir la trama de la obra. Aparentemente el centro de la misma, lo sería el asesinato de Carlos Castillo Armas y una supuesta intriga orquestada desde Ciudad Trujillo, en aquella época así se llamaba Santo Domingo, la capital de la

República Dominicana, bajo complicidad de un oficial del entorno del Presidente Castillo Armas, el Teniente Coronel Enrique Trinidad Oliva, hermano del entonces Coronel y Ministro de la Defensa, Juan Francisco Oliva —cuyo cumpleaños se celebraría esa misma noche, o sea la noche del crimen—, quien no está claro del todo fuera parte de los conjurados, aunque otras versiones sí lo implican, no así Vargas Llosa y su narrativa fantasiosa, acompañados por supuestos "sicarios" dirían hoy en día, bajo el control del dictador dominicano Rafael Leonidas Trujillo, quien se sintió ofendido y traicionado por Castillo Armas, al no cumplir con una supuesta oferta de invitarlo oficialmente a Guatemala, recibirlo con los máximos honores e imponerle la Orden del Quetzal. Los sicarios dominicanos, en plena coordinación con Oliva, burlan toda la seguridad de la Casa Presidencial y logran introducirse por la noche y asesinar al Presidente, quien caminaba en esos momentos hacia una cena o acto oficial, próximo a celebrarse. Tanto los hechores extranjeros y el único complotado guatemalteco, actuaron con una cierta bendición de la CIA y un supuesto agente a quien Vargas Llosa llama a lo largo del libro, *Mike o el hombre que no se llamaba Mike*. Alrededor de esta terrible historia, giran una serie de personajes, históricos, reales, que son mencionados con sus auténticos nombres, así como el de los hechores del magnicidio. Contrario a lo que Vargas Llosa afirma, en realidad solamente Castillo Armas es el único presidente asesinado en Guatemala a lo largo del siglo pasado, así como esa leyenda negra, incansablemente repetida, sobre el Apocalipsis de la supuesta "primavera democrática" guatemalteca. Jacobo Árbenz mismo se hizo elegir Presidente sobre un crimen, nunca del todo aclarado, de su rival —quien gozaba de una enorme popularidad indudablemente, lo cual siempre planteó dudas, si Arbenz ganaría unas elecciones, en las que tuviera que competir con Francisco Javier Arana, asesinado de manera muy misteriosa—, o sea, ese hecho, el cual algunos han tratado de ocultar, desvirtuar e incluso atribuirlo a supuestos complotados, sobre el cual existen serias evidencias, que plantean al menos una enorme duda, tampoco ha sido del todo aclarado y permanecerá siempre, como una enorme sombra, sobre toda esta terrible historia. Sin embargo, la protagonista de la novela es Marita, a quien extrañamente apoda Miss Guatemala, una mujer cuyo verdadero nombre es Gloria Bolaños, por razones no tan evidentes —nada es evidente en esta narración—, y quien es una o tal vez la única de las personas que evita llamar por su verdadero nombre. Una de las cosas más asombrosas es una especie de addendum o *"anexo"*, el cual lo titula simplemente, *"Después"*, en el que recoge una supuesta entrevista con Marta Borrero Parra, en la ciudad de Washington, a cuya vivienda acude acompañado de Tony Raful, quien le dedica, entre otros, un libro publicado hace poco, bajo el título *La Rapsodia del Crimen*, quien relata esta misma historia que Vargas Llosa modifica o agrega esencialmente. Pues bien, según el propio Tony Raful, Gloria Bolaños vive en New York. Tal vez asustada o cautelosa, a Vargas Llosa, a quien en esa supuesta entrevista, amenaza e incluso saca de su casa, Marta Borrero Parra/Gloria Bolaños, extrañamente le dice, "no se moleste en enviarme una copia del libro, porque no lo voy a leer, no obstante, mis abogados si lo harán". Y más aún, si nos fijamos en el siguiente párrafo, en la página 336 del libro, donde literalmente dice lo siguiente: *Llevo dos años imaginando a esta mujer, inventándola, atribuyéndole toda clase de aventuras, desfigurándola para que nadie —ni ella misma— se reconozca en la historia que fantaseo.* Y aquí es donde nos centramos en la cuestión fundamental.

En diversas ocasiones, al referirse a su nueva obra, Vargas Llosa ha enfatizado que se trata de una novela de ficción, no de

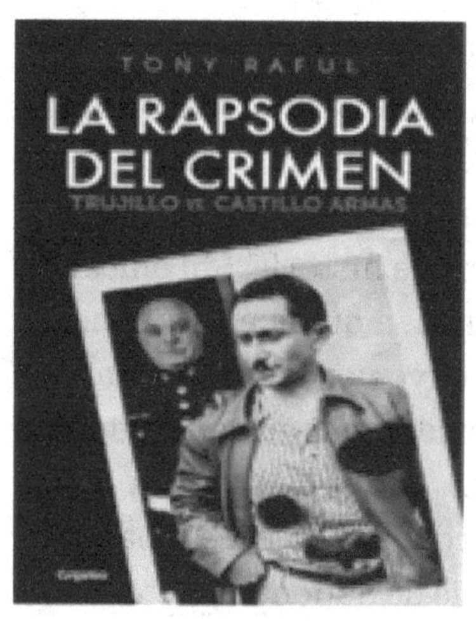

una novela histórica y los hechos no son narrados, contados, como los de un contador, de una manera estrictamente apegada a la forma real como los sucesos novelados verdaderamente ocurrieran. A lo largo y ancho del texto —para nosotros lo interesante es el texto, el cual emerge y se separa de su creador o autor, para constituirse en obra literaria o en otra cosa— Vargas Llosa narra con la irresponsabilidad de quien se siente afuera de ese submundo infernal; empero, su trabajo de investigación previa y la manera como *cuenta* los acontecimientos —que para los guatemaltecos tienen una enorme importancia— lo hacen alejarse muchísimo de la verdad histórica y más aún, ofrece una caracterización de una país que en momentos pareciera también de toda una gran región de la América Latina, aquella que Pablo Neruda llamaba *la cintura de América*, en el Canto General. Dada mi formación particular, cuando pienso en el arte y las obras artísticas, como la gran literatura, evito siempre no ignorar su relación con la verdad. La esencia del arte surge desde la manifestación o del desocultarse de la verdad, que éste trae a la tierra y al mundo. La obra de arte instala una tierra y habita un mundo. Y en este caso hay una muy deliberada construcción de unos personajes siniestros y sombríos, una historia diabólica e infernal, surgida en los laberintos nocturnos del poder y del misterio de una naturaleza humana deformada y torcida. Incluso la cita de Churchill en inglés y sin traducir, que se lee al inicio del libro, no está puesta allí por casualidad. Al referirse a *...this bloody place Guatemala...* Haber elegido esa expresión típicamente inglesa, coloquialmente inglesa, nos da un marco referencial, en el que casi como Dante, el narrador y ahora su lector, están por entrar en los círculos del infierno y la lectura de esta obra, para mí fue eso, como un descenso a lo más infernal y oscuro de lo humano. Para cualquier guatemalteco, sea de la orientación o tendencia política que sea, partidario de uno u otro bando, es un auténtico tránsito, en un delirio y alucinación, casi inexplicables.

La muy curiosa estructura dialéctica de la novela es sumamente interesante. No cabe duda, que el pensamiento dialéctico aún prevalece y Vargas Llosa no lo ha abandonado del todo. La apertura o inicio de la novela es tan asombrosa como lo arriba mencionado, anexo o pseudo agregado. La entrevista con la protagonista imaginario-desrealizada, para recordar un tanto el lenguaje sartriano, de esa extraordinaria obra final incompleta, sobre Flaubert, que bien vendría a cuenta, L'Idiot de la famille. Los pares de oposición, a la manera estructural, se repiten en la construcción y arquitectura, internas y externas de la obra. Jacobo Árbenz y Carlos Castillo Armas, Sam Zemurray, un judío este moldavo, emigrante y exitoso empresario; Edward L. Bernays, un judío vienés, emigrante también; por cierto el fundador del prestigioso Zamorano, hoy día una Universidad Agrícola. En 1941 fue Zemurray, con el invaluable apoyo del Doctor Wilson Popenoe, cuyo trabajo y dedicación son ampliamente recordados y muy valorados en toda la región. Zemurray incluso presidió la United Fruit Company. Las oposiciones o relaciones de oposición dialécticas son muchas, y en muchos momentos, parecieran implicar incluso cuestiones de supuestas superioridades e incluso estéticas. Esto merecería análisis posteriores y más profundos, pero nótense las constantes referencias *al hombre más feo del mundo*, casi implicando una relación entre el horror, la fealdad y el mal. Todo esto precipitará una narración lenta y cargada de opiniones expresadas a través de los personajes construidos, bajo ciertos prejuicios o ideas preestablecidas, alrededor de estos trágicos hechos. Las confusiones, incluso anacronismos son muy notorios. Escogemos algunos al azar, para conformar un argumento, sobre lo que pueden ser no solamente los excesos en la creación, sino tal vez, más preocupante, el abandono de la verdad. A lo largo de la página 25, después de reconstruir una reunión imaginaria del Directorio de la United Fruit Company, hace decir a Bernays, en oposición al más rudo y directo Zemurray —Schmuel Zamurri era su nombre original, conocido como el Bananaman—, que implementaría una narrativa mediante la cual influenciaría la opinión americana y crearían las condiciones para justificar una estrategia dura y agresiva frente a un comunismo en expansión. Allí lo hace afirmar lo siguiente: *Mediante la prensa, la radio y la televisión, la fuente principal que informa y orienta a los ciudadanos tanto en un país libre como en un país esclavo.*

La televisión, realmente compuesta de programas de penetración propagandista al estilo nazi, promovidos por un judío americano, es muy dudosa; de cualquier manera la televisión se introdujo en Guatemala a finales de los años cincuenta y principios de los sesenta. No solo parece anacrónico, sino poco real. A Bernays se le pueden atribuir muchas cosas —la invención de Madison Avenue, si se quiere exagerar— pero es muy cuestionable esta línea de pensamiento. Los pares de oposición se ven allí plenamente configurados. Las confusiones históricas también se suceden: fincas de café en Chichicastenango y, algo particularmente curioso, además de describir y construir una larga y extensa galería de personajes degenerados e infrahumanos, los hace tener unas costumbres particularmente desagradables. Si quiere practicar el neorrealismo, pues es una elección de su condición de creador literario; pero, hacer beber Ron Zacapa en los años cincuenta a esta galería de monstruos, es realmente una total barbaridad. El Ron Zacapa surgió y se estableció en Guatemala —ahora una de las marcas más prestigiosas del mundo y uno de los mejores, sino el mejor, ron del mundo y con énfasis, creado y producido en Guatemala— al menos cuarenta años después de todos estos hechos. Y así, sigue una serie de libertades creadoras, muy separadas de los hechos históricos como tales, prevaleciendo anacronismos y confusiones en su narración y recuentos de la historia misma de Guatemala. Particularmente confusa es la referencia a la embajada americana ubicada en la zona 14 de la ciudad. Además de describirla como la más lujosa y afluente, es totalmente anacrónico, puesto que en los años cincuenta no se había desarrollado aún dicha área de la ciudad y todos los guatemaltecos saben en qué parte de la ciudad se encuentra la residencia de la embajada estadounidense y no es donde la fantasía de Vargas Llosa la instala.

Hay un hecho en particular que me interesa personalmente rescatar. Los dos episodios centrales son la ejecución del crimen y la caída-renuncia de Árbenz. No me ocuparé de la cuestión de la gesta liberacionista, francamente mucho se ha escrito sobre esto y aún hay guatemaltecos vivos que pueden y seguramente lo van a hacer, referirse con precisión histórica a la verdad de cómo se sucedieron los distintos momentos que atravesó este complejo proceso. En ese mundo de dictadores *tropicales* que Vargas Llosa ha elaborado, no es el único se ha ocupado, en hablar y narrar estos horrores que nuestros pueblos han vivido. Me interesa destacar algo, para mí de relevancia fundamental y pocas veces referida, de esta terrible tragedia. Castillo Armas no hizo la liberación solo y tampoco la CIA y Peurifoy; ahora bien, la influencia y presencia norteamericana ha sido y continuará siendo enorme y es difícil pensarla de otra manera. Lo curioso es el giro que está tomando actualmente. Hubo una muy extensa participación de personas, no solamente de la élite guatemalteca, sino también de otros estratos sociales, que participaron y sí, también hubo extranjeros. Como en todos los casos. En esto no se puede ni debe ser ingenuo. Castillo Armas no se pensó a sí mismo como otro Ubico o Estrada Cabrera, no se vio nunca como Presidente Vitalicio, esa nunca fue su intención y las personas a su alrededor tampoco auspiciaron semejante fantasía. Es muy importante destacar que las listas de su gabinete, los miembros de la Asamblea Constituyente, que redactaron y aprobaron la Constitución de 1956 están llenas de los más ilustres y connotados guatemaltecos, muchos de los cuales eran ya personalidades de enorme prestigio, sino lo siguieron siendo a lo largo de sus vidas profesionales. Por cierto, se equivoca el autor al referirse al Ministerio de Justicia, como lo hace, término propio de otros países, en el Perú por ejemplo. En el caso guatemalteco era y es aún Ministerio de Gobernación, y lo ocupaba el Licenciado Don Miguel Ortiz Passarelli, quien incluso años después presidió una de las Cortes Supremas, con una serie de nombre y juristas de un enorme prestigio y respeto. Fue Ortiz Passarelli quien perdió las elecciones, con el General Ydigoras Fuentes, elecciones que se hicieron bajo ese marco normativo, de una Constitución llena de enormes rasgos de modernidad, y que con algunas cuestiones menos felices, facilitó de cualquier manera la sucesión presidencial, posterior al asesinato del Presidente. Dicha constitución contemplaba la figura de los Designados, normado en los artículos 165-167 de la misma y de esa forma se llevó a cabo la sucesión, no mediante un nuevo golpe, como lo sostiene Vargas Llosa. Castillo Armas no podía reelegirse y no lo buscaba tampoco. El artículo 162 de la referida Constitución, estableció contunden-temente la no reelección directa y establecía una espera de dos períodos presidenciales, para poder buscar una nueva reelección o sea, doce años. Incluso contiene unas cláusulas muy claras sobre la manera cómo se podrían modificar esos artículos y las limitaciones que existirían. Esto es muy relevante para entender que la historia de Guatemala es y ha sido una lucha interminable por construir una República Constitucional de Derecho. Eso y no las dictaduras está en el corazón de los guatemaltecos. Nada más alejado que los dominios interminables de tiranos y dictadores. Esa es y ha sido la lucha real, frustrada, truncada, inconclusa, siempre en march; esa y no otra es la vocación de la manera cómo el guatemalteco quiere vivir y organizarse. El autoritarismo es una aspiración de pequeñas minorías.

Para concluir y cerrar este muy limitado comentario, no tanto análisis, que bien merecerá ese trabajo posteriormente, quisiéramos mencionar algunos asuntos, que es mejor destacar al final. En este tema, existen claramente dos posiciones confrontadas e irreconciliables. Vargas Llosa ha hecho esa extraña afirmación, sobre el surgimiento del fenómeno castrista y el ascenso y establecimiento del comunismo en Cuba. Incluso afirmar que sin la Liberación y la "odiosa" intervención estadounidense, vía la CIA y el Departamento de Estado, por razones siniestras y obscuras, proteger a una empresa dedicada al banano y las frutas, cuyo poder mitológico era capaz de cambiar gobiernos y corromper vidas y personas. La Guerra Fría sucedió y fue crudamente real. Y se libró por todas partes, no solamente en el Occidente, ni en el Oriente comunista, también en la América Latina. Con extraño dejo de piedad, Vargas Llosa busca redimir a Árbenz y lo hace una víctima del enorme poder, de sus opositores. No lo rescata, lo explica o al menos eso nos intenta hacer creer. Al manipular y cambiar los hechos históricos, crea una ficción literaria sumamente desagradable. Trata de hacernos ver el horror de los monstruos que han gobernado y abusado a todos los países de esta región. No quiere decir —eso seria insostenible, que tales infiernos no existan en otros latitudes y muy cercanas a nosotros—, los demás países están y no son o han sido inmunes a estos trágicos destinos. No es ese el principal argumento. Lo que francamente es difícil, muy difícil de aceptar, es esa pseudocausalidad de los hechos alrededor de esta terrible tragedia —el final trágico de la vida de Árbenz ha sido ampliamente documentado y es eso, una horrible tragedia—, en la cual los principales protagonistas sufren destinos enormemente perturbadores. Lo mismo es el final de Castillo Armas, un magnicidio el cual aún hoy en día es casi imposible de comprender cómo pudo pasar y la explicación de los *recios tiempos*, es francamente insuficiente, ficción por decir lo mínimo. El fenómeno de la liberación no es el origen causal del *castrismo*. Fidel Castro surge bajo otras condiciones y en otras realidades, que aunque cercanas, son esencialmente distintas. Y allí la mano estadounidense también estuvo presente, como lo continuará estando, constante e ininterrumpidamente.

De una manera muy íntima y personal, casi totalmente privada, quisiera cerrar este comentario a *Tiempos Recios*, con una nota sumamente emocional de Odilia Palomo Paiz, hermana de mi padre. Entre los dos existió siempre una relación entrañable y que testimoniamos a lo largo de nuestras vidas y la de ellos. Los dos descansan en paz. Tía Lila, para todos nosotros, fue siempre una invaluable y querida presencia, muy cercana siempre. Incluso durante los años en los cuales ella tuvo una participación política pública, hasta su retiro de todas las actividades políticas, mantuve una estrecha relación con ella. Largas conversaciones, secretos compartidos, sugerencias, consejos, en fin, me fue lentamente contando una gran cantidad de sucesos y hechos, alrededor de toda esta tragedia, que conservaré y guardaré conmigo siempre. No me interesó y menos ahora, la *civilización del espectáculo*, la cultura del entretenimiento, como la llama Vargas Llosa o la época de la imagen, como preferiría denominarla. Mi madre, Julia Silva Beteta, también fue testigo presencial de mucha o casi toda esta terrible historia. Ella nació en New Orleans, una ciudad muy querida y con la cual mi familia ha mantenido un largo vínculo. Mis abuelos maternos, los padres de mi madre, incluso, se casaron en New Orleans. Mi madre llegó a Guatemala a casarse con mi padre, muchísimos años después. No era guatemalteca aunque logró vincularse con suma facilidad, mi abuela materna era guatemalteco-mexicana y tenía una familia bastante grande en la Guatemala de ese entonces. Eso facilitó mucho la integración de mi madre a un núcleo familiar. Nosotros pertenecemos a una generación que aprendió a amar con respeto. Mi madre tuvo que huir de Guatemala hacia Honduras, teniendo yo apenas cuarenta días de nacido, un bebé de brazos decían en Guatemala antes, logró cruzar la frontera y con extrema cautela y precaución culminó ese azaroso viaje y trayecto, bajos circunstancias sumamente delicadas. El comunismo era real, no era una ficción novelada o inventada, por Peroufoy y otros agentes de la CIA o políticos del Departamento de Estado, para justificar o inventar una agresión. Muchos lo vivieron y lo sufrieron, no eran fantasías, había familias divididas por estas causas. Muchas de estas cuestiones, de gran importancia para mí, pude lentamente confrontarlas y enriquecerlas a lo largo de mis muchos años de Servicio Diplomático, y me ayudó poder acumular muchísima información y descartar otra. Mi carrera diplomática ya ha concluido, ahora es el tiempo de las lecturas y la reflexión y, sobre todo, de la escritura. Entre mi familia se contaba la historia de que al producirse el asesinato de Castillo Armas, dejé de hablar por mucho tiempo, largos silencios, hasta que de pronto, lo volví a hacer. Ahora prefiero guardar silencio y esperar que Guatemala no tenga más *recios tiempos*, sino tiempos de paz y alegría, tiempos de prosperidad y no de lágrimas.

4
LIBER AMICORUM: ARMANDO DE LA TORRE Y SU LEGADO. EL GRAN AGRADECIDO

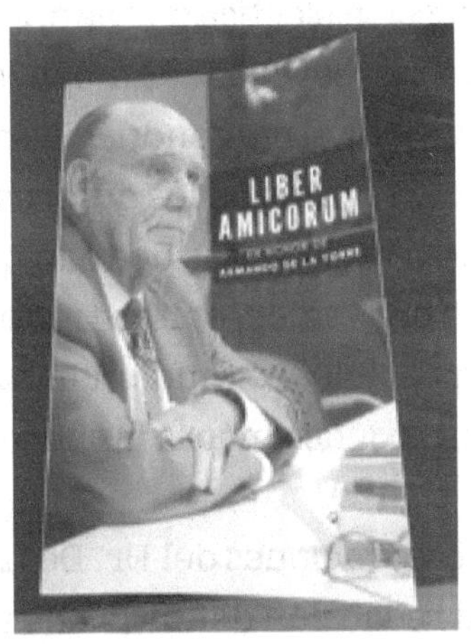

Conocí al Doctor Armando De La Torre durante mi examen privado de licenciatura, en la Universidad Rafael Landívar, cuando sometí mi primera tesis —después escribí otras más durante mis años de estudios doctorales—, sobre Heidegger. Era una cuestión bastante complicada, aún recuerdo vivamente toda la historia de la elaboración de la misma, el asesor era el Padre Antonio Gallo, a quien todos sus alumnos y seguidores admiramos profundamente y, en mi caso particular, lo recuerdo siempre con un muy profundo cariño. La terna la integraron el Dr. Luis Lara Roche, un muy importante filósofo guatemalteco, con una larguísima trayectoria académica; el Dr. Vicente Arranz Sanz, por quien dicho sea, guardo una enorme admiración y cariño mantenidos a lo largo de mucho años, y, por supuesto, el Dr. Armando De La Torre. Escribir una tesis sobre Heidegger en aquellos años era una enorme audacia, aunque todos eran plenamente conscientes de la enorme importancia de su pensamiento, no tanto de su vida. Quizás por la propia influencia del mismo Heidegger nunca me interesé demasiado en las vidas de los autores que estudiaba o leía, lo cual tal vez con los años pasados, me obliga a reflexionar, si francamente podía practicarse dicha excepción, reducción eidética quizás o, usando una expresión de la fenomenología tan cercana a mi pensamiento, "poner en paréntesis", einklammern siguiendo a Husserl o hacer epojé, ἐποχή, de las vidas personales de los autores estudiados. De allí pues, para mí el texto regía antes de todo, incluso llevado aún más lejos, los textos originales, evitar traducciones, en tanto y en cuanto ello fuera posible. Lo fundamental era sumergirse en el texto mismo incluso ponderando la influencia de los intérpretes y traductores.

Los aportes y observaciones del Dr. De La Torre fueron muy importantes para la redacción definitiva de un trabajo complejo y lleno de cuestiones filológicas y giros particulares del alemán. Él fue quién me hizo la llamada de atención, que el término Gelassenheit, era femenino en alemán y deberíamos conservar esa redacción, lo cual incorporamos inmediatamente al corregirlo y presentarlo ya definitivamente para el examen público. Allí se generó una relación llena de respeto y cariño, que se ha mantenido hasta estos años. No hace mucho, tal vez un par de años, lo visité en su casa de La Cañada, estando de visita en Guatemala. Mi querida amiga, Ana María Timpanaro, tuvo la cortesía de llevarme a verlo. Platicamos extensamente de muchos temas, mi interés en la política y los fenómenos de poder, no es central en mis intereses; más bien están dirigidos al pensamiento filosófico y a ese encuentro con el Derecho Internacional, y eso nos acercó al tema del Diferendo sobre Belice, una materia que al Doctor De La Torre le interesaba mucho, y que conoce profundamente, hay que decirlo. Hablamos extensamente de ello en muchas ocasiones y claro está, la filosofía y la Cancillería, mi otro gran interés, centraban nuestras conversaciones.

El libro, publicado en Guatemala por la Universidad Francisco Marroquín y el Instituto Fe y Libertad durante el 2019 y cuyo título completo es *Liber Amicorum: En honor de Armando De La Torre*, reúne una colección de ensayos e incluso unos poemas, de ese extraordinario talento, Amable Sánchez Torres, quien a lo largo de su vida ha cultivado una poesía excepcional, con un cuidado y pulcritud únicas. Sus sonetos son de una métrica y construcción ejemplares, y con esos poemas se abre el libro. Y luego hay una serie fascinante de ensayos, que abarcan muchas *formas del saber* —me gusta emplear la antigua expresión de Max Scheler— y tienen una unidad interna y un horizonte teorético y conceptual que los une y vincula, desde la teología, la economía, la reflexión jurídica y, sobre todo, el public choice, lo más atractivo del texto, probablemente para la mayoría, ya que el movimiento iniciado por Duncan Black, consolidado por Gordon Tulluck y Buchanan, para analizar los fenómenos del poder y la política, desde las herramientas y principios, de las ciencias económicas, cubren el texto, con una perspectiva muy ilustrativa, sobre cómo se fue construyendo lentamente un pensamiento, que proviene de esa otra y antigua tradición anglosajona, del pensamiento libertario y sus variantes. La tradición no solamente respira y es palpable a lo largo de toda la obra, sino más aún y quizás esto sea lo más relevante, une, ata y genera una continuidad al pensamiento, que le configura una impronta muy seriamente elaborada, a partir de una antigua tradición establecida.

Aunque ordenados de una manera distinta, en el texto podríamos utilizar otro criterio, tal vez por disciplinas o materias, mejor aún, formas del saber. Así, tenemos que los ensayos teológicos de Gabriel Zanotti, Guillermo Méndez, Gonzalo Chamorro y el texto filosófico de Günther Meléndez sobre Karl Jaspers, podrían ser leídos como un bloque; los ensayos sobre los temas económicos o de economía política —aunque este término no me agrada demasiado por sus connotaciones históricas—, empezando por el lúcido y muy ilustrador texto de Caroll Rodríguez, un magnífico *"anecdotario"* alrededor de los orígenes y constitución del pensamiento del public choice y su muy interesante debate entre de la Torre y Ayau, por la traducción al español del mismo, es francamente fascinante. No puedo sino recordar la célebre expresión de Buchanan al referirse al public choice, *politics without romance*, la cual un poco anima ese extraordinario debate, sobre la incorporación de la ciencia económica y sus métodos y técnicas, a la comprensión del comportamiento político y de los políticos; el trabajo de Walter Castro y Luciano Villegas a partir del análisis de Marshall alrededor de las visiones de corto y largo plazo, podrían incluirse dentro de este grupo de reflexiones, bajo el espíritu de contribuir a superar e iluminar toda aquella confusión, aspirando a ir más allá de aquello que John Rawls llamaba un salir allende y *...behind the veil of ignorance...*; hay algunos textos que son únicos y diferentes, por ejemplo, el de Mireya Molina de Castillo, casi un guión para una obra de teatro, que bien podría llamarse, "Los enemigos de la libertad", una especie de guía al pensamiento libertario o neo-libertario inclusive, es un ensayo que borda con la creación literaria y hace uso de una aparente experiencia semi-biográfica, para construir una hermosa reflexión, aunque llena de metáforas, y nos sitúa en el corazón de una discusión abierta e interminable. Por eso se me ocurría la referencia a las amenazas a la libertad, concebida aunque más allá, de la mera libertad de mercado o de mera elección; están también los ensayos-textos con un tono intimista y pedagógico. La labor y legado docente del Doctor de la Torre es enorme, su influencia y legado están plenamente atestiguados y relatados por tantísimas personas de todos los niveles; por lo que tenemos que Dina Castro y Karen Cancinos nos dejan sendos ensayos sobre la labor docente y la dimensión ética de la libertad, acercándose más al tono personal y tocando profundamente ese misterio de la generosidad y gratitud de una persona excepcional, poseedora de una extraordinaria capacidad de extender la mano y el corazón, entregar y dar tanto. Por eso y aunque en cierta forma, también vinculado a esta línea de reflexión y, por qué no decirlo, de emoción también, el prólogo redactado por la hija del Doctor de la Torre, Virginia, nos deja una reflexión intimista. No puede ser de otra forma, la filialidad y el cariño, lleno de admiración, fluyen a lo largo de esa hermosa introducción a esta colección de estupendos trabajos. No puede ser de otra manera el reconocimiento al Gran Maestro —Karen Cancinos lo llamó el *Gran Agradecido*, lo cual es profundamente conmovedor— y el forjador de una pensamiento, conservador y continuador de una tradición, que viene desde muy lejos; destaca por su fuerza y convicción, la contribución de Anton Toursinov, que nos retrotrae a las cuestiones del autoritarismo y el enigma del poder, sus advertencias sobre los abusos y excesos en el ejército del poder, y son muy profundas y nos obligan a no olvidar ese enorme riesgo, que aún se mantiene sumamente activo, amenazante y tratando de socavar los fundamentos de la cultura judeocristiana a la cual se alude constantemente a lo largo de estos muy valiosos ensayos.

Dejo para el final dos reflexiones, que me parecen relevantes, sobre el trabajo de Steve Hecht y David Landau, así como unos breves comentarios, sobre los ensayos teológicos, los cuales me generaron no solo recuerdos, sino un interés singular. Es fácil preguntarse cómo se pueden empalmar las tradiciones teológicas católicas y cristianas —esencialmente enfrentadas—, con una tradición anglosajona, más ligada a los movimientos teológicos generados, en la Reforma *protestante* europea y sus versiones estadounidenses. Probablemente ese encuentro se gesta a partir del amplio despliegue del ecumenismo surgido a partir de los Concilios Vaticanos I y II sobre todo, que contribuyeron a la construcción de un ambiente, de mucha apertura, especialmente durante los años sesenta y setenta en adelante, para generar puentes y diálogos, superar diferencias y contribuir a encuentros y coincidencias, que las hay y muchísimas. Tal vez los resultados no sean tan evidentes, sin embargo, los frutos están allí. Y es dentro de ese espíritu, que estos trabajos teológicos parecen suscribirse. Los ecos de las posiciones derivadas de la denominada *teología positiva*, a partir de Karl Barth, las visiones existencialistas que se aprecian notoriamente en Paul Tillich o más aún, la hermenéutica de la *desmitologización* —el Entmithologysierum— de Rudolph Bultmann, a partir de la visión teológica del Kerygma y Mythos o el retorno a la re-interpretación de los textos teológicos; en fin, una enorme tradición, que pudo de alguna manera caminar con las interpretaciones de Karl Rahner —el más importante teólogo católico de aquellos años—, quien incorpora no solo la analítica existenciaria y la fenomenología hermenéutica a la construcción de una nueva teología. Baste recordar las nociones de *oyente de la palabra*, construida a partir de la analítica existenciaria de Heidegger o su anterior histórica tesis doctoral, sobre la conversio ad phantasma; la célebre elaboración de Santo Tomás, en la Summa, 1q.86 a.1, donde se abre el distanciamiento con la neo-escolástica, todo este extraordinario conjunto de grandes teólogos, que generaron un notable resurgimiento del pensamiento católico-cristiano, recuerdo particularmente la noción de la *evolución del dogma*, construida por Rahner de manera sistemática y cuyo influjo posterior ha sido enorme.

Así tenemos pues esos magníficos aportes de Zanotti, en su análisis sobre el pensamiento teológico de Ratzinger —el Papa Emeritus Benedictus— y sus visiones sobre el encuentro entre la razón y la fe; Méndez nos lleva a la teología de la intersexualidad a partir de una neo-hermenéutica; finalmente, Chamorro nos ubica, dentro del contexto reciente, a partir de von Balthasar y la recuperación de una muy antigua tradición gestada dentro del tomismo y la escolástica clásicas —con un más que conocido origen aristotélico—, sobre la visión del Ser Perfecto, en quien coinciden esencialmente la Verdad, la Bondad y la Belleza, esta última acota Chamorro muy oportunamente, dejada un tanto de lado y reflexiona sobre el pullchrum, proponiendo la continuidad de una *teología de la belleza*, partiendo del pensamiento y propuesta de von Balthasar. Fascinante. Un punto que es importante tocar de pasada, es que estos aportes nos hacen ver consistentemente que hay un pensamiento teológico que no quedó "encerrado" por la cristología política y la teología de la liberación, en el debate entre una Iglesia de los Pobres y una Iglesia Antigua, superada, cargada de un peso insoportable, derrumbándose internamente, sumida en una crisis insuperable, de dimensiones catastróficas, que se resiste a la reforma y al cambio o peor, contaminada internamente por una corrupción y decadencias plenamente humanas, no abordadas y pospuestas interminablemente; más bien, la propuesta del retorno a los textos mismos, las lecturas construidas a partir de sólidas metodologías histórico-exegéticas, pueden aún contribuir a una reflexión teológica racional y seria, que se nutra desde su propia tradición y a su vez, esté abierta al mundo, o para usar el dictum del propio Rahner, llena de verdaderos *oyentes de la palabra*.

Para concluir, unos muy breves comentarios alrededor del trabajo de Hecht y Landau, elaborado en inglés, lo cual me parece sumamente pertinente, en un mundo donde la necesidad de un uso constante de otras lenguas, es no solamente una necesidad, sino una exigencia. La posición mantenida en el ensayo de Hecht y Landau gira alrededor de la oposición entre individualismo y colectivismo, y parangona casi como sumergidos en la misma crisis o mejor dicho tal vez, en una extensión de una crisis originaria, librada alrededor del mundo entero. La defensa de las libertades individuales y la colectivización de la vida humana, no solo la organización social y económica. Más allá de economías planificadas y autoritarismo estatal, o sea, dictadura colectivista, de lo cual hay muchos ejemplos, los autores intentan una muy sólida defensa del individuo y de las sociedades constituidas dentro del respeto del estado constitucional de derecho —the rule of law—, frente a una masificación y destrucción tanto de la persona humana como de las instituciones fundantes, sustentáculos de la vida en libertad.

Abunda en ejemplos y es extensa —lo cual es plenamente congruente con la vida entera de Armando de la Torre— la crítica de los gobiernos colectivistas, que se pueden encontrar por todas partes. Son los enemigos de la libertad. Hecht y Landau son unos apasionados —tal cual lo es el Doctor de la Torre— de la defensa de las llamadas sociedades abiertas, donde el individuo es el centro y eje de la acción humana misma. Lo tal vez más estremecedor del texto, es la advertencia y denuncia, que se hace a lo largo de este trabajo. Hecht y Landau escriben continuamente sobre esta materia, y es esa doble paradoja, la cual se puede resumir de la siguiente manera: los enemigos de la libertad operan desde adentro de los Estados Unidos, sostienen una lucha contra la actual administración, por razones oscuras y muy complicadas, y la misma se ha trasladado a Guatemala y muestran el otro lado de esa extraña paradoja; aquellos que ellos llaman las *antiguas oligarquías guatemaltecas*, recurren a esa expresión y término, han sido colectivistas, por razones de corrupción y auto protección. La salida es una lucha real contra la corrupción liderada, no por instituciones internacionales, sostienen, como Naciones Unidas, sino por individuos y el decidido establecimiento del estado de derecho, the rule of law, sin ambages y manipulaciones corruptas. Ese es el camino que llevará a la libertad individual. Me parece si recogemos los dos primeros artículos de la Constitución guatemalteca, los número 1 y 2, podemos introducir otra terminología —la constitucional— estos dos principios meridianamente formulados en la misma, *el estado se organiza para proteger a la persona humana* y es deber fundamental del estado *el desarrollo integral de la persona*. Si entendemos al individuo como persona humana podemos estar plenamente de acuerdo; pero, solamente si la persona humana es concebida como sujeto portador y realizador de valores humanos. Esa es la esencia misma de un estado constitucional de derecho, que tan elusivo nos ha sido a los guatemaltecos y es esto lo que Armando de la Torre nos ha querido enseñar, señalar y hacer ver a lo largo de su ejemplar vida y obra. Su auténtico legado como el Gran Agradecido.

5

FROM DON QUIXOTE TO ARTHUR: MARIA ODETTE CANIVELL'S NATIONAL HEROES

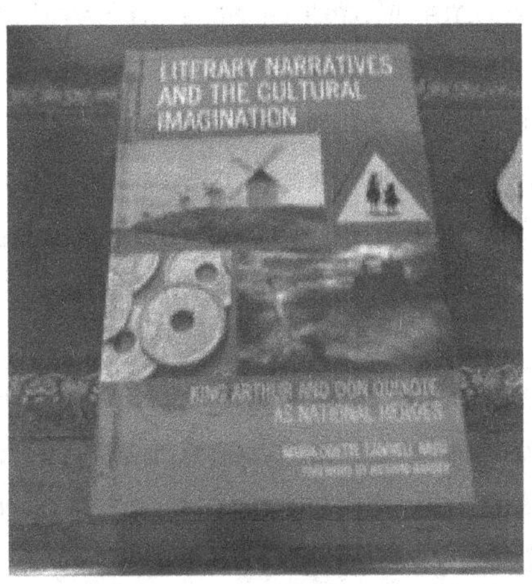

The publication of Maria Odette Canivell's recent essay on Lexington Books, from Rowman & Littlefield, 2019, under the title *Literary Narratives and The Cultural Imagination*, brings out to the public a very complex and beautifully written book on a subject dear to many, not only in Spain and the United Kingdom but all over the world. For generations and then some, Camelot has been an inspiration and a dream, even to the media and to the wide public, there is an American period of history generally acknowledged as *Camelot* thus referring to the times of the late President John F. Kennedy and his White House. We all remember the rise and tragedy of the Kennedy Family all too well. And so it will remain. But we also remember the music and the joy, we like to think of Camelot as that marvellous place where *there's no legal limit for the snow* and where justice and law rule, to employ the terms extensively used in our current political jargon. But Don Quijote calls from another place also. The dreamer of all dreamers, the one who challenges us to dream *that impossible dream, to quest for that start no matter how hopeless, no matter how far*, striving towards that evasive and elusive goal that remains ahead or beyond but from where the meaning of life springs and blossoms. Maria Odette Canivell gives us not only a marvelous analysis of the myth and the history that grounds the colossal characters, following a very carefully crafted essay, built with the proper and extensive research accompanied by a strong methodological strictness and the development of a conceptual framework that gives the study solid theoretical support.

The book as such is built around five chapters, *is the hero still worship able? to be or not to be Arthur: is that the question; in a place of La Mancha whose name I cannot recall...; the path to herodom* and *how to win friends and influence others* plus a very long Introduction named *35 million kings*. Each chapter has a very extensive bibliographical and different sorts of sources as support for the extensive argumentations crafted around every specific subject. The research conducted to complete the book is remarkable it shows and proves an extensive and long in-depth process to back the theories and positions taken throughout the analysis. It ends with a Conclusion where the author exhibits both knowledge and creativity. The book is about two very well-known characters, namely, King Arthur and Don Quijote portrayed as *national heroes*, which is a concept she employs to put before our eyes, the souls of both peoples as seen when we consider the fundamental importance of the construction of national identities as a long and complex process that emerges from the roots of the peoples and those who dare to view themselves and think on how a nation is built. No simple task

by any far stretch of the imagination. Two utterly different charac-
ters-heroes and two different people. Linked together and forced
to confront and fight against each other due to an incredible
history that even shaped the future not only of Europe but the
entire world. Empires clashing in the face of global domination
are forced by their elites to walk the path of confrontation rather
than that of peace and friendship. Oddly enough if we consider
that both *national heroes* —to employ Canivell Arzu's methodological concept— strove for peace and civilization. Arthur and
Quijote, as different as they may seem, are both constructors of
nations and searchers of peace.

Canivell Arzu engages in an extensive and detailed argumentation on the long, complex process of transforming a hero
from his humble and local origins into a general or a national
figure of identification. The lengths by which both, Quijote and
Arthur, endure it's becoming or emerging as symbols of national
unity or transcend the status of their local mythological condition
into that of the identification or bringing into one figure of a
whole people, is incredibly difficult to achieve or even more, to
comprehend or describe. Whether it is something altogether
spontaneous or carefully constructed, is what she brings before
our eyes. It doesn't seem to be the same on the paths of Arthur
and Quijote. One seems to be a long and subtle, well-designed,
quest for the other it springs from the interaction of history and
circumstances. When she presents us with the facts of the naming
of names or choice of names, amongst British royalty, leaves
out any doubts about sheer coincidence and roots history and
descendence on a common and ancient origin. The public and
open claim read "we are the descendants of the Great King Arthur
and our goal is the rebuild of Camelot in the shape of a global
Empire". On Quijote's side, we have another reading, that of the

poets and philosophers, intellectuals, that claim for their country a "national hero" who champions values, ideas, and principles regardless of any prowess and war victories. It is the birth of a "New Spain", as many of the great Spanish poets claim. That of justice, equality, and progress. The "New Spain" is like, the one that the great Andalusian poet Antonio Machado called upon, the one that walks tall under the inspiration and guidance of Quijote. Fearless in its trust in right, equitant and new beginnings. That which the Dreamer of all Dreamers taught the Spaniards, in general, to conceive, dream on, and achieved. Quijote ultimately teaches and entrusts to his descendants, the ability to dream all dreams.

The book concludes with a very well-poised and presented construction of different arguments and thorough exposition of historical facts and an in-depth reading of a long line of sources, ranging from literary works to even, economic, and social sciences studies of great relevance. Views on politics and history summon the dialectics of the Spanish/Anglo-British relationships, through a history of war, deceiving, backstabbing, and cultural aggression, this being of no lesser importance if we consider not only the historical roles played by Raleigh, Drake, or even the so-called Bloomsbury Circle and the notorious episode, as related by Canivell Arzu, very accurately and punctually, one may add by one Gerald Brenan. Canivell Arzu calls with exquisite precision on the review of the Black Legend in contrast to the heroical positioning worldwide of the Arthurian narrative of dominance. This is a very sensitive and delicate subject one that has political implications, that date not only from the times of the clash of the Empires but to the building of the New World or better employ another term, an encounter of civilizations. The birth of British Colonialism —doubled by many and lauded by the same as the most perfect model for nation-building, rooted in many of nowadays greatest and some, unsolvable, conflicts, i.e. the Middleast— as opposed to the Spanish approach, labelled as a medieval and unfunctional alternative, that engenders poverty and misery in the New World which is a very unfair, unjust dominant narrative that pays no tribute to historical reality and truth. The tale of the triumphant Empire or history as told by the vanquishers.

To conclude this brief commentary on Canivelle Arzu's recent essay, the opposition established, between Quijote and Arthur might seem challenging or even surprising, national heroes, where a literary character is transformed into a national hero due to a long process, carried out by generations of intellectuals —Spain has to be said, is a great nation of poets, thinkers and writers and this must be stated unequivocally— even from and within the Latin American domain not exclusively from the Iberian Peninsula as such while the global presence of Arthur and Camelot transcends the British Isles to become a worldwide phenomenon. Arthur nonetheless emerges from the ancient times of the Welsh, Scottish, Saxon, or Norman peoples that blended after fighting terrible wars to become one Kingdom unified by fire and law. Arthur is a warrior no doubt but is also a nation-builder and inspiration, a leader, and a creator of nations. Quijote is an aspiration, the best of mankind, a horizon of hope and generosity. Quijote inhabits that which is the most human of humanity, that which we call the essence of man. So this is the tale of two Empires, very different, two national icons and symbolic forces that cannot be compared without touching on all that bears the meaning of life and of being humans so this and then some, more, is addressed by Canivell Arzu as she travels and follows the path of these two extraordinary characters and most likely, both of them, where never real individuals but the sum of what is best of the dreams of mankind.

6
BRUCE CHAPMAN'S "POLITICIANS"
A JOURNEY INTO THE
GEOGRAPHY OF POLITICS

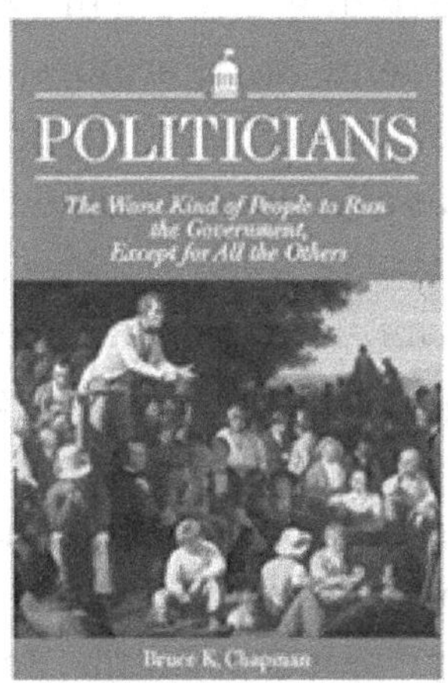
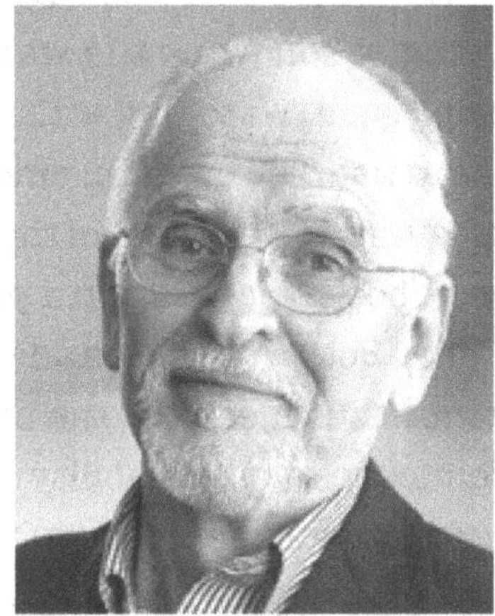

With the recent publication of his extraordinary insight on the American world of politics, Bruce Chapman, Founding Member of the Discovery Institute and his President, produces a remarkable and lifelong journey that blends both his personal and professional career and life from his times in Harvard, academical formation, political praxis, journalism, theoretician all encompassed by his wonderful natural skills. The book is beautifully written and the prose that Bruce Chapman employs is of the highest level, the language and wit throughout the whole text generates admiration, and an easy-to-read book that deals with grave and very serious issues and maintains not only this exquisite form of writing —even introducing new word-concepts— but adding a touch of humor with an elegant twist of irony.

My approach to Bruce's book is through the eyes of Foucault reading and viewing the famous and mysterious marvelous painting by Diego Velasquez, The Meninas, Las Meninas, developed on Les Mots et Les Choses of 1966. The painting is well known for its extraordinary complexity, not only formally but thematically. The painter is standing before a very large painting and at the back, there's another figure standing on a small staircase observing or following the whole scene. So, therefore, seeing and being seen. Watching without being watched. The observer and the artist. The creation emerges at a crucial moment while the remaining images, that of the *Meninas*, seem to take a second stance. A book of layers and a painting with different epistemic moments. Both Foucault and Chapman search for *historical coherence* thus meaning, the utter difficulty in reading reality and politics rests on the ability of the observer, seeker, analysts, or maybe, middlemen, to use Chapman's word concept, to peel through these layers to achieve some sort of episteme, Foucault wouldn't use terms as *levels* due to the immediate reference to Structuralism and this notion won't be present at all on Chapman's work. Nonetheless, they would share the epistemic sought-after. The creation of knowledge as such. The penetration into both eluding realities is shaped to confuse and even introduce chaos and arbitrariness. Politics and art have many common features.

If we continue traveling under Chapman's guidance —travellers that venture or dare to enter uncharted worlds, without a clear leading hand or authority, like in the present case, tend to get lost or wander lacking any reference to where the path takes us, Bruce's book provides this illuminating experience— the first corner is turned by the reference and need of a good and sound education grounded on a constant tradition. Lamentations of the collapse of education and the system as such can

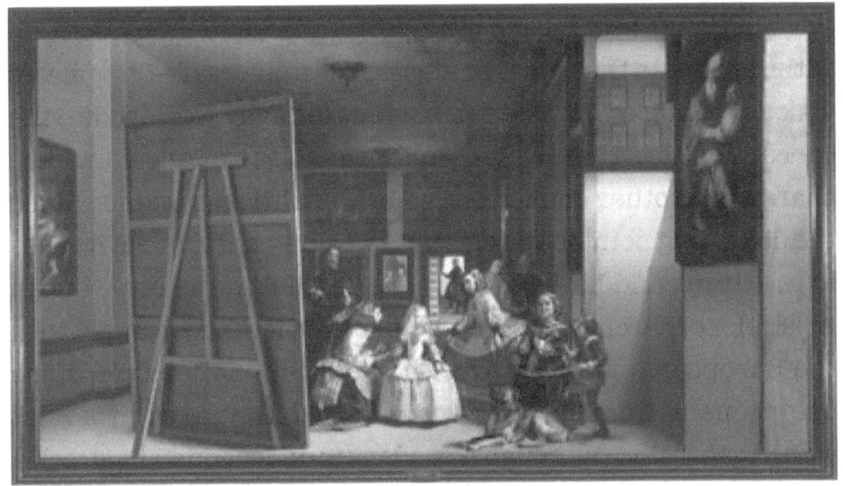

be heard even outside the United States even so in Europe itself, the cradle of all the forms of organized knowledge in the West. Transformation or neo-reformation is overwhelmingly present in all corners not of the West only but in other regions and countries everywhere.

The journey begins with a *geography of politics*, education, and tradition initiating the traveling. It is no mere casualness that the introductory element of the sought-after enterprise starts on the perhaps central topic. A sound and grounded education lead to the politics of virtue, which is described at length in the Second Part of Politicians. The real politician —not the corrupt or the opportunistic type— will conceive his goals and objectives as emerging from a profound education and political knowledge and this can only be achieved if the institutions and universities pursue education and shape it on an axiological core coming from the foundation of science and humanities also thus creating individuals that will not only acknowledge but shall practice politics according to a certain hierarchy of values.

This is the best means to avoid scandals and mongrels. One of the elements that must be stressed is universal —Chapman's vision is centered on America but is essentially worldwide— the conception that these values and principles are and should be shared with other countries and even political systems. Since the departing point is the classical world —constant references to the Greek and Latin classics are present in the book— from Aristotle to Marcus Aurelius and many others accordingly with the European and Latin American educational models, since one emanates from the other and both are a continuation of what we call generally —although nowadays is under constant attack— the Western Civilization. And that is the deep reason, following John Adam's wording, we think of the real politician as the one that has this enduring *passion for distinction.*

But the current world of politics everywhere it seems, regardless of the country, faces similar conditions and adversities, due to the lack of confidence and trust or the widespread conception and generalized corruption where even corruption optimi pessima, can be found and established —there's a strong and sound argument in favour of International Courts and therefore international justice and that is the reason the so-called principle of complementarity has been created, not after an important struggle— suffice to say here that although corruption is a universal tragedy, some other highly sensitive issues that permeate and influence political activity and politicians, the demanding and sometimes blind administrative systems in place, regulation, and overregulation, which leads to the never-ending process of reforms and reformers thus the rule or to use better wording, the well-known Cesar Wife Rule. At the same time, these constant and permanent ways of turning the world of politics into something different as was generally developed bring into life new roles and more, newly crafted professions or an assembly of power influencers and political operators, agents of the times of scandals, deceiving and truth-hiding. Facts don't matter anymore are just the way they are presented, twisted, or spun, to generate political advantage or impose the total cruelty of destruction of the other, the opponent, or opponents.

Triumph at all costs regardless of the damage inflicted. This the reality of the middlemen, lobbyists, PAC operators, consultants, and pollsters versus the end of the politicians —in the original and pregnant sense— and the establishment of the internet of things, like Jeremy Rifkin once called this complex new set of political, economic and technological realities. It is the rule of the media and bureaucracy or as Chapman calls it, *the age of containment*. Maybe we are all witnessing the return of pure muckraking in the times of the pure image and his tyrannical realm.

Chapman's closing chapters are truly remarkable. A strong and accurate constructed argumentation in favour of the axiology of virtuosity that leads to the leaving and conducting of all political actions and compromises having always the clear horizon that genuine virtue guides every step that the politician takes all within the search and maintenance of a profound historical coherence. His Personal Postscript is a wonderfully worded recount of Bruce's political life a dedication to the defense of the individual, free market economy over the despotic rule of collectivism and State intervention in all spheres of human existence, the constant threat to the inner virtuosity of the individual and the sacredness of the personal and intimate privacy, core and center of dignified human life. Safeguarding these sanctuaries is the highest call to the politicians who can restore the values and virtues that must prevail in this utmost activity of humankind. Bruce Chapman has lived not only a remarkable political life but also an exemplary one. His success and legacy shine through like should be for all devoted warriors and champions of the individual or as we prefer to name it: the human persona.

Let us close this post that his aspiration is none other than an invitation to read and study this outstanding contribution to the fields of Political Theory, Social Sciences, and even more, to the politician as such, the aspiring, or the active ones. We cannot find a more correct form of closing this invitation than quoting Chapman's words: *It is the role of politicians, then, to harmonize the passions and interests of humanity with the higher standards and goals of civilization. Politics looks to success but ultimately must aim for virtue. Success without virtue, ironically cannot persist. The human soul will not stand for it.*

ANABELLA GIRACCA O EL NEO-NATURALISMO EN "PARA SERVIRLE"

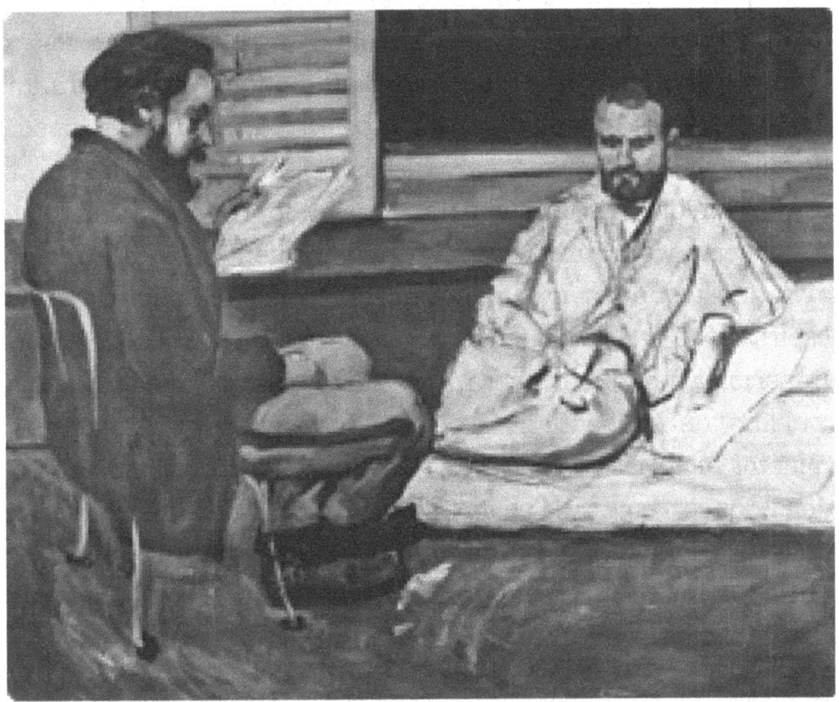

Paul Cezane: "Paul Alexis lisant à Émile Zola", 1869-1870. Museo de Arte de Sao Paulo.

La reciente novela publicada, por Alfaguara, de Anabella Giracca, bajo el muy sugestivo título, *Para Servirle*, México 2018, es una fascinante inmersión en un mundo complejo y doloroso, el del llamado *servicio doméstico, asistentes* o incluso *asesoras del hogar*, según el lugar o país y no está extento de una cantidad mayor de otros nombres, que nombran y describen una realidad semi oculta y evidente, que en la Amérca Latina tiene unas condiciones casi irreales, y que lindan con todo lo mágico, esotérico, macondiano incluso, y sobre todo, donde lo real se confunde con el misterio y la magia. Anabella Giracca nos lleva a deambular, como sumidos en una niebla de irrealidad, la cual bruscamente nos instala, casi de golpe y sin anuncio, en el corazón mismo del dolor y la tragedia de la pobreza. Tal cual Zola relatara la historia de los Rougon-Macquart, durante el Segundo Imperio, o sea la transformación de Luis Napoleón de Presidente en Emperador de los franceses, autoproclamado Napoleón III, después del conocido autogolpe organizado, para instaurar el Tercer Imperio, ante la prohibición constitucional de su reelección. Son también tiempos de grandes desarrollos intelectuales y científicos, tanto como artísticos, que forman parte de ese extraordinario mundo espiritual de la Francia del Siglo XIX, hasta el colapso del Segundo Imperio, la derrota francesa, durante la guerra franco-prusiana y el final del siglo, tan lleno de grandes nombres y de acontecimientos históricos de una gran relevancia. En ese mismo mundo, donde los escritores y la política se ven sumidos, en la inevitabilidad de una conversación fundamental, especialmente cuando los períodos históricos, pasan por esos momentos decisivos, que marcan y definen unas transiciones y cambios, pospuestos,

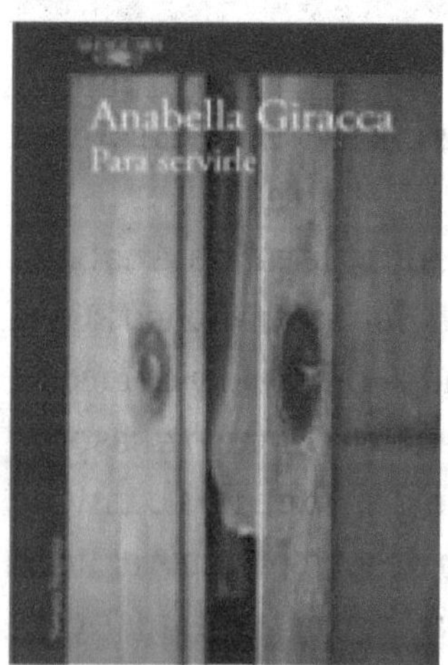

postergados, los cuales emergen desde adentro de los gritos angustiados de todos aquellos "que no tienen voces para gritar" y demandar justicia y equidad. Tiempos de guerras, aunque de naturalezas distintas.

Las historias de la familia Aguablanca son francamente extraordinarias; pero, no son narraciones de realismo mágico, son todo lo contrario y a la vez lo mismo. Por eso hablamos acá de un neo-naturalismo a lo Zola. No son los cuentos fantásticos de los grandes narradores de la literatura de lo real-imaginario. Más bien son historias del dolor más duro, de la pobreza sin esperanza, de la desnutrición y su terrible condena, del olvido y del abandono. Y de esa formidable capacidad de sobrevivir de sus protagonistas. La novela abre con un crimen y se cierra con otro. A lo largo y ancho del relato, otros más se suceden, crímenes secretos, escondidos, debajo de la piel y la carne de sus protagonistas; asesinatos de amor y de pasión y otros, simplemente por venganzas, algunos meramente insinuados y otros como apariciones fantasmales, las cuales parecieran perseguir y acechar constantemente a todos los protagonistas, de este drama poblado por lo extraordinario, aquello que ocurre casi sin comprensión alguna. El Caimán —en una parte del texto, el pueblo así nombrado, pareciera tener un otro nombre, El Chol, cuyas derivaciones serían más que evidentes— es un lugar paradójico. La leyenda del extraordinario animal, que habitaba en alguna parte y en todas partes, re-bautiza al pueblo. Los nombres que los nombran. Tal vez de allí esa tan curiosa alegoría explicaría algunos de sus múltiples misterios.

El lenguaje del texto y sus técnicas narrativas escapan a los objetivos aquí contemplados. Merecen una mayor y dedicada configuración, como las anteriores novelas que Anabella Giracca ha publicado, *Demasiados secretos*, *Sanjuana*, *El enigma del santuario* y la anterior, *Gitana mía*, del 2014. No cabe la menor dudaque las publicaciones y estudios de su novelística, serán muchas y muy nutridas. Sin embargo, hay una poesía interna dentro del texto mismo, frases que parecieran escaparse, cuidadosas, penetrantes y sumamente reveladoras, que insinúan oportunamente, con una métrica casi perfecta, su uso muy mesurado y sumamente oportuno.

Tomemos unas de ellas, casi al azar, por ejemplo: *Es lo único que tenemos, un sitio donde escupir tranquilas.*; *Dicen que la miseria te roba las palabras.*; *Imagino que no es nada fácil para usted comprender la magia de ciertas cosas, pero sería bueno que haga el esfuerzo porque la vida no es tan clara como se cree.*; *Para mí la muerte no es un castigo sino un favor.* Mucho del lenguaje pareciera ser como producto de una observación y catalogación sistemáticas, casi etno-lingüística, frases extraídas del lenguaje diario y coloquial de muchísimas personas y tal vez hasta propio y peculiar, dentro del mundo no solamente de las Aguablanca, sino incluso más abarcador e incluyente, de un uso más extendido. No son meros giros o estilos, formas del habla popular; son como fotografías, que contienen y detienen, en sí mismas, la realidad de la que este neo-naturalismo nos pone delante. Es la falta y carencia de casi todo, donde *escupir* se transforma en un derecho inalienable, el enmudecer ante tanta pobreza y limitación, donde la muerte misma es vista como una salida, una solución al interminable sufrimiento y dolor. Y sin embargo, hay una esperanza o un refugio, una magia, presente a lo largo de todos los relatos, en una constante. Es vista como una herramienta o instrumento, cuya posesión es un secreto y cuyos conocimientos son completamente reservados; es el arma contra el poder, lo que pone límites al poder aplastante y duro ejercido constantemente, sobre todos los otros, aquellos que no son más que esclavos o sirvientes, de todos los que pueden pagar.

Hay otras formas de evasión también, aunque vienen con un altísimo precio. Hay un erotismo siniestro relatado de manera brutal, neonaturalística, como *Germinal* o *Nana*, por eso la alusión a Zola y sus personajes, de la decadencia y destrucción, transformación, de un mundo en pleno proceso de mutación. Un mundo que termina y otro que emerge o nace de la destrucción del otro. Tal vez ese neonaturalismo es más patente en su descripción de ese erotismo violento, agresivo, vandálico, denigrante, donde la víctima y el victimario sufren por la destrucción de todas las formas de ternura. Las víctimas son tantas y tan inocentes. Y de esa pérdida de inocencia surge la venganza y el odio. Un rencor sordo y silencioso, capaz de esperar por y durante años, para ejercer su justicia reivindicadora. La fuerza de la debilidad ultrajada convertida y transformada en la más brutal forma de castigo. El mal inflingido al convertirse en una manera de sobrevivencia engendra también, incomprensiblemente, un poder secreto, que llevará eventualmente a la imposición y condena del victimario. Nunca habrá olvido.

Son muchos los lugares de encuentros rituales en El Caimán. La pila, tal vez una sola, donde las mujeres se reúnen, para limpiar y aprender, descubrir, trasmitir y compartir secretos y conjuros, aunque también para ritualizar las muchas formas del amor y sus misterios. Y probablemente el personaje central de la obra, aparentemente sería Candelaria; visto más de cerca, la larga sombra de Lila Aguablanca está presente en cada uno de los detalles de la vida de todos las habitantes de El Caimán y la de aquellos, que llegan a tener alguna relación con la Aguablanca o el pueblo. Lila es como la poseedera de todos los secretos y la guardiana suprema de una forma de saber, de conocimientos, capaces de provocar, desencadenar, unas fuerzas ocultas, las cuales solamente ella y sus más cercanas iniciadas, poseen y pueden controlar. Los secretos de la protección y de los castigos. Aunque como en las formas clásicas de drama, hay un gran colectivo, quien es el verdadero protagonista de la totalidad de la obra es el pueblo de Aguablanca, tal y como concluye, con una referencia hierática, al apuntar todas las sospechas, de los hechos ocurridos, "al pueblo entero".

La cuestión no está en describir detalladamente la trama de la novela, sino más bien provocar e invitar a su lectura y estudio. Es un texto sumamente relevante. Habla de una realidad dolorosa. Dura e impactante, se trata de un mundo por todos conocido, aunque de mayor o menor manera, muy superficialmente, es una realidad existencial, presente constantemente en la cotidianidad.

Impacta decisivamente las vidas de muchísimas personas, el tratamiento dado por Anabella Giracca, quien en su más reciente trabajo, cuestiona, pregunta, narra y cuenta, y con una habilidad muy especial, reconstruye detalles, de una forma de existencia esencial y central, para tantísimas personas. Y francamente, impacta a millones, dentro y fuera de El Caimán. No es solamente una experiencia limitada a una pequeña región del Macondo tropical —por eso no es solamente real-imaginario, es neonaturalismo puro—, existe en todas las latitudes del mundo entero y sabemos bien, que el mundo es ancho y ajeno.

8
"AN ENGLISHMAN IN NEW YORK": BULMER-THOMAS AND THE "RETREAT OF THE AMERICAN EMPIRE"

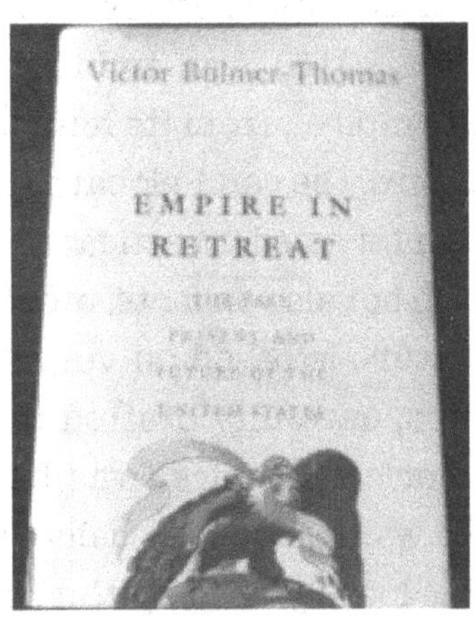

"...why do you dress me In borrow'd robes?" Macbeth. Act 1, Scene 3, 108-109

"Oh, I'm an alien, I'm a legal alien/I'm an Englishman in New York", "...you can hear it in my accent when I talk/I'm an Englishman in New York..." so goes the famous lyrics of the Sting song, inspired on the emigration to the United States, namely New York, in the latter stages of his extraordinary life, of the cultural British icon Quentin Crisp. John Hurt rendered 2009 a remarkable performance on Crisp's emigration. The immensely complex relationship between the United States and the UK tells us a story of origin and transformation. It goes far beyond coffee and tea. Or the "special relation". Even language. Victor Bulmer-Thomas a distinguished British scholar and Professor Emeritus of London University and a world-leading authority on the fields of economics and international relations, former Head of Chatham House and perhaps the most recognized expert on the history of economics in Latin America and the Caribbean, also author of a series of very impressive books that had an enormous impact amongst social scientists and economists throughout the region as well. His latest publication, "Empire in Retreat. The Past, present, and future of the United States" (Yale University Press: New Haven & London, 2018) is an ambitious study of what he calls the "American empire", from its foundation, the creation of the territorial empire, the semi-global to the retreat.

A wonderfully constructed investigation grounded not only on extensive research but also on facts, numbers, and statistics. Its internal architecture is based on very strict and rigorous methodological steps, carefully crafted to demonstrate and argue that the "American empire "was built" as such by its Founding Fathers but was also conceptually thought to be a world empire the term was loosely used by the Founding Fathers in spite of genuinely aiming for a Republican form of government, according to Bulmer-Thomas' affirmation, after taking the position of former Spanish colonies and even till the end of the Cold War and its aftermath. This assertion might be a little troubling and not only due to the historical facts that the United States emerged from a colonial war against an Empire, a real empire, against whom fought and won a "war of liberation" and established the contrary to the British Empire, that of a Republic, "We the people" is radically different than the "Royal We" of the European Monarchs or Emperors. But let us avoid superficiality because Bulmer-Thomas' book is in no way shape or form, superficial. The question is whether the term or concept of empire and all its implications, anti-imperialism, can or could be employed to refer to the United States. His journey is to prove that not only was a real Empire but amazingly so, is now in retreat. This retrieval is according to the author, due to mainly internal reasons and this is leading to the constitution of a nation-state as opposed to the semi-global empire.

There is a possibility to use the term or concept "empire" with a benign or even neutral connotation. Empires are associated historically with the extremist forms of authoritarianism even with "evilness". The "evil empire" is not only described in the visual language of the cinema or nowadays of video games. Sometimes "emperors" are even depicted as illustrated or enlightened leaders, Alexander was allegedly educated by Aristotle himself but Nero's closeness to Seneca is by not far stretched of the historical imagination, a model of such relationships. The list is long and not a very fruitful one, there are some interesting exceptions, maybe Frederich the Great and Voltaire, to think of an outstanding historical figure, most of the time intellectuals or thinkers would oppose despotism. In the case of the so-called "American empire" it is very hard to think of Jefferson, Madison, Franklin, Adams, or even Washington, as authoritarian emperors or aspiring to be. Their quest was another one. At least this is randomly taken from the dominant narrative. "We the people..." is the essence of democracy. No place for the ruling tyrants. Constitutional Law is the modern conception that will put an end to the old doctrine of The Divine Right of Kings and what better British way to think of it as Macbeth, usurpation by killing the chosen one by right, Duncan, or birth, finds no place on American history. Rulers are also subjects before the law and shan't be above it, never. Human power is fundamentally a subject of mere mortals nor of the divine ones, one will rule as a representative of the "We the people...". Not as representative of God. Here we find the path to the modern-democratic world.

The argumentation in the book is extensive and deep. From its historical origins, Bulmer-Thomas takes on the history of the foundation of the United States and all the different moments it went through. And there are some very dramatic moments, not only the Civil War that thorn a nation apart, the expansion period and the claiming or even buying of territories until the shaping of the geographical conformation that we came to see and acknowledged as the United States of the 50 members of the Federation. Nothing can replace reading this fascinating and intriguing work. Suffice it to say that the author goes to great lengths to analyze and discuss almost all the principles that support not only the historical policies of the United States but also questions its usage and invocation under several historical-critical periods of ideas such as "American exceptionalism", "manifest destiny", "the Monroe Doctrine", "Exemplarism" and many more. From imperialism as "extraction of revenue", and "territorial control" via expansionism as tools for security control. Hard-soft-smart diplomacy. His reading is very demanding and is hoping a controversy should be open eventually —am thinking here on Dascal's Theory of Controversies— on the subject of the conception of imperialism to begin with. It will be fascinating to see if what Dascal describes as the Solomon Model can serve to articulate this extraordinary controversy and its expansion.

But the part of the retreat of the empire is the most challenging and interesting one. The book is built to come to this conclusion. The numbers and the study of the "decline of leadership", the huge and incredible problem of the debt and its tenors to the transformation of the retreating empire, put before our very eyes, the taking form of an unthinkable situation, debt to levels beyond imagination, colossal numbers and the dangers involved in taking such enormous risks. Let us follow Bulmer-Thomas's own words: "The stock of external assets (i.e., those US assets owned by foreigners) is now much larger than the country's

GDP. Best known is the US federal government debt obligations held by foreigners. At the end of the fiscal year 2016, these were valued at $6.3 trillion roughly one-third of the total. Then there are the debts of the financial system to foreigners together with the debts of the nonfinancial sector and intercompany loans to give a total of $19 trillion for the gross external debt position of the United States."

So, this is an outstanding contribution to the study of Foreign Policy and international relations especially if we view them from the horizon of trade and economics. The book as such is worthwhile for deep study and discussion. Am sure the debate is already taking place and the Model Solomon awaits the deconstruction of the controversy and all its elements. The debate surrounding the "imperialistic behavior" of some superpowers is not a new one, looms from every corner of history and the constant struggle that feeds and nurtures the sprouts emerging from the interactions amongst nations and men.

9
SOBRE LOS TIEMPOS QUE SE FUERON: ÁLVARO ARZÚ, MÉNDEZ-VIDES Y LAS LECTURAS DEL MISTERIO DE LA TEMPORALIDAD

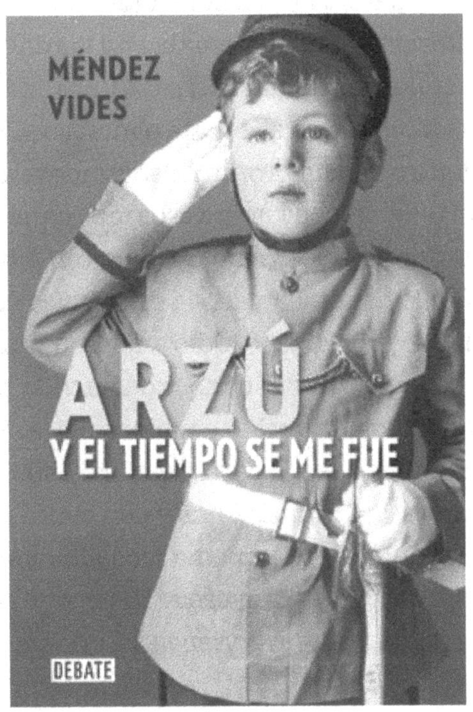

Mucho y más se escribirá sobre el recientemente fallecido alcalde de la ciudad, Don Álvaro Arzú Irigoyen. Alcalde emeritus, sobre todo si repensamos el origen del vocablo, cuya raíz es el verbo latino emeri, cuyo significado más pertinente es servir, y si alguno sirvió a la ciudad y la transformó fue Álvaro Arzú. La reinventó, generó espacios humanos, modificó e introdujo una gran cantidad de cambios e innovaciones, que muchos admiran y reconocen y otros critican y condenan. Ante la muerte procede el respeto y el reconocimiento, aunque no ignoro algunos invocarán la crítica y el ataque, bajo muchísimas formas, algunas deleznables, aunque la moderación y la contención no abundan estos días, donde la generosidad está tan ausente. Este fenómeno no solamente es recurrente en Guatemala, sino prácticamente en todos los lugares donde los márgenes de libertad son suficientemente amplios. La ironía y el insulto han sido cultivados incluso como formas literarias. En Guatemala hay verdaderos maestros de este tan peculiar estilo narrativo. Nunca lo he practicado. Creí, desde mis inicios, que el debate e incluso el mero disentir, se deben dar dentro de una profundidad de ideas, conocimientos y conceptos, sin tener que recurrir a esos medios de descalificación y alternativas, donde el lenguaje del odio toma lugar de forma tan evidente. Eso lo hemos llamado la epistémica del odio. Porque es odio, muy hondo y arraigado. Odio anónimo y también abierto y sin disimulos. Álvaro Arzú luchó toda su vida política contra estas formas de violencia verbal e incluso física. Y las enfrentó, contundentemente, y daba la cara y estaba dispuesto a desafiar a sus contrapartes, sin limitaciones y con claridad. No siempre sus detractores asumieron la misma forma hidalga y quijotesca de conjurar el debate y la controversia. La obra de Adolfo Méndez-Vides recoge varias de estas experiencias a lo largo de un discurrir lineal.

Desde sus inicios, hasta ese extraño final, premonitorio tal vez, o sencillamente anticipado. La leyenda sobre su posible conocimiento del final del tiempo tanto en el título, como en esa larga conversación, que abarca toda su vida, es probablemente una manera muy propia de contarla y quién sabe, sino substituir unas Memorias, las cuales siempre fueron esperadas. Aunque a muchos no les guste, fue el político más relevante de la Era Democrática. Curiosamente su carrera política empezó durante el final de los llamados *gobiernos militares* y concluyó en el actual momento histórico, en el que, incluso, se cuestiona a esa misma Democracia tan dolorosamente construida, incompleta. Hoy día términos como *cooptación, colusión, corrupción, refundación* y varios más, ampliamente usados por el sector cuestionante de la formalidad de nuestra Democracia, se agota y requiere de unos profundos cambios, planteados alegremente —esto siempre lo he encontrado de una audacia casi suicida—, para cambiar o modificar totalmente la actual Constitución, convocando ese fantasma llamado *Asamblea Nacional Constituyente*, para re-escribirla y edificar un nuevo mundo, que superaría al que la Constitución presente ha sido incapaz de arribar. Es más, defender la Constitución pareciera tarea de las llamadas *fuerzas antico-rrupción*, que el alcalde ahora fallecido, encabezaría. Una profun-da insanidad y un riesgo enorme. La Constitución actual es tal vez lo más virtuoso de la Era Democrática. En más de una ocasión nos ha salvado del abismo y en la narrativa de la temporalidad, que Méndez-Vides magistralmente construye al darnos el relato de la vida política del ahora difunto alcalde, quien fue un compro-metido defensor de nuestra Ley Suprema. Claro que vivimos en un país profundamente injusto, inundado de una pobreza dura y aplastante y de unos contrastes casi indescriptibles y menos aún, pensables como realidades. Arrastramos un pasado del cual no hemos podido separarnos. No hemos sido capaces de construir bondad y amistad. Estamos sumidos en atrinchera-mientos radicales e incluso absurdos; sin embargo, muchísimo se pudo lograr, una paz casi inesperada, el final de un largo conflic-to, que parecía ser interminable y un naciente crecimiento —aun-que no desarrollo— económico, que continúa evolucionando, a pesar de tantísima inestabilidad y crisis permanentes y constante. Y el mérito es de todos, no de unos pocos. Construir justicia es sumamente complicado. Y se ha logrado. Álvaro Arzú es parte de todo eso y fue uno de sus constructores. No sólo realizó obra pública; sino también la invisible, la que no es publicitada, fue una constante en sus sucesivas gestiones como alcalde de una ciudad que creció desmesuradamente y a una rapidez casi inexplicable.

Méndez-Vides fabrica una narración lineal, por medio de la cual, bajo el recurso de preguntas muy bien elaboradas, nos pone ante los ojos una historia que empezó en la Avenida Simeón Cañas y concluyó, inesperadamente, en San Isidro. Un largo camino desde una parte de la ciudad atada a sus orígenes e historia y una nueva parte de la ciudad, devenida de la modernidad y el crecimiento. Y en medio de ese camino, la figura protagónica de una importantísima parte de la historia de la modernidad guatemalteca. Un recorrido que fue haciendo historia. Un caminar que cambiaba paso a paso, una ciudad saliendo de los barrios, hacia un mundo nuevo, peligroso y desafiante. Hay varias cons-tantes a lo largo del relato-entrevista, por llamarlo de algún modo ya que tiene de ambos, relato porque es un contar, entrevista porque formalmente, contiene preguntas y respuestas, que abarcan un largo período de tiempo, es decir, va más allá del formato típico de la entrevista "periodística". No es un ejercicio de comunicación mediática, sino más bien la construcción de una forma de biografía-memoria, sin agotar a ninguna de las dos modalidades e intentando emerger, bajo una nueva forma de decir historias. En ese *decir historias* hay varias constantes que se detectan a lo largo de la vida misma de Álvaro Arzú, casi como presencias matemáticas; una su autodefinición, como *prag-matista-nacionalista*, alejándose de las posiciones conceptuales o visiones de la política y del mundo, en tanto que se puedan referir a *ideologías políticas* —me siento incómodo usando este término— intentando ubicarse en un téorico centro, en medio de las injustas acusaciones de *neoliberalismo*, de un sector y del otro sector, como demasiado complaciente, con la inclusión de una *izquierda*, a la cual le abrió espacios, principalmente, en su gestión como Presidente; una segunda constante es la de privilegiar el hacer sobre el decir, o sea lo que cuentan son las obras hechas, el legado está en lo tangible y objetivo, en todo aquello que pueda afectar las vidas, para bien, de los habitantes de la ciudad y en un contexto mayor, de todo el país, en su doble función de Presidente y Alcalde; en las convicciones y principios, hay una larga coherencia en su trayectoria, buscó el centro y se alejó de los extremos; solo así se pudo firmar la paz y encontrar en Ricardo Ramírez-Rolando Morán, un acompañante inesperado, para lograr cerrar un período trágico de la historia moderna de Guatemala.

Navegante de crisis y mediador eficaz, enfrentó muchísimos dilemas, que se consignan con pinceladas incluso de humor, durante sus interminables esfuerzos por lograr solucionarlos. Él mismo se refiere a algunos de los más complejos y difíciles de resolver, nos quedan así versiones precisas de cómo se dieron algunos acontecimientos decisivos, a los cuales le tocó enfrentarse, en momentos sumamente delicados y sensibles. Incluso denuncia nombres y personas, cuyas actuaciones públicas y privadas, no coinciden y en algunos casos, se confirma esa visión oscura y siniestra que se les ha adjudicado. La lista es bastante larga. Hay una expresión que me llamó mucho la atención, referida a las mejores formas de gobernar o si usamos o recurrimos al término *estrategia*, me refiero al dictum *la política solamente se puede llevar adelante con amigos*, se puede gobernar únicamente con amigos. Supo construir equipos, trabajó con equipos, tanto como Presidente como Alcalde, tal vez por eso la Alcaldía seguirá funcionando a pesar de su enorme ausencia. El equipo que él dirigía queda allí, para continuar la obra, seguir haciendo y tal vez, decir poco o casi nada. Pura *acción humana*.

En varias respuestas a las preguntas de Adolfo Méndez-Vides, en lo tocante al tema, de la improvisación o a la reacción ante lo inminente de resolver problemas, que surgen inesperada o sencillamente son inanticipables. Se definía repetidamente como un *improvisador*, opuesto al planificador. Las urgencias permanentes y constantes, las cuales demandan atenciones inmediatas, las referencias a cuestiones capaces de distorsionar lo acordado y tal vez si, previamente planificado, un infame secuestro, por ejemplo, que estuvo a punto de tirar al suelo un proceso delicadamente constituido, para llegar a la firma definitiva de la paz, en las respuestas hay otros ejemplos que hablan abundantemente de ese *improvisador*, dotado de una extraña capacidad de intuición, que produjo soluciones y que también, él mismo reconocía, en sus respuestas, en determinadas ocasiones no funcionó. No cabe duda que la política demanda y obliga, en más de alguna ocasión, respuestas improvisadas o reacciones inmediatas, ante situaciones enormemente delicadas y sorpresivas. Allí es donde los estadistas emergen y los políticos de menores envergaduras, naufragan. Hemos visto muchísimos casos de hundimientos casi anunciados, donde otros factores precipitaron caídas estrepitosas de políticos poco racionales y fríos, incapaces de superar barreras intempestivas, que de pronto y sin anuncio o peor aún, no previstas, generaron precipicios y sepulturas insalvables. Es muy difícil, tal vez imposible, adivinar estas sorpresas, sobre todo en un mundo político, en el que las crisis se suceden interminablemente, casi sin interrupción, o sucesivamente.

Hay un misterio que siempre rodeará al libro y está precisamente en su final, que algunos querrán ver como premonitorio: el título del libro mismo, ...*el tiempo se me fue...* apunta a un final, al acabarse del tiempo, y pareciera más aludir a una cuestión de tiempos políticos u oportunidades de generar más innovaciones y cambios. Lo cierto es que el alcalde Álvaro Arzú falleció de improviso, cuando los tiempos así lo decidían. La tragedia humana de la vida y de la muerte. No hay duda que dejó un legado enorme, una obra vasta y más que evidente, aunque sus detractores se empeñarán en contradecir y negar esto. En el tránsito de una paz firmada —hay que decir, negociada, edificada, por varios guatemaltecos, cuyo trabajo preparatorio fue fundamental y decisivo, aunque parezca aún hoy día, insuficientemente reconocido— y escrita a una paz real, de convivencia sincera, apenas estamos iniciando el camino, las heridas no cierran del todo. Aprender a transitar del mundo de los silencios al mundo de las voces, sendero lleno de tropiezos y caídas, ciertamente nos ha dejado un escenario urbano, por el cual podremos continuar, en ese extraño y complicado andar de la generación de amistad y generosidad a la vez, que también proseguimos, en la ruta de la construcción de justicia, en el más originario de todos sus significados.

10
ASTURIAS, SALAZAR Y LA LITERATURA DEL MAL. EL RETORNO DEL HOMBRE FÁUSTICO

…¡Alumbra, lumbre de alumbre, Luzbel de piedralumbre! Como zumbido de oídos persistía el rumor de las campanas a la oración, maldoblestar de la luz en la sombra, de la sombra en la luz. ¡Alumbra, lumbre de alumbre, Luzbel de piedralumbre, sobre la podredumbre! ¡Alumbra, lumbre de alumbre, sobre la podredumbre, Luzbel de piedralumbre! ¡Alumbra, alumbra, lumbre de alumbre…, alumbre…, alumbra…, alumbra, lumbre de alumbre…, alumbre…, alumbra…, alumbra, lumbre de alumbre…, alumbra, alumbre…!

Miguel Ángel Asturias, El Señor Presidente

La extraordinaria novela de Oswaldo Salazar, recientemente publicada por la Editorial Alfaguara, *Hombres de Papel*, nos muestra una vez más la continuidad de la llamada literatura del post conflicto. Los guatemaltecos han encontrado una forma de enfrentarse e intentar comprender este, entre muchas otras vías de expresiones estéticas: arte, poesía, aunque no exclusivamente las mismas, siendo, por supuesto, la novela, una de sus formas más buscadas. Sin embargo, la complejidad de la novela de Oswaldo Salazar rebasó de muchas maneras los límites que otras obras, dentro de esta tendencia, habían marcado. Es cierto que, por su temática, la obra es literatura del conflicto, ello es más que evidente, también es cierto que es una novela política; pero, muchísimo más que una novela política, es una reflexión o meditación muy profunda sobre la esencia del mal. Una fenomenología del mal. De allí la referencia, en el título de este comentario, al retorno del hombre fáustico. Del principio al fin, la obra tiene como corazón, en el lenguaje guatemalteco, vernacular, un empactamiento. Es decir, Miguel Ángel se transmuta —estamos hablando de una cierta ficción, que el mismo autor destaca, aunque a la vez, refiere usar a lo largo de su obra, textos o expresiones, del mismo Asturias—, en una especie de Fausto latinoamericano. Aquí hay dimensiones universales también, nada ajenas al verdadero Asturias, quien aspiraba ser un autor universal y a la universalización de su obra. Y lo consiguió. El Fausto-Asturias es tal vez a quien buscamos deconstruir, el personaje creado por Salazar, quien despliega no solamente una erudición enorme, sutil y elegantemente usada, sin caer en la banalidad, del que anuncia su sabiduría, sino más bien la emplea, con una profunda calidad.

La novela consigue un estado casi religioso, hierático y poseedora de una liturgia latinoamericana, transmutadora de la realidad, lectora e intérprete, de un mundo que se le da a Asturias, aunque también a otros más, ese mundo circundante, lleno de símbolos, metáforas y alegorías, de todos tipos, de su condición de circundante y de abarcador e incluyente, a todos aquellos que compartieron y tal vez aún, a otros que continúan haciéndolo, hoy día, en un mundo post-conflicto, el cual intenta definirse, en una apertura, que como tal, es titubeante y muy proclive a los excesos.

El encuentro con el Luzbel de piedralumbre. Durante una noche de alucinación, en medio de una legendaria borrachera, sin tenerse claro si buscándolo o siendo buscado, o sea elegido, Asturias tiene un encuentro y un diálogo, con un personaje siniestro, de aspecto demoníaco, aunque de palabras suaves y elegantes. Seductor, el Lúzbel-Mefistófeles, poseedor del talento, de embrujar la realidad, aquella realidad aparente y pragmática, convence con extrema facilidad, al saber muy bien no sólo la debilidad de su víctima, sino también, capaz de corromper aún más la podredumbre. Un hombre caído. Debilitado por su propia debilidad. Casi entregado a la renuncia de la esperanza. Sucumbe fácilmente ante lo que tiene que oír, como entregado al pacto de sangre, al sacrificio por lo buscado; en este caso no es el amor de una jovencita, sino la eternidad de la fama, el reconocimiento, la certeza del cumplimiento, de un destino y con algo más, el sacrificio de su propio hijo, quien incluso, sin saberlo, es ofrendado también, para completar y cerrar el demoníaco acuerdo, casi inevitable.

A lo largo de la obra se presenta varias veces, incluso habla con Rodrigo, cuando este se acerca a un hospital para pacientes mentales, en búsqueda de su madre, usando por primera vez el nombre Legión. Otra vez es El Inquisidor, en el interrogatorio o en lugar de torturas en Buenos Aires y finalmente, vuelve a ser Legión al bailar, con Bárbara, la noche de la entrega del Premio Nobel en Estocolmo. Las referencias son muy conocidas y citadas, provienen del Nuevo Testamento, en especial, Lucas 8,30; también, en Mateo 26,53 y Marcos 5,9. El texto griego dice: Λεγιών, ὅτι [1]εἰσῆλθεν δαιμόνια πολλὰ εἰς αὐτόν. Es la respuesta dada a Jesús al inquirir por el nombre del demonio, que ocupaba un cuerpo humano o sea la referencia a la multitud innúmera de demonios, en la que no solamente son legión, sino son lo mismo, en una multitud. La unidad múltiple del mal. Y aquí es pues, donde la transmutación, casi divina, se lleva a cabo, Miguel Ángel-Fausto. El que puede hablar con los demonios, cuestión propia de las mujeres, de Eva y su descendencia, quien fue la primera en hablar con la serpiente ya que comprendía la lengua y pudo responderle al ser invocada por la misma. Ahora, Miguel Ángel-Fausto ha conocido el lenguaje secreto, y es capaz de hablar con Legión. Entre las concesiones que le otorga, destaca la de dictarle dos libros, el resto tendrá que hacerlo él mismo. Intercambios de sabiduría o de secretos, iniciaciones, viejas deidades, que son las mismas, bajo muchas formas, aunque siempre las mismas. Secretos antiguos, poseídos y compartidos a los empactados, iniciados, bajo oscuros y negros propósitos, indescifrables y misteriosos. El mundo faústico.

Uno de los trabajos más excepcionales de Asturias el joven, fue una traducción del Popol Vuh, la cual intentara, con Georges Raynaud y González de Mendoza, durante su primera estadía en París. La lista de los nombres de los demonios de Xibalba es insuperable, el uso y creación de un lenguaje, los nombres que los nombran, abre e instala esa extraordinaria capacidad poética y manejo de la lengua que llevó a Miguel Ángel a ese nivel único, que le permitió abrir y deparar ese mundo, que hoy llamamos libremente, Maya, acercándolo al conocimiento y asombro de todos los que descubrieron a través de su obra, una realidad desconocida en aquellos momentos. En ese panteón de Dioses Mayas, con miles de nombres también —no olvidemos que El Señor Presidente fue antes Tohil—, donde la obscuridad parece prevalecer, en esa lucha interminable, entre lo humano y el mal, en el juego interminable, en el que perder la cabeza era el costo de la derrota, si pensamos en el Juego de la Pelota; en el occidente faústico, la pérdida de la eternidad de la luz, la factura del pacto al cobrar el alma, al final del juego, no son similares aunque en esencia, a pesar que Mephisto se le presenta a Fausto, vestido como un escolástico, siguiendo el relato tal y como no los dice —los grandes poetas nos dicen, no nos narran— Göthe, ante la pregunta, quién eres, la respuesta es el famoso acertijo, Ein teil von jener Kraft, Die stets das Böse will und stets das Gute schafft (Faust). La conversación entre el Miguel Angel-Faústico y el Luzbel de piedralumbre, transcurre en términos similares, la intención es la misma, el pacto cede ante la idea de la continui- dad, claro está se trata de la continuidad del mal, el engaño es evidente, ambos tienen ideales universales, desean una humanidad mejorada, luminosa, llena de generosidad y de justicia. Mephisto y el Luzbel buscan el olvido. El abandono, la renuncia. La indiferencia resignada, ante la imposibilidad de alterar todo aquello, que se nos da de manera inhumana. Fausto sueña con una humanidad vuelta a la naturaleza, redentora, el ideal romántico. Y Miguel Angel busca la utopía de la revolución o el camino de la salida del olvido, el regreso del fracaso. Aunque es aquí sumamente importante señalar que esa liberación, según Miguel Angel, vendría por la palabra y el lenguaje, ese es su magnífico legado liberador. El narrador es en cierta forma, poseído por el gran poeta, que estaba antes y siempre, y Miguel Angel es un poeta de una fuerza portentosa. Luzbel y Mephisto buscan la continuidad y de allí que la entrega sacrifical de Rodrigo, en el relato de Salazar, es la metáfora de la violencia y la destrucción, como forma de liberación o solución de la maldad.

Su olvido y permanencia enmascaran esa visión luminosa, en la que el lenguaje liberador es la mejor respuesta. Miguel Angel se opone vehementemente a la violencia de la revolución armada ya que esencialmente quiere interrumpir el ciclo establecido por los Dioses de la noche. No se resigna a la determinación de lo inevitable. Por eso sus diálogos con el Luzbel son de una enorme violencia verbal, y si cae en la seducción, es por el engaño y la mentira. No es del todo inocente y tampoco culpable. El mal está en el tránsito ese, entre lo que el hombre tiene de divino y está preso, entre los dos, tal vez es el misterio de la libertad humana. Rüdiger Safranski, en su notable reflexión, sobre el mal, Das Böse oder das Drama der Freiheit (Fischer Verlag, 2001), nos dice que el mal no es otra cosa sino la lasitud o la parálisis de la capacidad creadora de la naturaleza del hombre (...die Trägheit oder Lähmung der shaffenden Natur der Menschen.).

Hay dos amplios dominios de la novela, que no los voy a tocar, pues buscaba no solo generar interés en la lectura de la misma, sino también y, tal vez, aun más relevante, evitar la polémica sobre la cuestión del tema de la llamada paz en Guatemala y su construcción, que Salazar toca seriamente a lo largo del relato. Es más, es parte constitutiva y central. El conflicto padre-hijo, por las visiones divergentes sobre los caminos de liberación; las influencias, que sobre ambos recaen, el caso de Cardoza y otros personajes más es sumamente interesante, así como los recursos narrativos empleados en la construcción, tal vez mejor, la re-construcción del drama y la tragedia. No por causalidad estamos ante hombres de papel, que en tanto intelectuales, son diferentes y múltiples. Sujetos a la poderosa influencia del mal. Condenados a sostener, mantener y enfrentar, ese diálogo interminable, con todas las formas del mal. De allí la referencia bíblica a la legión. El otro dominio, más objeto de los críticos literarios o de los estudiosos de la literatura, es la ponderación de la estructura y el manejo de técnicas narrativas; por ejemplo, la cuestión de la temporalidad o el uso de la primera persona; en otros casos, su apego o no a la realidad histórica o a una orto-doxia asturiana, eso nos dice y nos habla de esa enorme y gratamente enriquecedora lectura que nos ha otorgado Oswaldo Salazar. Hay toda una dimensión estética presente. Tal vez a manera de provocación o de insinuación, Salazar nos ha dejado una novela más cercana a Beckett o Joyce; a Kafka, incluso, que a las narrativas centroamericanas o guatemaltecas.

Eso no es casualidad. Su búsqueda de expresión es totalmente otra. Para cerrar un comentario final sobre el asunto soslayado, la paz y su proceso, la complejidad del mismo, pensando con Salazar, quizás nos acerque más a los procesos irlandeses, aunque claro está hay diferencias enormes y de bulto. Luchar contra un imperio no es lo mismo que un conflicto interno; sin embargo, sostener eso es riesgoso, parte esencial, entre los irlandeses, fueron sus luchas familiares interiores, no se trata solamente de facciones enfrentadas o concepciones religiosas antagónicas, católicas y protestantes. Eso es solamente un ángulo de ese complejísimo enfrentamiento, si podemos ver de cerca a los llamados "fineans" y cómo todo ese movimiento sufrió mutaciones y desgarramientos, convirtiéndose después en una fuerza enormemente decisiva, pues bien, en muchísimos casos, pasó por luchas, entre familias, primos y hasta hermanos. Nos falta aún como guatemaltecos, ver el drama de la paz, fuera de la perspectiva exclusivista y cerrada, de dos facciones luchando entre sí; por eso tal vez, la antinomia, como la plantea Salazar, padre-hijo, no la hemos podido del todo recoger. Real o ficción, no nos pronunciamos sobre esto, la disputa está cerrada; antes que se generara, el autor mismo llama a su novela, un trabajo de ficción.

11
THE METAPHOR OF HISTORY OR MARÍA ODETTE CANIVELL'S "JULIA"

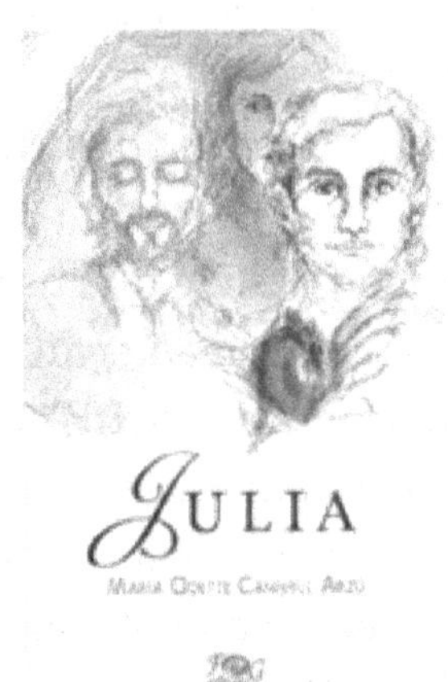

During the last few years, Guatemalans have been trying to write their recent history and they are using different means, tools, and narratives to come to terms with what is fundamental to their meaning and significance. Of course, social scientists and journalists following the footsteps of politicians and other important actors of the past fifty years events, tend to create a corpus historic forum that mainly falls prey to ideologies, conceptions, or simply political positions. They are telling their own stories to interpret or merely tell what took place. Following Foucault's wording, they have established *systems of knowledge*. Parallel narratives or metaphorical constructions. They aim ultimately at an effort to explain what happened and how it all shapes up or constitutes itself on the cruel reality that almost destroyed a nation. An outside conducted and guided social experiment or an immense human tragedy. Writers have been part of this construct and some of the novels written about or related to the so-called, *Literature of the conflict* (Literatura del conflicto) have created some very interesting contributions. Maria Odette Canivell's Julia is a recent example of this ongoing trend.

Written in beautiful Spanish prose and published in 2014 by F&G Editores has all the elements of a historical novel and yet a strong tolstoian épos. Love in times of war. All great love stories take place in the extremist of conditions for mankind, the experience of war. Using a highly developed technique, Canivell tells us a love story caught during a great tragedy, both human and historical. She uses masterfully, the language spoke in real life, the colloquial language with the nuances and almost dialectical spins of the Guatemalan every day the street's way of talking, goes to the soil itself where this language emerges from the warmth and heart of a long-standing tradition. Is the language of real persons. People do speak like that. Humour impregnates the whole telling tempo and the reconstruction of the tale that moves in different levels of time and space. Although, as fluid, the stream runs deviates to touch on lateral topics and introduces other elements as a reflection alternative to the story as such.

Like other writers of her generation, Canivell reflects on the historical events that surround this story. Breathing from real lives the narrator recounts events and stories that come from the factual history of the country. Guatemalans from all sorts of positions have recurred to novels, plays, and poetry to bring before the eyes of the world and especially the younger generations, how this enormous tragedy took place. Can we call it *post-conflict literature*, most probably the answer is much more complex than ascribing or pinning names but serves the purpose of naming what seems to be a period of Guatemalan history itself?

The characters of the story mingle with monsters of many sorts. On the underground movement, and this one is no exception, the borders of good and evil become blurred, not easy to distinguish nor to draw a line between them. On wars or conflicts-Guatemalans refer to their struggle as *conflict* —death is always the everlasting presence. Lures and watches from every corner, disguised and constantly threatening without any real effort to mask themselves, is there constantly and the characters walk with her. Death and the maiden become Death at our tables. Seats at bars, drinks with all of them, and finally shows up in its darkest shape, that of the lack of mercy. Death happens.

The book must be read, I am not bringing any spoilers to the story. It is indeed a unique and dramatic tale of *love and despair*. Other elements might carry a polemic tone, namely that of reality and fiction, the writer's right to recreate the journey, because here we are facing the circle of the journey of return this takes place, the second half is called *El regreso a casa*, Homecoming, which is a crucial dilemma for Guatemalans who went abroad, had to flee or simply decided to leave the country for greener pastures or better worded, in search of hope and freedom. Guatemalan contemporary literature has been dubbed or labelled, as occurring in other countries, exiled intellectuals, artists and writers have a long tendency to move away to think, rethink and create works of art and then come back, not all of them, but a large majority have done so while others remain and continue to create wonderful works of art that transcend their historical periods and become masterpieces. Julia remains loyal to this tradition, written abroad, but deeply rooted in history from where it blooms and emerges.

12

"AIDA, THE BEAUTIFUL" OR A VISIT TO THE HOUSE OF FRAGRANCE

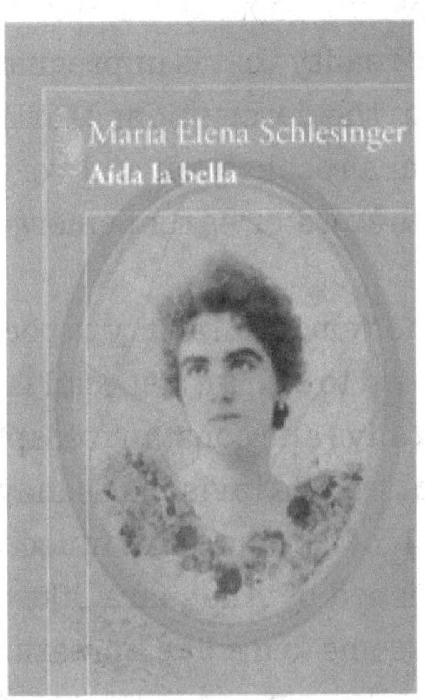

A language that describes scents, smells, tastes, and flavours amongst others, dares us to visit the House of Fragrance. Maria Elena Schlesinger de Méndez-Vides, the second novel is about that and more. A world built around memories is one that still leaves inside those who share it. Maria Elena's private world is shared by some of us and as well as the colours, the birds, the winds, and the different faces forming the earth, a special place where we walked together while growing up and becoming older versions of ourselves and all the others that we loved and left with. *Aida, the beautiful*, the name of her second novel, the first one called, *The Night of the Comet*, both written and published in Spanish, tale tales and speak about this world of scents, colours, smells, and tastes that called the House of Fragrance, a mandarin name, and concept, where one inhabits and dwells. A certain sense of serenity comes from visiting and simply being in The House of Fragrance.

But in the world of Maria Elena, human beings, persons, real individuals, leave and populate this extraordinary rethinking and reconstructing reality that is impregnated from memories and visions. Most of the descriptions Maria Elena puts before our eyes, come from a recollection and very carefully detailed recounting of events and stories that emerged from her private world.

She brings to us a wonderful ability to portray with a delicate, palatable one tempted to affirm, a special language that comes to life from keeping alive and constant recapturing of an elusive series of an element that as invisible as may seem, can only be seen with the touch of candour and innocence that only love can generate. Published by Alfaguara, like the previous *Night of the Comet*, Aida seems to me like a creation coming out of the times of the Nouvelle Romain, the short story filled with sensorial descriptions with almost a graphic virtuosity placing even the smallest of cracks on the walls. But don't think or imagine that these are happy tales sucked in honey and where the characters dance till the morning the day after, some are covered with a tragic destiny where death is the great healer of such intense and quiet suffering. Even the dog in the last story, *Antonia, Paul, and the dog*, leaves this world with a certain silent cry of outrage: *...when the animal barely crawling manages to get near the bread sweated with raw milk, that Antonia would put on a plate by her nest. (Page 149)*

When thinking about a translation of Maria Elena's language one might find it an insurmountable task. Not only constructed with and under very sensitive memories but filled with the local and temporal uses and experiences of a world that has disappeared before our eyes. There is indeed an internal movement that may be engineered by the dialectic of pain and food. Food is the ultimate nourishing power, but the pain is always present and the stories throughout the book are constructed in this way. The feeding archetype is ever-present as a female character, not necessarily a mother but a loving and affectionate presence even Salvador or Pablo despite their secret tragedies, found the comfort of the loving hand, the one that possesses the secret of nourishment and healing. The healing power of food is eternal in the fight against pain. In this world of scent and fragrance, the eternal carrier of the sacred secrets known and reveal only verbally to the chosen ones who were handpicked or through eye contact, like Maria Elena's mother whose deep knowledge and command of the secrets, gave her the ability to see through persons or read their eyes, as one said in this times: ...*It was enough, like in older times, to see the face of the other person*, and that's how Antonia is introduced into their world.

To conclude there is one very important element that is ever-present in Maria Elena's narrative. Animals of all sorts. Birds, dogs, cats, and the fantastic ones as well. Nature is still alive and encompassing. Earthquakes and the rains, the eternal rains, it's cyclical visiting. Awaited and at the same time feared. Guatemalans coexisted with nature and sickness. Maria Elena tells the stories of the way to contract certain maladies and even how to cure them, with the help of natural remedies, sometimes they don't guarantee any success at all. Aida is a victim of this semi-magical reality; her destiny is cruel to our postmodern eyes, but *nature takes its curse* and curses us as well. The circular and even ritual arrival of the *great rains* also brings a cycle of purification and change, some sort of renovation or revival or better worded, the return of the same and that is the reason why the cyclical and ritual repetition takes place at the same time and parallel to a calendar year. At the end of Aida's story, despite the iron rule of never mentioning her name again, takes a strange twist, the little girl also named Aida, like her aunt, was forced to be called, Isabel dropping her original name. So, the story ends, with the girl lamenting being forced to take another name, in her own words …*call me Isabel like the crazy and loony Meme.*

13
JUAN MONGE O LA UNIVERSALIZACIÓN DE LA SUBJETIVIDAD

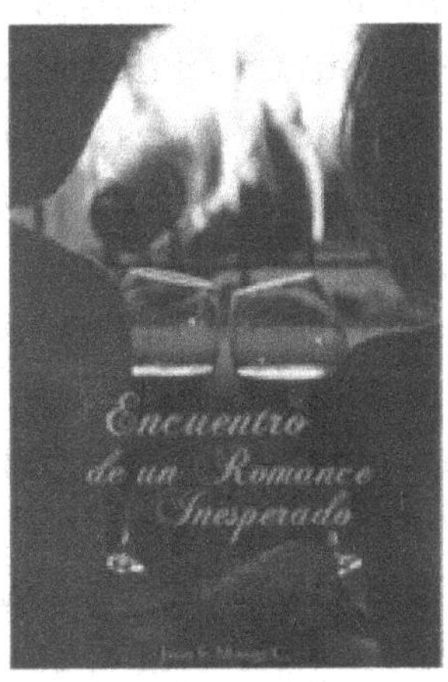

La recientemente publicada novela de Don Juan Monge Calderón, titulada *Encuentro de un romance inesperado*, bajo la Editorial Chaak Balam, en Guatemala y bajo la distribución de ese magnífico *lugar de encuentros*, Sophos, además de acotar que el autor ha donado cualquier tipo de beneficio a fundaciones caritativas, lo cual lo enaltece y agranda aún más, por su legendaria generosidad y capacidad extraordinaria de compartir e incluso, distribuir, término peligroso, sumamente peligroso, en los contextos locales y políticamente *complejos*, de nuestra Guatemala.

La novela es realmente notable. Sin arrugas ni disimulos. En ella encontramos una muy precisa radiografía de lo que pasa en la Guatemala actual: esperanza frente a la indiferencia; privilegios frente los límites de los nuevos poderes y abusos cotidianos, que diariamente los guatemaltecos enfrentan. Nadie se escapa y nadie puede esconderse o protegerse suficientemente, ante la avalancha del terror y del horror, que lentamente nos está devorando. El autor no deja ocasión para expresar sus criterios personales y sus visiones de las atrocidades a las que constantemente se enfrentan todos los guatemaltecos: después de una evolución argumentativa y narrativas notables, el autor nos sitúa frente a un secuestro irracional y oportunista, que roba uno de esos momentos mágicos, fundamentales a la naturaleza humana y que llenan de sentido nuestras existencias individuales. Nos pone ante el límite: la muerte misma, la completa impotencia, sin importar el origen de los protagonistas, ese encuentro extraordinario con ese personaje, brevemente pincelado, que el autor llama *"Don Mingo"*, auténtico profeta de la esperanza, de la capacidad de admirar y respetar lo más fundamental de la condición humana, que no es otra cosa, que la vida misma.

Narrada en primera persona, la novela nos relata la historia de un hombre solitario, dedicado a su familia totalmente, a su trabajo, que en un momento particular de dolor, ante la pérdida de un amigo entrañable, inicia un viaje, que él llama *sabático*, para darse a sí mismo un tiempo de reflexión y reposo. Así conoce a *su Princesa*. A partir de ese inolvidable coqueteo, búsqueda, conquista o tal vez sencillamente, destino, conoce a una maravillosa mujer y juntos viven un romance intenso, que los lleva a través de la geografía mágica de Guatemala, hasta que intempestivamente se ve interrumpido, no terminado; tal vez mejor, solamente suspendido, después de un choque brutal, con la realidad aplastante de nuestro país, que lentamente nos consume y destruye.

Juanito Monge no disimula. Recurre a la eterna capacidad del escritor —y aquí es cómplice, con los grandes—, de denunciar, no solamente narrar, y no renuncia a la crónica, opina y abiertamente señala, advierte, como aquel único cuya capacidad de decir, está fuera de cualquier duda. Estamos al borde de un abismo. O lo paramos o nos caemos y nos llevamos todo lo construido dentro del mismo. Pocos tienen la capacidad de denunciar y a la vez, relatarnos una hermosa historia de amor. Trabajo importante y que nos instala delante de un hombre extraordinario, que no solamente conoce el mundo empresarial y del éxito, sino que tiene y nos revela una enorme sensibilidad humana. Esta novela será seguramente continuada por algunas más; sus obras serán esperadas y leídas, con enorme interés y muchísima curiosidad, por muchos lectores, encantados con una narrativa muy clara y directa, sin mayores disimulos, fresca y fácil de seguir. Un estupendo relato, construido alrededor de una historia trágicamente común y llena de sorpresas inesperadas, las cuales se siguen dando, una muy fina pluma, que reconstruye detalles y observa con mucha atención y está llena de atractivas imágenes, que se prestan a transmitirnos vivencias y realidades cotidianas, tornadas en encuentros y situaciones plenamente inesperadas. Obra de madurez y seriedad. Muy recomendada para cualquier lector intrigado,por un país lleno de muchos secretos y descubrimientos sorprendentes.

14

LUCA, DE LAS PATOLOGÍAS AL DRAMA DE LA CORRUPCIÓN: LOS LENGUAJES DE ADOLFO MÉNDEZ-VIDES

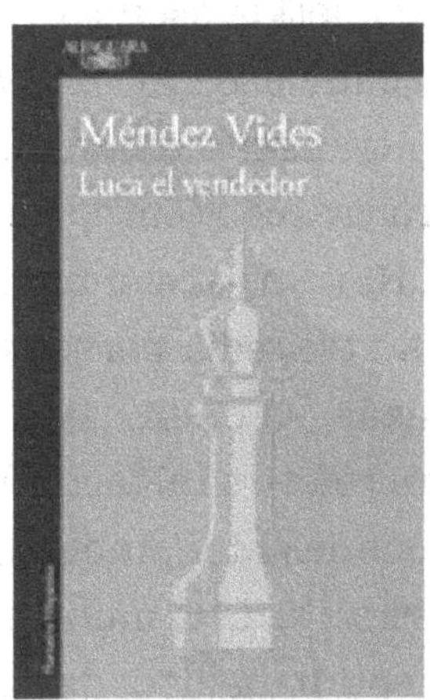

La recientemente publicada última novela del escritor guatemalteco, Adolfo Méndez-Vides, Alfaguara, Grupo Editorial Penguin Random House, en agosto del 2020, nos trae de nuevo a esa especie de neo-naturalismo, del que hemos narrado con anterioridad, sobre las nuevas tendencias de la literatura actual guatemalteca. Obra fundamental y que depara unos espacios importantes a las maneras de contar y relatar de los autores y creadores actuales, constructores de lenguajes y críticos relevantes; de esa realidad dura e impenetrable dentro de la que los guatemaltecos han tenido que vivir, existir y luchar diariamente, debatiéndose, en un hercúleo esfuerzo, por comprender lo invisible y lo no evidente. Méndez-Vides crea un personaje muy particular, no es ni un héroe o menos aun, símbolo de unas generaciones desgarradas por la inequidad y las carencias de todo. Es un personaje siempre en tránsito y siempre metamorfoseándose en algo nuevo y distinto, mutando y transmutando, deviniendo en tragedia y castigo. Un Orestes macondiano, que se inventa y reinventa, se descubre y se pierde en ese tránsito interminable de su deambulante vivir. Luca nos habla desde una realidad terrible y profundamente real. La gran literatura a fin de cuentas está comprometida esencialmente con la verdad y desde allí nos observa o incluso, tal vez, contempla Luca, en la fuerza de su misterio y transmundanidad, porque en cierta forma, Luca es una figura trascendente, que va más allá, mucho más allá, de sí mismo. Hay un cabe-sí-mismo, que es ineludible, su historia personal, su tragedia personal y particular, hasta que se convierte o quizás, se muta, para emplear un término sumamente usado, para referirse al terror actual que nos acecha por todas partes. Nos pone delante del abismo, de lo incomprensible y del miedo mas ancestral: el de la muerte; pues bien, Luca al ir más allá de su propia cotidianeidad, de su condición eminente personal y anecdótica, deviene en una especia de *todo poderoso constructor y destructor*, de todo lo que no debería ser. Una especie de consciencia ética, sedienta de equidad y orden, anticorruptor extremo, casi un semi-héroe de las distintas literaturas gráficas, del cómic, ahora transformadas en dimensiones metafísicas, que vuela allende de la imaginación e incluso de lo posible. Semidioses sin límites, superhombres, invenciones fantásticas, de una fantasía ilimitada, ansiosa de crear nuevos mundos, desde los cuales se podrían explicar las miserias humanas y sus fracasos interminables. No hay mejor momento para introducir acá, el celebre dictum de Becket, contenido en Worstward Ho: *Ever tried. Ever failed. No matter. Try again. Fail again. Fail better.* A pesar de las múltiples y diversas interpretaciones vertidas, sobre ese cuasi-mantra o transformado en tal, acá valdría la pena retener unos de sus múltiples significados. Viene muy a cuenta el absurdo del fracaso, la absurdidad de continuar fallando al repetir lo mismo interminablemente.

Luca es un poco todo eso, alguien que fracasa y vuelve a fracasar, vuelve a intentarlo, solamente para volver a fracasar e incluso, fracasar mejor, el *fail better* de la condenación al absurdo que Beckett nos devela. Así seguimos a Luca, el creador y el destructor, como el viejo Abadón del Gran Sábato, ilustre compañía, con la que camina Luca.

La obra no es fácil de leer tanto por su estructura interna, como por la manera bajo la cual encara una narración en primera persona, directa y clara, precisa, en muchos momentos, tal vez impulsada por la búsqueda de esa elusiva comunicación carente de ambigüedades e imprecisiones, giros lingüísticos inadecuados o poco claros, en la vieja tradición del ingeniero —Adolfo lo es de profesión— y, como tal, hombre de números, donde el evitar las contradicciones o falta de claridad es norma, sin dejar espacios para esos territorios de las sombras en la intención comunicativa; se pierde o deforma o se encubre, deliberada o intencionalmente, para imponer esa mala polisemia múltiple y engañosa. Esos lindes, dominios de las letras y los números, están ontológicamente ligados, la Gematría, cada letra y cada nombre, cada palabra incluso, tienen un número, origen de sus significados, múltiples ab initio. Nombre y número son básicamente inseparables.

La mayor parte de la narración está dominada por un lenguaje elegante e inequívoco, puntual, inconfundible. Méndez-Vides elude, deliberada y conscientemente, caer en la "literatura" del habla coloquial, que fuera muy popular entre muchos autores, especialmente de los desmitificadores y con primarias visiones políticas y ante todo, ideológicas; ese no es su camino, no deja de utilizar recurrentemente, incluso, lisuras, giros de expresiones provenientes de una tradición popular y de un habla generalizada, sutilmente introducidos, casi medidos, llenando una función concebida para emerger, con un texto que despierte y un lenguaje capaz a su vez de transmitir emoción en todas sus formas. Luca deambula por una existencia extrema y dolorosa, es un gran auto-recuperador de su propia esencia, constantemente amenazada, de múltiples y agresivas formas. Incluso físicamente, sufre un atentado al final de la novela, que refleja una realidad casi diaria lastimosamente.

En la primera parte de la obra, referidos acá como los capítulos o parte iniciales, al arrancar con la descripción de los orígenes familiares de Luca y el lugar desde el cual o a partir de dónde el viaje se inicia, nos encontramos con la noción de patologías sociales y culturales, casi orgánico-biológicas, la condenación del origen, la marca profunda que definirá e imprimirá unas características definitivas, sean como "comportamientos adquiridos", o como un ineludible destino o pathos trágico. Luca-Orestes nace en el interior de país, crece en la ciudad, se escapa y casi huye, en búsqueda de respuestas y soluciones, al imperio. Allí toma decisiones que lo acompañarán constantemente. Definirán su condición y situación existencial y su ethos cultural, así como su sistema axiológico. Luca es el protector de su madre. Idealizada y a la vez temida.

Admirada al extremo y centro, eje, de todo lo que intenta construir y destruir, Luca, como Orestes, derriba muros y ejerce venganzas inenarrables. Al viajar al imperio lo hace de manera regular, no es un caminante del desierto o un migrante oculto y aventurero; su riesgo es otro y más que todo motivado por una profunda búsqueda de una identidad sumamente elusiva, casi inalcanzable. Lo que no pareciera ser su motor propulsor es el ingreso de subsistencia, aunque con el tiempo, logrará una enorme fortuna y un inmenso poder. Ese tránsito lo llevará de frente a la experiencia de la guerra, de la muerte y del límite de la vida misma. Lo marca con esa carga del sobreviviente, del que vio los máximos horrores y pudo aprender y redefinirse, hacerse ingeniero, como su autor-creador. La impronta de la guerra lo conducirá a lo largo de su azarosa y complicadísima vida. Los niveles de los lenguajes empleados son verdaderamente fascinantes, frente a una fluida y pulcra narración de los diálogos de los personajes, que están llenos de esa coloquial simpleza de expresiones, impregnada de multisemias indirectas, las cuales precipitan las confusiones y los diálogos perdidos.

Las innumerables incomunicaciones o simplemente, malos entendidos, es un navegar no solamente en el absurdo, sino también en la confusión que dan pie a las íntegras y repetidas traiciones e inevitables cadenas de mentiras y canalladas. Los personajes alrededor de Luca son muy poco rescatables, se nos presentan como una galería de oportunistas, abusadores, incluso violentos, delincuentes y criminales, políticos y empresarios corruptos y carentes de valores o menos aún, o peor aún, sin ningún somero atisbo de principios y valores. Es y resulta inevitable e ineludible la referencia a formas de patologías sociales y culturales, determinantes de sociedades y culturas enfermas, profundamente enfermas, donde la empatía y la generosidad casi no existen; el lucro y la ventaja han substituido a todo aquello que tenga fragmentos de humanidad, piedad o cualquier mediana presencia de caridad o magnanimidad. Luca sí la posee y la muestra en diversas ocasiones; por eso su característica notoria, de salvador e incluso de una gratitud enorme, por aquellos que alguna vez le mostraron un corazón abierto y generoso. Implacable con sus enemigos y pletórico de manos abiertas y entrega, hacia aquellos que le mostraran sensibilidad y formas de afecto.

Mención aparte y de especial importancia y relevancia, es el tratamiento de la corrupción. Aunque al inicio presentado como consecuencia de una moralidad fragmentada y rota, al final de la novela —concluye de esa forma— el tema es narrado y descrito de una manera contundente. La corrupción no es solamente un fenómeno de la política y de los políticos, aunque estos aparecen al centro de la misma, es una realidad integrada y formando parte, de la condición humana. Empresarios y políticos son presentados como los grandes monstruos de la corrupción. Las últimas paginas de la novela, en las que se relata el proceso de privatización o compra de una empresa de telecomunicaciones, mediante los mecanismos conocidos, nos sumerge en el corazón mismo de este drama humano. Luca, en el medio, debatiéndose, para alcanzar un sentido dentro de la oscuridad.

La cuidada descripción del complejo proceso de adquisición de la empresa de telefonía, que Méndez-Vides llama, con una fuerza de ironía muy especial, Tel&Tel, es relatada detalladamente; las mentiras y engaños interminables, las traiciones y al final, los juegos develados, como siempre suele suceder. La verdad emerge desde su ocultamiento y se manifiesta con toda su fuerza. Sin muchos disimulos, alude al mexicano autor y conductor, Felix Delgadillo, desde las sombras de toda la operación y el subsecuente drama y profunda traición, o más bien la consagración de la corrupción maniobrando y moviendo todas las piezas o cartas del juego, controlado sempiternamente por la banca, que reparte y dirige el juego y, la banca, nunca pierde. Luca apostando y jugando un juego que lo desbordaba, que casi lo lleva a la muerte, claudica al final, ante un jugador mayor, lleno de recursos e insaciable, en su ansia de poder y de acumulación de riqueza. Todos le dan la vuelta comprados y manipulados por el Gran Inquisidor. Luca estuvo cerca; sin embargo, no entendió el juego en su base fundamental. La novela tiene una conclusión francamente alucinante y no la vamos a revelar acá. Se trata probablemente de toda una enorme sorpresa, que como todo gran drama, no puede sino concluir con todos los elementos clásicos de las grandes óperas o los grandes dramas. Luca es cíclico y el eterno retorno de lo mismo; la repetición interminable y circular del absurdo y la ausencia completa de sentido, se reitera y redunda a lo largo de este notable trabajo que nos ha dejado Adolfo Méndez-Vides.

15

EL DEBATE SOBRE SOBERANÍA Y NO INTERVENCIÓN, FRANCISCO VILLAGRÁN DE LEÓN Y SU MÁS RECIENTE OBRA

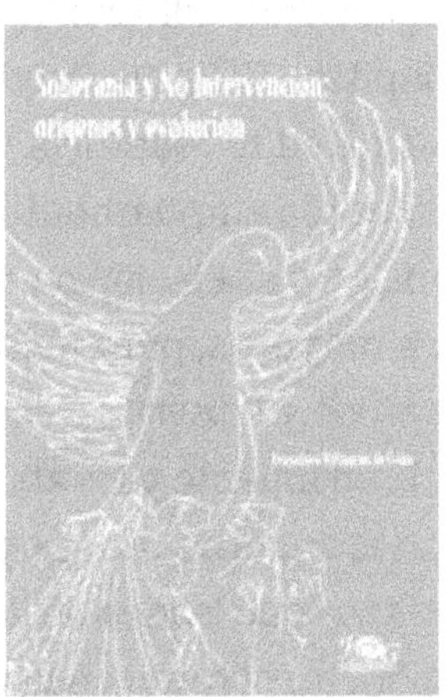

Se trata esta de una obra muy bien investigada y con una amplísima base documental y bibliográfica, del distinguido Embajador Villagrán de León, miembro de una generación importante de diplomáticos guatemaltecos, que combinaron la academia y las visiones teoréticas con el ejercicio de la diplomacia. Sus contribuciones no se redujeron al trabajo diplomático y de representación, sino que generaron importantes contribuciones al estudio e investigación del Derecho Diplomático y del Derecho Internacional General. La publicación del trabajo al cual hacemos referencia es una clara muestra de tal aserto. Publicada en Guatemala bajo el titulo *Soberanía y no intervención: orígenes y evolución*, F&G Editores, 2021. En nuestro país, el tema de la Soberanía y de la No-intervención, son y han sido objeto de debates casi de carácter semi-religioso. Los lenguajes empleados son apasionados y llenos de exaltaciones de muchos tipos, desde un posicionamiento nacionalista hasta las tendencias globalistas, términos empleado en un sector para cuestionar las posiciones, que buscan limitar los espacios de las soberanías nacionales. Dentro de ese enfrentamiento de términos y lenguajes, hay concepciones opuestas, hay un tránsito largo de la consagración de la no-intervención a la defensa de la injerencia "humanitaria", para utilizar el lenguaje derivado del celebre Capítulo VII de la Carta de Naciones Unidas.

Las consecuencias de su invocatoria y aplicaciones, condicionadas por procedimientos ampliamente conocidos, han generado incluso una expansión y apelación a unas supuestas pseudo-facultades de potencias mayores, para justificar acciones militares, bélicas y de otros tipos, en territorios de otros estados, con el fin aliviar o mitigar el sufrimiento y los abusos de seres humanos y poblaciones enteras, víctimas de la agresión y del uso excesivo de la fuerza. Aunque se sabe que la idea de la injerencia humanitaria tiene una formulación importante en la política internacional, principalmente a partir de la llamada Guerra de Biafra (1967-1970), ante la neutralidad de la no-intervención, la necesidad o mejor dicho, el deber humanitario, forzaron una injerencia directa, con tal de solucionar definitivamente una cuestión totalmente inaceptable y que demandaba la atención inmediata de otros Estados y aquí también desencadena y gesta el fenómeno moderno, de organizaciones humanitarias y otras creadas ante tales tragedias, para superar la pasividad neutral que la no-intervención imponía a los Estados.

El camino hacia la injerencia tomaba una forma, ante la cual el Derecho Internacional y la Política Internacional, no podían permanecer indiferentes. No es una idea realmente nueva. La idea o noción de auxiliar, ayudar o apoyar a una nación extranjera es realmente muy antigua. Camina paralelamente a la de la no-intervención, incluso Grotius la emplea, en su obra histórica, *De iure belli ac pacis*, de 1625, al referirse a la posibilidad de intervenir ante actos abominables cometidos por una tirano y cuyos abusos desbordan los limites aceptables y tolerables del comportamiento humano digno, que sobre todo era visto como violaciones al derecho natural, dando nacimiento a las ideas clásicas, de un ius naturale y un ius gentium, entendiendo este último como un derecho positivo, que obliga a un Estado a castigar, intervenir o injerir en asuntos internos de otro estado, cuyo comportamiento se separa de las grandes normas y principios del Derecho Natural. Aunque claramente dicha noción ha perdido su vigencia introdujo y preparó el debate, hasta que la llamada *teoría fiduciaria* cobrara fuerza. Es deber de un estado intervenir en asuntos graves, cuando las violaciones de los derechos de las personas o de los pueblos se encuentran siendo conculcados, y crímenes de distintos tipos se cometen y se requiere de una injerencia directa, impostergable, para aliviar y detener las violaciones de los derechos de los pueblos y las personas. Estamos pues, en el mundo del Derecho Internacional Humanitario y en el Derecho de los Derechos Humanos.

El Derecho Internacional General Consensuado ha evolucionado dramáticamente durante el último siglo. El Embajador Villagrán de León nos narra, con una muy copiosa referencia a documentos, obras y autores, la manera cómo se transitó desde los inicios de la formulación y adopción del principio de no-intervención, hasta sus limitaciones actuales, producto del desarrollo paralelo del Derecho de los Derechos Humanos y la consolidación de un Sistema Americano y uno universal, bajo el amparo de una red de instrumentos internacionales, surgidos dentro del multilateralismo y el desarrollo tanto del Derecho Internacional Americano, como el de Naciones Unidas, inclusive, de mecanismos, de observaciones y cumplimiento del pleno respeto e incluso exigencia de su cumplimiento, por los Estados miembros. Un largo camino recorrido, sin embargo, en el Derecho Internacional tradicional, la ausencia de la persona humana es notoria, es un viejo derecho entre estados.

El voluntarismo no ha desaparecido del todo. Los neo-conservadores aun debaten y defienden esa visión estatal de las relaciones internacionales como de ser exclusivamente entre estados. La realidad jurídica ha evolucionado en una dirección muy distinta, del antiguo principio de la injerencia humanitaria, hoy en día, el principio pro persona humana, pro victima está cada vez más consagrado, piénsese en la enorme e impresionante contribución del distinguido jurista brasileño, Antonio Augusto Cançado Trindade, actual miembro de la Corte Internacional de Justicia, antiguo Presidente de la Corte Interamericana de Derechos Humanos y quien a lo largo de su vida y con una obra riquísima, ha propulsado con un enorme valor y consecuencia, la inclusión de la persona humana, como sujeto del Derecho Internacional General Consensuado. Sus opiniones y votos razonados, incluso cuando disiente, son auténticas piezas indispensables para el Derecho de los Derechos Humanos. Rescato una particularmente notable, se trata de su Opinión Separada, en el Caso *Aplicación del Convenio Internacional para la represión del financiamiento del terrorismo y la Convención Internacional sobre la eliminación de todas las formas de discriminación racial*, cuya sentencia se pronunciara en La Haya, en la sede de la Corte Internacional de Justicia, el 8 de noviembre del 2019. En la misma hay una extraordinaria cita y referencia de una obra de Séneca, *De Ira*, siguiendo una reflexión de los estoicos romanos, aludiendo a los tiempos desde los cuales se invitaba a una acción regida por una recta ratio, donde los jueces y los hombres se respetaban y los vulnerables eran protegidos. Ese largo camino que va desde Séneca y pasando por muchas partes, Derrida alguna vez, lo llamó "la temible cuestión de la soberanía", en sus memorables seminarios sobre la bestia y el soberano, repensando un poco la idea del "soberano que habla con la voz del león", en la galería de las bestias políticas y sus soberanos de la guerra y el silencio, el que la ordena la guerra y el que invoca la paz, aquello que en los principios del siglo XXI, Derrida llamaba la *zoopolítica*, la idea de *La Bête et le souverain*. Por eso, en su afán de mostrar la bestialidad de la soberbia absoluta de la capacidad temible de invocar el silencio de la paz, así pues, la preocupación y consideración del pleno acceso a la jurisdicción universal internacional, en términos actuales, ha sido preocupación constante y permanente, postergada por siglos, centro del Sistema de Protección y Observación de los Derechos de las Personas Humanas; no solamente como principio de derecho general, las Constituciones americanas, todas, contienen referencia a la persona humana y sus Derechos inalienables. No se trata de declaraciones o formulaciones teóricas, sino que están plasmadas plenamente en un Sistema que aspira a la universalidad.

La llamada injerencia humanitaria desencadena sobre inmensas tragedias y horrores inenarrables, una respuesta obligada, incluso forzosa, que concretó en más de una operación internacional, intervención, bajo forma de *guerra autorizada* al invocarse el Capítulo VII de la Carta de Naciones Unidas, para detener actos de genocidio y otras atrocidades, perpetradas por déspotas y tiranos, cometiendo crímenes de lesa humanidad, en contra de sus poblaciones y habitantes, donde la jurisdicción interna no es aceptable ni suficiente, ante la perpetuación de actos barbáricos y de exterminio, ante los cuales no cabe el silencio y menos aun, la condonación.

Lo relevante para nosotros o al menos lo más atractivo, es la evolución de las normas jurídicas, esto es, claro otra perspectiva que busca transitar, entre los límites del derecho y la política, las relaciones internacionales y las políticas exteriores, y navegan sumergidas totalmente en el dominio de lo político y los políticos, como fueran sus formas. La condición de abstractas de las normas demanda otra manera de estudiarlas y analizarlas. No es cuestión tal vez, establecer una preeminencia, aunque claramente las normas deberían —aunque esto sería mera deontología o aspiración de justicia, al menos en el Derecho Internacional General—, especialmente aquellas que tienen condición y carácter de *ius cogens*. El Derecho de los Tratados, ese esencial como instrumento formulado no solo de grandes normas codificadas, sino de su establecimiento y reconocimientos plenos. Su observancia y aplicación se convierten a su vez en una cuestión que determina la naturaleza misma de la evolución de las principales normas. La invocación de la *injerencia humanitaria* es una contribución —aunque no del todo normada y regulada, como otras normas plenamente consagradas y reconocidas— importantísima para poner al Derecho Internacional General, en condiciones de responder contundentemente ante los extremos de la soberanía absoluta y más, específicamente en su capacidad de convocar al silencio —imponerlo bajo formas y figura falsas— y sobre todo, de hablar con la *voz del león* y demandar bajo la fuerza de una dudosa autoridad, que no solamente esclaviza sino, más grave aún, destruye vidas y aniquila esperanzas.

Hay una especia de obligación ética de intervenir, según sean las circunstancias. Sumarse al silencio impuesto por la fuerza del dominio absoluto es intolerable e inaceptable, la necesidad de responder y actuar, es una obligación y un derecho pleno, que se debe ejercer sin vacilaciones y dudas. Claro está, que acá hay posiciones y visiones divergentes, confrontadas incluso; sin embargo, a pesar de la posición neo-conservadora, el silencio ante el sufrimiento humano y los excesos y abusos de una autoridad soberana que viola todos los derechos humanos concebibles y pone en riesgo incluso las relaciones mismas con otros estados, obligará a respuestas y reacciones consensuales, tal vez primordialmente, colectivas, si fueran necesarias. La obra del Embajador Villagrán de León nos ofrece un despliegue de documentación, así como unas referencia a autores, obras, resoluciones de Organismos y Organizaciones Internacionales, enormemente rica y sumamente útil para los estudiosos de estos temas. Es un aporte importante a la discusión y tratamiento de una materia esencial, para la vida de los Estados actuales y sobre todo, aborda las cuestiones históricas y los orígenes y formulaciones de los dos grandes principios acá aludidos, tanto del Derecho Internacional Americano como el General Consensuado.

Tenemos pues unos principios consagrados en instrumentos internacionales, siendo también reconocidos dentro del Derecho Internacional Consuetudinario; sin embargo, su evolución y transformación han sufrido un proceso notoriamente divergente. La injerencia humanitaria, aunque no ha alcanzado el nivel de norma imperativa absoluta, en la manera el Derecho de los Derechos Humanos continúa su marcha progresiva, mientras siga creciendo y lo seguirá, no nos cabe duda, el sistema mismo la terminará incorporando a una práctica cada vez mas expandida y, en materia de Derechos Humanos, su observación e incluso la condición de respeto y cumplimiento, es en nuestros tiempos una realidad plenamente establecida. Los fallos y demás resoluciones dentro de la jurisdicción internacional o en tribunales regionales, cuentan con una vasta jurisprudencia en esta materia; podría incluso decirse se han convertido en instancia internacional remedial, de cara a ciertos casos donde el derecho interno no puede dar una respuesta o incluso los sistemas jurídicos de ciertos estados resuelven en contra de los mismos derechos reclamados, por personas, víctimas, de horribles violaciones y crímenes reconocidos, dentro del sistema internacional de protección y garantía de la persona humana.

Las Cortes de Derechos Humanos han sido contundentes en estos casos y en particular, el Tribunal de Estrasburgo o Corte Europea de Derechos Humanos, facultado para ejercer jurisdicción en materia propia de los estados miembros del mismo, facultado por los estados miembros del Convenio y sus Protocolos, a resolver, con absoluta independencia, en contra de resoluciones de la justicia interna de las estados parte del mismo, amparado en el Convenio para la protección de los derechos humanos y de las libertades fundamentales, al cual es posible acceder una vez agotadas todas las instancias jurisdiccionales, no discrecionales y extraordinarias, incluyendo amparos, dentro del estado donde se haya litigado el caso y no existan vías u opciones procesales pendientes, el Tribunal actuará y conocerá el caso una vez se hayan cumplidos los requisitos ratione temporis, loci, materiae y personae. La Corte Interamericana ha desarrollado también una amplísima jurisprudencia y ha conocido y fallado, en muchos casos de violaciones a los derechos humanos de las personas, aunque su mecanismo de acceso no es similar al del Tribunal de Estrasburgo, permite el acceso de las víctimas y claro está, ha fallado en casos de amplio impacto a lo largo y lo ancho de la región latinoamericana.

Sirvan pues estas reflexiones y opiniones acá contenidas, como análisis y comentarios a la importante obra que el Embajador Villagrán de León nos ha presentado y su contribución será reconocida por su valor y calidad. Aunque siguiendo la expresión de Derrida, con pasos de lobo, lentamente nos acercamos a un sistema universal de protección en el Derecho Internacional General, en el que la persona humana pueda ser considerada como *sujeto de derecho internacional*. A fin de cuentas, la mayoría de las constituciones de las democracias occidentales y republicanas, no occidentales, la tienen como centro y fin de su organización, en cuanto que Estados.

16
LOS LIBROS DE MARIO PERMUTH Y EL SUEÑO DE LA PAZ

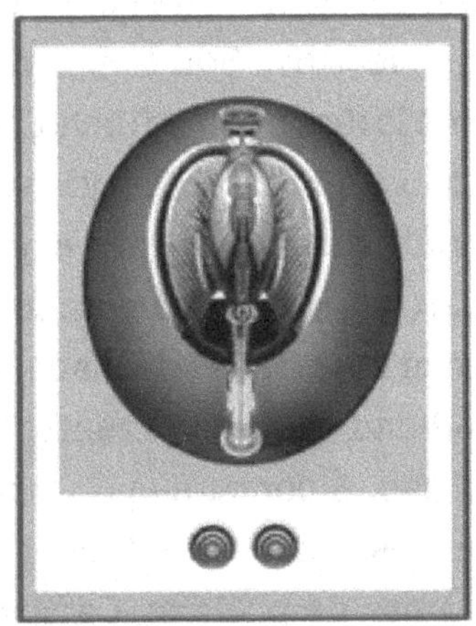

TOMO I DE LOS INFORMES CONFIDENCIALES DE MARIO PERMUTH LISTWA

Los Cinco Volúmenes, en los que Mario Permuth Listwa reúne sus notas, memorias, diarios, incluso crónicas, en el sentido antiguo del cronista, como constructor de relatos, sobre los cuales no solamente guarda memoria, sino que es parte y protagonista a la vez, se sentaron a la mesa, directamente, con los principales actores del drama de la paz guatemalteca.

En *Pax Guatemalensis*, su lectura y reflexión será obligada, no solamente ahora, sino en el futuro, como textos de referencia, para comprender tanto las causas como la historia misma desde adentro, íntima, de una construcción ardua y compleja. No era solamente y menos se buscaba silenciar las armas; se buscaba transformar un país entero, reconciliando, acercándolo a sus raíces, orígenes y contradicciones. Aprender a vivir, en lo diferente, en la diferencias, que debían unir y no destruir o separar.

Los libros están ya disponibles en Amazon, en versión digital, en cierta forma —aunque no soy ningún simpatizante de esta manera de edición-publicación, probablemente si alguna obra o libro se adaptara a este tipo de formato, podría tal vez ser este tipo de textos, y bien vale la pena intentarlo, sin abandonar la idea de la impresión tradicional, en el libro impreso— e incluso, a lo mejor facilitará su lectura. Son tomos densos y detallados, minuciosamente, sobre lo dicho y lo no dicho, sobre las estrategias y los fracasos, las posiciones endurecidas y la voluntad consistente, de una parte claramente decidida, desde el principio, por lograr alguna forma de acuerdo. Tal vez la forma como concluyera este crucial proceso, no es ni fue la más adecuada. Un camino se cerró y se abrió una posibilidad casi inexistente, se pudo empezar a soñar el sueño de la paz. A continuación y como una forma de estimular su lectura y estudio, sobre todo, reproduzco el texto, que preparara a manera de prólogo, Carlos Rivers Sandoval, quien escribió un extraordinario prefacio a la misma, "Opus Magnum", de Mario Permuth Listwa —fotógrafo insigne y cuyas maravillosamente misteriosas fotografías son carátulas de cada uno de los volúmenes. La arriba reproducida —cortesía del propio autor y abuso de mi parte al destacarla, en la plenitud de su misterio— tiene cuatro compañías adicionales y cada una de ellas, merecería un estudio por separado, portadoras de mensajes e iluminadoras de misterios.

Ese misterio de la tan elusiva paz, condenada a ser permanente y engendrando así, en ella, esa elusividad constante, de la imposibilidad de la permanencia, y la guatemalensis, particular- mente. Siempre es mejor dejar que la obra hable por sí misma, como efectivamente lo hace, y navegar por sus páginas e intentar comprender todo aquello que llevó a la firma de los Acuerdos de Paz.

TODOS LOS CAMINOS PASAN POR OSLO

LOS SENDEROS DE LA PAZ

La extraordinaria aportación histórico-política de Mario Permuth Listwa, sobre los orígenes, transformación-evolutiva y finalmente concreción de un largo proceso por alcanzar una elusiva paz, firme y duradera, como se le adjetiva a lo largo de las negociaciones y la larguísima serie de documentos, preacuerdos, acuerdos parciales, limitados y una serie interminable de contribuciones para culminar en la firma de una aspiración y sueño. Esa Paz, con mayúscula que depara, una reconciliación y una construcción, de un país nuevo y transformado. No solamente se trataba de un cese al fuego, de una interrupción de las cadenas de muertos, así como de la supresión definitiva de una cantidad de actos ilícitos, delincuenciales y, por supuesto, de las violaciones de los derechos humanos.

Todo proceso o fórmula de negociación pasa por una serie de momentos que le son comunes a muchísimas de las controversias planteadas y establecidas, que buscan superar, de alguna manera, las diferencias y construir acuerdos amplios, sólidamente sustentados y los cuales puedan no solamente implementarse, sino cuyos efectos sean reales y profundos. De allí los términos empleados en los Tratados y Acuerdos, que históricamente empezaban bajo la sombrilla, de "tratados de paz y amistad", a la más recientemente acuñada, "paz firme y duradera", empleada a lo largo de las referidas negociaciones de paz, entre ese ente al cual se le denominó URNG y un gobierno constituido, el guatemalteco, que actuaba bajo la plena legitimidad de una marco constitucional republicano y una arquitectura legal, que le fijaba los espacios y posibilidades de cualquier negociación. Si bien es cierto que el desacuerdo armado se daba sobre una clara confrontación teórico-conceptual, la negociación debía pasar por complejísimos tamices y capas que ocultaban cuestiones mas delicadas y difíciles. Había coincidencias no reconocidas y simpatías no expresadas, aumentando la enorme complejidad de la confrontación y a su vez, la manera de dar por terminados los enormes desacuerdos. El Arte de la Negociación es una facultad no esparcida generosamente, requiere de ciertos individuos capaces de ver y leer por encima lo no evidente. Es muy fácil transcurrir de la base originaria de la disputa o controversia, obviando, en beneficio de un llamado "pensamiento estratégico" o de unos métodos para resolver temas no esenciales, en favor de aspectos periféricos o a manera de avanzar en las negociaciones complejas, partir de lo más simple a lo mas complejo, descartando así por número, o si se quiere, importancia, hasta llegar a los aspectos más complicados, generalmente resueltos al final de los procesos de negociación. Noruegos y suecos desarrollaron a lo largo del pasado siglo una serie de métodos e instrumentos para abordar correcta y si se quiere, "científicamente", este tipo de controversias, a partir de la objetividad del rigor metodológico y evitando caer en las discusiones teoréticas irreconciliables. En el Volumen IV, Mario Permuth narra detalladamente ese momento en que las partes y los facilitadores o mediadores —como se prefiera llamarlos— convocaron a una de las últimas negociaciones y firmas de Acuerdos fundamentales, en el proceso de paz conducido, entre tantísimas adversidades. El tema del lugar donde se iniciaron las reuniones secretas entre israelíes y palestinos, que eventualmente desembocarían en los llamados Acuerdos de Oslo I y II, los cuales finalmente se firmarían en Washington, en la famosa ceremonia en la Casa Blanca del 1993, poco después de que las extraordinarias y sumamente secretas y reservadas negociaciones y que concluyeran exitosamente, se efectuaron bajos los auspicios de un modelo especial de negociación indirecta. Bajo una constante vigilancia y supervisión constante, se condujeron en Boorregaard Manor, en Sarpsborg, donde curiosa y para nada casualmente, unos Acuerdos similares entre Guatemala y la URNG, con amplísima participación internacional, tanto a través de Naciones Unidas y un denominado Grupo de Países Amigos, firmaran otro más de estos Acuerdos de Oslo, bajo esa inspiración y acompañamiento, que buscaba no solamente resolver controversias, sino generar formas de paz, plenamente transformadoras y estabilizadoras.

Una de las cuestiones más relevantes dentro de estos procesos de negociación son los asuntos de las visiones del mundo sostenidas por las partes y que desembocan en los conflictos. No me gusta emplear el termino ideologías, porque eso realmente significa otra cosa. La vieja sociología del saber nos mostraba el carácter y condición propia de "enmascaramiento" que el concepto conlleva. Algo ideológico es básicamente una elaboración o un constructo complejo de formas de saber o de un pensamiento, deformante y ocultante de lo verdaderamente real. De allí la noción de enmascaramiento; en este caso lo que se daba en esencia, era el enfrentamiento abierto y sin disimulos, de dos visiones o concepciones del mundo. Y de allí la profundidad de la controversia; por una parte, la antiguamente llamada "concepción científica del mundo", el materialismo histórico, así como su muy particular principio revolucionario de la lucha armada, liberadora de las clases oprimidas, y la búsqueda del establecimiento de lo que se llamaba "la dictadura del proletariado". Esa revolución era necesariamente violenta y buscaba derivar un orden establecido; frente a ellos y esa concepción del mundo y de la historia, un Estado plenamente constituido, una República Constitucional, con una arquitectura legal, fundada y organizada como un Estado cuyos fines eran completamente diferentes y están recogidos en un *corpus iuridicum* y en una historia y una tradición, el cual funciona bajo leyes, reglas, principios e instituciones, que no podía sino reaccionar y defenderse ante una revolución, que inició un enfrentamiento armado, buscando revertir, subvertir e instituir ese nuevo orden revolucionario e implantar una realidad, en todos los sentidos, diferentes y antagónicamente opuesto al establecido y vigente. Construir una negociación para superar esas dos concepciones del mundo y de la historia, sin siquiera abordarla, evitar incluso tocar y analizar esa colosal divergencia, cubierta además de violencia y agresión armada, una lucha por derrocar y derribar, no solamente a un gobierno, sino a todo un estado y substituirlo, por un "mundo" radicalmente diverso, donde absolutamente todo cambiaría, desde la economía a la religión, se trataba de una misión o tarea titánica y plagada de dificultades insospechadas. Al no poder empezar por donde se debía, probablemente hubiese sido un ejercicio en plena futilidad. Quedaba pues abordar los temas que podrían superarse y alcanzar un "alto al fuego" o sencillamente, "parar la muerte", detener la violencia y establecer condiciones nuevas, para poder coexistir pacíficamente. En los primeros volúmenes se repite un "mantra" —recurriendo a una terminología exógena— atribuido al Cardenal Rodolfo Quezada Toruño, quien como se relata desde el inicio, en su función de Conciliador, se refería a la paz como "el bienestar del hombre guatemalteco" o de una manera más clara y contundente, era imperioso detener definitivamente las muertes. Las diferencias de visiones del mundo y de la historia probablemente eran insuperables y en muchos momentos, en los análisis y comentarios que Mario Permuth recoge y nos deja, como valiosísimos momentos de una historia y de un proceso, duro y sumamente cruel.Hay un episodio narrado y recogido en el volumen IV, precisamente durante una de las innumerables cenas y reuniones organizadas para contribuir a construir puentes y formas de acercamientos, donde se recuerda una conversación, entre Pablo Monsanto, cuyo nombre real es Jorge Soto —aunque sea de suponer, no lo emplea más; incluso es Diputado al Congreso y continúa utilizando el nombre de Monsanto, sin ningún equívoco posible) En esa conversación en la que participan varios de los negociadores, Monsanto acusa a los negociadores guatemaltecos, "de refugiarse en la Constitución, para no aceptar cambios", y la respuesta de la contraparte, no podía se otra, fue la de hacerle ver que ellos actuaban dentro de un orden jurídico establecido y vigente; eran observantes de las leyes y normativas que determinan la base y realidad de un orden republicano cons-titucionalista. No podía ser de otro modo. Esas divergentes concepciones subyacían en un proceso de negociación que no podía abordarlas, las mismas serían totalmente insuperables y francamente, nunca se resolvieron o superaron; siguen estando constantemente presentes. La ilusión de "la caída del muro de Berlín" generó una idea equivocada, profundamente equivocada, repetida interminablemente. El mundo bipolar había cambiado y la "vieja" confrontación cesado definitivamente. Nada más ilusorio. El marxismo ha conservado esa capacidad interna, auto-dialéctica, de transformarse constantemente, sin modificar ciertos principios y conceptos, inmutables, que tienen casi condición de dogma. Hay una especia de ortodoxia inmutable y constante. Si la revolución violenta podía ser detenida, sea derrotándola por las armas, la idea de la utopía revolucionaria y la aspiración a una sociedad sin clases, donde la vieja burguesía sería enviada a los más bscuros fondos de una historia irrepetible y purgada definitivamente, era una aspiración irrenunciable y continúa siéndolo. No existe más el Muro y, sin embargo, las dos concep-ciones del mundo siguen pugnando y luchando por establecer órdenes hegemónicos vía nuevos mecanismos y alternativas estratégicas, de subvertir el orden establecido. Aunque hoy en día prevalece la antigua idea o experimento de acceder al poder mediante vías pseudo-democráticas, ganando elecciones, muchas veces manipuladas, para establecer el "socialismo democrático" o sus modalidades actualmente prevalentes. Las revoluciones violentas y armadas parecen ceder ante las expectativas de triunfos en dudosas elecciones, acomodando los sistemas constitucionalistas republicanos a los dictadores tropicales de turno y, sin olvidar, las nuevas variantes de la incorporación de grupos corruptores y una rampante impunidad. A lo largo de las negociaciones, por eso es la necesidad de las modalidades invocadas: conciliador, mediador, intermediarios, facilitadores y facilitaciones, fórmulas conocidas y ensayadas y otras nuevas, intentando acercar a las partes, para poder hablar como guatemaltecos, en un primer momento y posteriormente, abordar las formas de terminar el enfrentamiento creando lenguajes, figuras nuevas e intentando generar formas aplicables, para establecer salidas a situaciones únicas y sumamente delicadas. Lo de los seudónimos o nombres, es un ejemplo dentro de tantos, en los que una realidad jurídica establecida, necesitaba ser tratada de formas ingeniosas e imaginativas, para superar cuestiones no tan evidentes. Documentar a los que no tenían nombre, crear registros y elaborar cuasi-censos, para identificar a quienes no parecieran incluso existir; es decir los rostros del conflicto, los desplazados, retornados, personas humanas, que sencillamente huían de la muerte o se resistían a tomar un lado del enfrentamiento. Los distintos Acuerdos intentaron abordar estos dramáticos problemas y darles respuestas y soluciones.

En el tomo V, Mario Permuth, durante una serie de largas reuniones en París, con la presencia del entonces Presidente de la República, licenciado Ramiro de León Carpio, organizada por el gobierno francés de ese entonces, con presencia de todos los participantes del proceso y, por supuesto, delegados de organismos internacionales y representaciones de los países del denominado entonces, Grupo de Amigos, en una de las tantas intervenciones —es de destacar, que es este uno de los mayores aportes de estas notables Memorias/Diarios, al conservar, para los textos de los discursos y exposiciones, presentaciones, hechas por prominentes figuras, dentro del proceso de negociaciones— el entonces Primer Secretario de la Paz, Héctor Rosada Granados, uno de los principales negociadores del proceso, relata de una manera muy peculiar y precisa, aludiendo a las visiones sobre cómo concebir al Estado, sobre una URNG que busca convertir al Estado guatemalteco en un *"Kohlkotzh y el CACIF en un Gerente de privatizaciones"*. Fórmula bajo la cual se podía resumir simbólicamente el conflicto existente. Se reconocían claramente las dos perspectivas enfrentadas. Curiosamente, Guatemala, después de firmados los Acuerdos y por muchos años, caminaría entre esa dicotomía o tal vez mejor expresado, relaciones de oposición, recurriendo al lenguaje del estructuralismo. Al estudiar detenidamente las largas y complejas redacciones de los diversos textos, siguiendo las modificaciones sufridas e introducidas, se nota una clara voluntad de evitar tocar o abordar esta diferencia fundamental, en muchos momentos de la negociación, y se nota palpablemente la enorme soledad de los negociadores del gobierno o de los sucesivos gobiernos, dentro de los cuales la larga lista de notables guatemaltecos es impresionante, en tanto que URNG maniobraba para posponer, demorar, o incluso evitar suscribir acuerdos y así llegar al elusivo "cese al fuego", en realidad el objetivo central del proceso. El primer paso trascendental es la firma del Acuerdo Global sobre Derechos Humanos. A partir de ese momento se hace casi imposible no terminar el conflicto. La llamada "comunidad internacional" —término no muy feliz— no siempre ejerció o se vistió de la necesaria neutralidad, en sus roles distintos de mediación, conciliación o sencillamente de facilitación. En grandes líneas los Organismos como tales mantuvieron una cierta neutralidad, no así algunos de sus distinguidos representantes, como es caso el de los Países Amigos, aunque no por las mismas razones; en unos casos de plena afinidad con URNG y su Comandancia, más que todo en el plano personal y los Países Amigos, salvo alguna notoria excepción, buscaban la conclusión y un fin del conflicto y poder, así, entrar en una nueva dinámica y relación con Guatemala y su población.

El libro, o sea, sus cinco volúmenes, están escritos no tan solo desde la evolución y transformación de los textos, sino también, y es muy bienvenido, desde un enorme sentido del humor, el negro, que me gusta mucho personalmente, y que está presente durante toda la narración. A saber, la reconstrucción de las reuniones, sus peculiaridades internas, las incontables convocatorias a reunirse privadamente en las habitaciones de los hoteles —según en que ciudad se estaban efectuando las negociaciones— las peripecias logísticas, los incontables aeropuertos y sus tormentosos procesos de abordaje y, claro está, sin faltar las cuestiones migratorias, resueltas vía diplomacia, de los distintos agentes guatemaltecos, quienes apoyaban las reuniones y facilitaban el transitar de los negociadores, cargados de por sí, con tareas titánicas y hercúleas. Durante los años de las negociaciones la Cancillería guatemalteca contaba con un grupo importante de Embajadores de un alto nivel y a su vez, de funcionarios notablemente preparados, los cuales coadyuvaron y fueron un importante soporte para los negociadores gubernamentales. Huelga decir que la Comandancia tenía sus propios equipos y los funcionarios internacionales, en sus roles de mediadores/facilitadores/intermediarios, no solamente hacían terapia psicoanalítica, sino que además sus funciones quedaban rebasadas al

tener que afrontar una situación y unos escenarios complicados
y delicados, que se podían romper en cualquier momento, lo cual
efectivamente estuvo muchas veces a punto de pasar. El hecho
que la posibilidad de acercamientos reales y personales estaba
sumamente limitado. Muchos contactos personales, casi casuales,
se daban con mucha frecuencia. Encuentros en pasillos o en
restaurantes, donde más de alguna comida o incluso algún importante espirituoso, fueron compartidos y sirvieron para acercar
posiciones o tal vez, sencillamente, para humanizar unos encuentros que realmente era de enemigos abiertos y confrontados,
sin disimulos y vacilaciones. La realidad imperante de parar las
muertes, detener una violencia insana y sin ninguna oportunidad
de solución, por las vías armadas y del enfrentamiento. Decidir
si esta confrontación era o fue una guerra civil o si el hiperbólico
concepto, *enfrentamiento armado interno*, era el correcto,
quedará abierto para la historia, la verdadera, no la narrada y
construida, para sustentar triunfalismo y falsedades. De estos
conflictos no hay auténticos ganadores, no hay victoriosos y
vencidos; solo hay muertos, dolor y un sufrimiento casi insanable,
y la llamada Comisión de la Verdad Histórica, la Memoria, y lo
que vino después, no ha sido suficiente para acercar grupos, que
en esencia no querían deponer las armas; no podían aceptar un
resultado por el que serían adjudicados al rincón de los derrotados,
por eso la llamada paz era en realidad un fin del enfrentamiento,
del conflicto armado, sin importar cómo se le denomine. Lo
imperioso fue detener las muertes y esa violencia deshu-
manizadora y a partir de allí, construir el camino de la paz, de
esa elusiva reconciliación y reencuentro, entre guatemaltecos
divididos por visiones del mundo antagónicas; por concepciones
del Estado divergente y por una violencia demencial, destructora
e infernal. Esa es la relación que Mario Permuth Listwa nos ha
heredado, esa fue la esperanza que ellos buscaban depararle al

guatemalteco, quienes, cansados de las muertes y la violencia irracional, anhelaban una vida con prosperidad y bienestar. La historia de la firma final de los acuerdos finales y definitivos —un término sumamente hiperbólico, también— se dio en medio de una circunstancia muy particular, que se nos cuenta en estos cinco volúmenes, los que concluyen con el final del gobierno del recordado presidente Ramiro de León Carpio. Los constructores de los acuerdos llegaron al final de un camino y abrieron un espacio enorme y generoso. Otros y tal vez no los auténticos constructores de los Acuerdos, concluyeron una negociación acelerada por un monstruoso error, crimen en realidad, de uno de los principales Comandantes de la insurgencia, quien no supo entender el momento y el sentido del espacio abierto; no supo ser un habitante real de esa paz y bienestar del hombre guatemalteco, sino que más bien no pudo frenar su insania y furia revolucionaria implacable, y cometió unos actos atroces y todas las partes dentro de la negociación, afuera y adentro, obligaron su salida del proceso y sancionaron su ausencia de esas firmas históricas, que deparaban ese nuevo mundo instalado a partir de esas incansables negociaciones y autenticas visiones, de una Guatemala con mañana. Esa parte no le toca a Mario Permuth narrarla, su exclusión de las firmas simbólicas, lo mismo es válido para los demás ilustres negociadores guatemaltecos, y no obvia el papel y contribución al nacimiento y germinación de otra nueva realidad para todos los que esperaban y confiaban en unos nuevos amaneceres. En cierta forma aún seguimos esperando el pleno cumplimiento no solamente de esos Acuerdos, sino sobre todo, de un auténtico reencuentro que nos acerque y reúna como guatemaltecos, y aunque las armas han sido casi totalmente silenciadas, hay otras que no derivadas de aquellas, generan hoy un inmenso dolor y nos hunden en abismos obscuros e insondables. Las viejas fuerzas desintegradoras mantienen una gran presencia y actividad, y aunque mutadas bajo otras vestimentas y formas, instan y alientan formas de agresión y destrucción. La distante reconciliación nacional continúa siendo una utopía lejana, aunque plenamente factible. No debemos renunciar al sueño de la reconciliación y de la paz, es la única manera de construir este país, donde la paz habite permanentemente.

17

MARÍA DEL ROSARIO MOLINA, DANTE Y EL OCTAVO CÍRCULO, ENTRE LA BELLEZA Y EL MAL

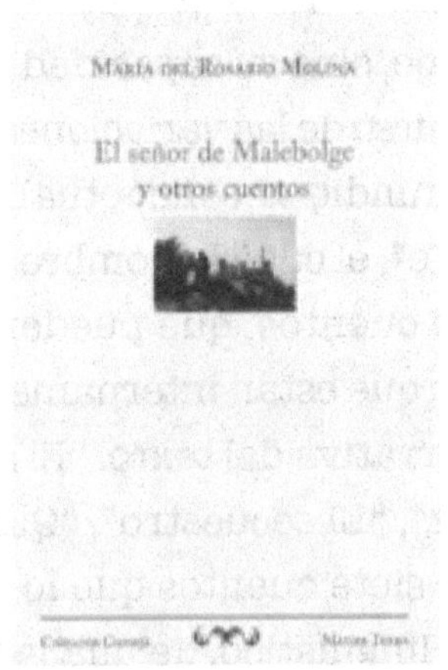

"Luogo è in inferno detto Malebolge, tutto di pietra di color ferrigno, come la cerchia che dintorno il volge.."

Inferno, Canto XVIII. La Divina Comedia, Dante Alighieri.

La apasionante lectura de la recientemente publicada obra de María del Rosario Molina, *El señor de Malebolge y otros cuentos*, Editorial C&M, Guatemala, en agosto del 2021, nos lleva por una magníficamente construida narración y por una auténtica y profunda reflexión sobre la naturaleza del mal. No es por casualidad la selección del título de la misma. El Malebolge es uno de las más tenebrosos lugares en el octavo círculo del infierno de Dante, quien incluso enumera —además de nombrar algunos de los personajes allí condenados— y lista detalladamente los pecados causantes de tal condenación, desde usureros, hipócritas, fraudulentos, rufianes y seductores, entre otros, se encuentran sumergidos en el bolge, una especie de foso concéntrico, donde yacen figuras históricamente reconocidas y otros meramente anónimos, sufriendo el interminable castigo de una eternidad de sufrimientos inenarrables. La obra conserva una unidad estilística y temática, interna y formal. Narrada en un lenguaje simplemente extraordinario, María del Rosario nos muestra no sólo su dominio del lenguaje, sino su capacidad notable de crear imágenes, de navegar el curso de las variaciones y giros no solamente poéticos, sino de profundidad conceptual. El cuento principal, "El señor de Malebolge", el cual da nombre al libro, es el primero de una serie de siete cuentos, que pueden leerse separados o como un conjunto, porque están internamente vinculados, y son parte de la unidad narrativa del texto. "El segundo círculo", "La tía Refugio", "Micifuz", "El secuestro", "Química" y finalmente, "La Jacinta", son los siete cuentos que lo conforman. Un viaje de un enorme placer lingüístico, de una lectura fluida y de una enorme elegancia, amarrados por el común denominador o mejor dicho, el hilo conductor de la visión del Infierno de Dante y complementado con un recurso narrativo muy particular, una combinación de surrealismo semi-macondiano y una literatura fantástica de terror. La oscilación entre luces y oscuridad que emerge desde la concepción y estructura del mismo, nos depara una arquitectura narrativa sumamente atrayente y casi intoxicante, que pareciera ser como una versión literaria de una sinfonía fantástica a lo Berlioz, impregnada de magia y fantasía.

No vamos a reconstruir ni analizar cada uno de los cuentos, todos vinculados, como decimos arriba, por el hilo conductor de Ariadna tal vez, buscando la luz y así logrando salir del laberinto o de los laberintos en los que habitamos, y deambulamos perdidos y ausentes, intentando encontrar sentido y significado a lo que hacemos o soñamos. Tal vez, un tanto desvinculado de los otros cuentos, el relato de Jacinta, tenga un valor particular, sobre todo después del intenso debate que la celebración o rememoración o tal vez, sencillamente recordación, del Bicentenario desencadenó —ahora pareciera menguar, en su intensidad al menos, por ahora— y curiosamente, sirvió para ubicar ideológicamente a la Guatemala dividida en sus grupos, facciones y hasta trincheras, confrontadas en una visión de lo que debió ser y nunca fue y lo que la realidad histórica —muy maltratada la mayor parte de las veces, en estos debates sumamente curiosos y algunas posiciones francamente, insostenibles, al menos en los niveles históricos y teoréticos—, deparó y desencadenó a esa Guatemala emergente o naciente después de la destrucción del mejor de los sueños y proyectos centroamericanos: una Confederación que se debió mantener y no destruir, en nombre de unos pseudo principios más personales y de intereses de grupos, personas mezquinas y como María del Rosario nos sugiere, habitantes del octavo círculo, donde muchos hipócritas, fraudulentos, seductores y más, están condenados a un eterno castigo y sufrimientos indescriptibles.

Claro es que la mejor metáfora de los cuentos es el encuentro de Isabella con el señor de Malebolge, en un castillo casi en ruinas, lúgubre, siniestro y oscuro, donde es convocada, invitada casi se diría, después de cumplir un encargo, cargado de maledicencias y profundas maldades. Hurto de reliquias sagradas, sustracción de obras de arte valiosísimas y consagradas, para servicios religiosos o sea, funciones y tareas de un muy alto orden y significado. Traficar con crucifijos, pinturas o esculturas, destinadas a los altares de observancia y de usos populares abiertos, para las asambleas o comunidades, delitos comunes, en el sentido de expandidos y frecuentes, como los de las extracciones y subastas de antiguas piezas de las grandes civilizaciones, que existieron y de alguna manera aun lo hacen, en Mesoamérica, con el fin de subastarlas, privada o públicamente, o ser adquiridas por coleccionistas privados y retenerlas para placeres individuales, como pasa con tantas obras de arte, son perseguidos afortunadamente, con vigor y consciencia, por todos aquellos que defienden estos patrimonios. No de alguna persona o familia, sino de naciones, las cuales son a fin de cuentas, las ultrajadas y vejadas por delincuentes y una usura desmedida, egoísta y diabólica. El señor de Malebolge recibe y castiga a Isabella y la envía a ese octavo círculo, del que María del Rosario nos relata a lo largo de su magnífica obra, donde de la mano de Dante —como un nuevo Virgilio— nos ubica en una profunda reflexión del mal y su profunda oscuridad. Valiosa, muy valiosa obra, que nos narra y reflexiona sobre ese terrible misterio del mal, que pareciera habitar por todas partes y del cual son testigos ese curioso gato, y una cuestión muy particular presentada casi como un inquietante cuestionamiento, existirá una genética del mal, porque parecieran existir familias enteras unidas y vinculadas, por ese espíritu de iniquidad, dónde las herencias se convierten en armas de destrucción y aniquilamiento, de sucesores y herederos. Se podría decir, estamos ante el mal manifestando su poder destructor. A veces la reflexión sobre los orígenes de ciertas fortunas, viene a cuenta, en estos tiempos de extraordinarias penurias. Si en el mal se pudiera encontrar los orígenes de la corrupción, probablemente Dante nos dejó un inventario y un camino para reflexionar, con la mayor seriedad posible, sobre un fenómeno totalmente global, presente en todas partes del mundo, ante el cual la incansable lucha librada, desde muchas esquinas del planeta, nos exigen un mayor compromiso y convicción, para su erradicación y castigo. Merece la presente obra de María del Rosario Molina una reflexión y análisis así como una lectura serena y dedicada.

CHAPTER IV
BELIZE/BELICE DE LA TEORÍA DE LAS CONTROVERSIAS A LA SOLUCIÓN DE CONFLICTOS

1
EL CASO DE BELICE Y LOS DOS SISTEMAS JURÍDICOS

En las últimas semanas, en Guatemala, la controversia por el tema del Diferendo Histórico está adquiriendo características de controversia. Incluso es palpable, como una de las leyes de la Teoría de las Controversias (Dascal), *las controversias crecen y se profundizan*, y esta va tomando forma e intensidad, o sea, se *profundiza*. Ha pasado de ser una forma de debate y discusión entre columnistas de medios impresos y digitales, a las redes sociales, adquiriendo los elementos típicos y propios de las discusiones en estos medios; a saber, intensidad, desorden, altos niveles de emocionalidad, desinformación, confusión deliberada, insultos, ataques maliciosos y otros aspectos ampliamente conocidos, cuando este tipo de polémica es introducida a estos niveles, donde filtros y moderación son poco exitosos y más aún, es un dominio en el cual la exageración y la confusión imperan. No veo cómo eso se podría evitar, dadas las implicaciones de la disputa, la cual abarca más de 150 años y si tomamos en cuenta el periodo histórico, es decir, el momento de los Tratados Anglo-Españoles, que es realmente, donde la controversia se origina, tanto formal como substancialmente, pues realmente, desde la Época Colonial, hasta nuestros días, ha estado presente, de una forma u otra y bajo distintas variantes.

De la búsqueda por Títulos Históricos, por parte del Reino Unido y su intensa procura de uno, sobre el Territorio Disputado, recuérdese sencillamente las infructuosas procuras e intentos secretos, tanto de Georges de Villiers, Duke of Buckingahm e incluso Lord Clarendon, o también Villiers, por obtener un Título por parte del Reino de España, existe documentación sobre dichas reuniones y altos dignatarios de la Corona Española. No es prudente dado el litigio existente extenderme demasiado sobre esta materia; baste aludir brevemente, que desde estos momentos, las concesiones para explotar madera, hasta la Independencia de las Provincias Unidas de Centroamérica, con la Confederación, como estado sucesor y emergente, de la Capitanía General del Reino de Guatemala, del proceso de Independencia, los territorios tal y como estaban establecidos, pasaron a ser parte territorial integrante de la Confederación. Acá incluso emergería la invocación a una de las mas conocidas formas y contribuciones del pensamiento jurídico luso-latinoamericano al Derecho Internacional General. Me refiero a la doctrina del uti possidetis iuris, la cual se encuentra contenida en el Derecho Romano. Su desarrollo y ampliación es una de tantas contribuciones al Derecho Internacional General, Público y Privado que América Latina ha configurado. Como sostenía arriba, no voy a revelar detalles que podrían afectar el caso y además, mi rol y participación en el mismo es completamente inexistente. Al terminar la negociación del Acuerdo Especial, me trasladé a Países Bajos, donde después de cuatro años como embajador y de seguir acuciosa y detenidamente los procesos incoados ante la Corte, me dediqué la mayor parte a mi trabajo como diplomático y profesional; a lo largo del proceso de la Consulta Popular, participé en algunas discusiones sobre la naturaleza del Acuerdo y los caminos venideros, y en mi condición de Embajador en Situación de Disponibilidad, hasta la fecha, hice algunas contribuciones adicionales, estudios y propuestas, para enriquecer las posibilidades de llegar a establecer los grandes pilares de la Primera Memoria, e incluso a un ex Canciller de la República, le entregué un extenso estudio sobre la eventual Arquitectura del Caso, con una propuesta de configuración, de la Memoria o si se prefiere, de los grandes temas y principios que esta debería de contener. En uno de mis viajes a Guatemala me reuní con la extinta Comisión de Belice, COMBEL, unos días antes de que fuera suprimida o cerrada, decisión la cual siempre cuestioné abiertamente. No es pues mi papel referirme extensamente al tema o a los detalles de la elaboración de la misma, porque entiendo existe un excelente equipo internacional de abogados, de un enorme prestigio y sumamente calificados, conocedores de todas las ramas del Derecho Internacional General Consensuado, quienes podrán y deberán elaborar un documento y anexos, con la mayor corrección y propiedad, de lo cual no me cabe la menor duda. En el tema de los equipos nacionales, prefiero guardar el más respetuoso y prudente silencio, puesto que tampoco se quiénes son sus miembros, salvo uno o dos nombres de personalidades, que respeto mucho.

Una de las mayores dificultades que el Diferendo Histórico enfrentará al someterlo a la Jurisdicción de la Corte, como es ya el caso, es la naturaleza y conformación de la Corte y sus grandes tradiciones. Aunque es una verdad totalmente reconocida, se trata de una Corte de un altísimo y ejemplar nivel; sus fallos y resoluciones, han sido y son aportes de un valor inmenso al desarrollo del Derecho Internacional, en todas sus formas y variantes. Sin embargo y quizás esto se hace más evidente, al recordar la exclusividad de las lenguas francesa e inglesa, como únicos idiomas de litigio o sometimiento de los Casos, es verdad que se pueden hacer excepciones, presentar alegatos, documentos escritos y durante la fase oral, argüir en el idioma original, de la parte ponente o presentante, no obstante, tal procedimiento, demanda con claridad la entrega a la Corte, al Registro de las correspondientes traducciones y ese es un enorme reto. Todo lo anterior está normado en el Capítulo III, Procedimiento, artículo 39 del Estatuto de la Corte. Hay un grave problema de fondo, además de que la Corte dictará sus resoluciones y sentencias, solamente en francés o inglés, algo más sutil y complejo subyace en esta práctica establecida y consolidada. Los dos grandes sistemas jurídicos dominantes son el francés y los sistemas codificados y el Common Law, o sea, el sistema de los países angloparlantes. Si bien es cierto que los sistemas jurídicos latinoamericanos están evidentemente más cercanos al Derecho Romano y de allí a la tradición francófona, claramente inspirada en el Derecho Civil y la tradición napoleónica, la realidad es que la evolución de los sistemas jurídicos latinoamericanos hace que hoy en día ya no sean tan cercanos al Derecho napoleónico o de los sistemas francófonos. La evolución extraordinaria del Derecho Constitucional está cambiando aceleradamente las visiones jurídicas y sus prácticas a lo largo y lo ancho del Continente. Es este pues el dilema, vamos a someter la disputa o dos sistemas jurídicos, que no son practicados en Guatemala y cuyo conocimiento de los mismos es limitado y reservado a ciertos especialistas, que los hay. Recuerdo con una gran claridad ciertas discusiones que se dieron durante la negociación del Acuerdo Especial, fueron muchas y sumamente enriquecedoras y no solamente me refiero acá a los procedimientos alternativos que se plantearon, ex aequo et bono, que tenía sus adherentes, siguiendo los trabajos de dos grandes internacionalistas guatemaltecos, Carlos García Bauer y Luis Aycinena Salazar, proponentes de esta alternativa y aun más quienes buscaron la alternativa del Arbitraje o el sometimiento de la disputa ante Cámara Especial, nunca hubo consenso sobre ellas y primó el sometimiento ante la Corte en Pleno, francamente la alternativa de Cámara Especial y que cinco Jueces resolvieran el Diferendo era sumamente difícil de aceptar. El tema del ex aequo et bono siempre me dejó intrigado, aunque hubo quienes claramente y sin dubitaciones, decían que debía ser un Juicio de Derecho. El procedimiento ex aequo et bono —usado en casos de arbitrajes— jamás ha sido empleado o aplicado por la Corte, era como una experimentación y una primera prueba, y aunque tenía y tiene sus muy sólidos méritos, resultaría políticamente inviable.

Allí surgía esa profunda inquietud y preocupación, vamos a buscar resolver el Diferendo Histórico, un asunto que pasa por el corazón mismo de la historia de Guatemala, a través de sistemas jurídicos, que nos son ajenos. Cuyos lenguajes no coinciden, sus prácticas son diferentes y aunque los principios sean los mismos y las fuentes coincidan, las distancias son claras y evidentes. Esa línea de argumentación siempre me la cuestioné profundamente y nunca encontré una respuesta satisfactoria. El problema está en la naturaleza misma de la Corte, la exclusión de ciertos idiomas —y el español es un idioma oficial de Naciones Unidas, lo cual engendra una paradoja muy seria— es más que la imposibilidad de hablar nuestro propio idioma como herramienta de comunicación y argumentación, tanto oral como escrita: es la exclusión de una enorme cultura y de una de las zonas o regiones, en tanto que un gran conjunto, es una de las que más han contribuido al surgimiento de muchas formas del derecho, entre ellas el ius gentium, que amarra toda la gran tradición luso-hispánica, desde la Península al Continente. Y los nombres son muchísimos. Muchísimos y de un enorme valor. Desde Vitoria hasta Eduardo Jiménez de Aréchaga, Bernardo Sepulveda, Antônio Augusto Cançado Trindade, actual Juez de la Corte y tantos más, que resulta imposible citar y recordar acá, en este breve espacio. Y dicho sea de paso, Guatemala tuvo y tiene una muy importante tradición, en esta materia también.

Como fácilmente se notará y podrá apreciarse, estamos y estuvimos ante una muy difícil decisión. Y esos temores y sombras flotan en las visiones jurídicas de importantes guatemaltecos, que silenciosamente siguen el proceso y se cuestionan, con discreción, muchísimas cosas y la prudencia y discreción, no el temor o la presión, hacen que muchos de nosotros hablemos poco y callemos más, para evitar perjudicar elcaso, posición común y compartida, con mi querido amigo Héctor Rolando Palomo González, notable jurista guatemalteco y profundo conocedor del caso y uno de los verdaderos expertos maritimistas, apasionados desde siempre del Diferendo y el cual seguimos religiosamente, tratando de evitar, en todo momento, perjudicar el caso, al hablar sin la propiedad necesaria. Sin embargo, se trata de la Historia misma de Guatemala y eso no lo debemos perder de vista.

Uno de los más graves obstáculos que enfrenta la Diplomacia en general, fenómeno global y no particular nuestro, aunque entre nosotros es muy acentuado, es el de la sobrevaloración e imposición de los Sistemas de Administración sobre la Diplomacia y sus prácticas. Ni siquiera la Academia se escapa de estas formas de control y supervisión. Los modelos y métodos corporativos están por todas partes. Los diplomáticos se ven literalmente condicionados por no usar y recurrir a expresiones o adjetivos contundentes por las administraciones. Y el caso y su administración y manejo no es una excepción, aunque algunos busquen excluirlo y asilarlo de tales realidades. No es ningún secreto, que las Cancillerías son grandes cementerios de papeles, informes, cartas y una serie de comunicaciones que se proliferan desmedidamente, sobre todo en la era digital y de las comunicaciones inmediatas, y de las respuestas inmediatas también. Ese falso sentido de urgencia es un catalizador de errores. Lo inmediato y lo urgente se mezclan y confunden. Los administradores de papeles demandan constantemente un mayor número de documentación, nunca termina y no tiene final. Y en medio de esos laberintos —no es solamente uno, son varios y se entrelazan— la búsqueda es interminable. La exigencia es incontenible. El llamado "empapelamiento" es un plan sistemático de generación de olvidos, extravíos y excesos. Y, sin embargo, no es posible navegar estos mares agitados sin medios coadyuvantes. Incluso, asuntos como confidencialidad y reserva, son y serán causantes de una preocupación constante en una época que demanda traspa-rencia y apertura. Las actuaciones deben ser públicas y de conoci-miento de cualquier persona. Los modelos de la secretividad, especialmente en América Latina, tienen tonos y evocan antiguos autoritarismos y formas dictatoriales, ante las cuales han habido innumerables luchas y rebeliones. Nuestros sistemas republi-canos demandan esas transparencias y aperturas, esfuerzos por ocultar o condicionar accesos a cuestiones que afectan a la totalidad o al dominio de la Nación, y chocarán con reacciones contrarias, que buscarán y lucharán por detenerlas y limitarlas. Intentar acogerse a fórmulas y remanentes,de los autoritarismos y formas de control por vías siniestras, hablará de unos tiempos y de un pasado nada deseado y cuyas consecuencias han sido claramente improductivas e, incluso, innecesarias. La lucha por obtener información clara y transparente, en asuntos de esta relevancia, donde la historia misma de Guatemala se ve encon-trada, carecen de sentido y no son consecuentes con los actuales esfuerzos por consolidar las democracias republicanas e incluso los Estados de Derecho. Guatemala eligió enfrentar a una poten-cia colonial, con las armas del Derecho Internacional y la verdad histórica. Mal sería que esa hermosa gesta no sea también algo que internamente se ha librado bajo ese espíritu y valores, que nuestro constitucionalismo ha ido lenta y pausadamente, incorporando a las esferas tanto públicas como privadas.

GUATEMALA Y BELICE: EL CAMINO A LA CORTE INTERNACIONAL DE JUSTICIA

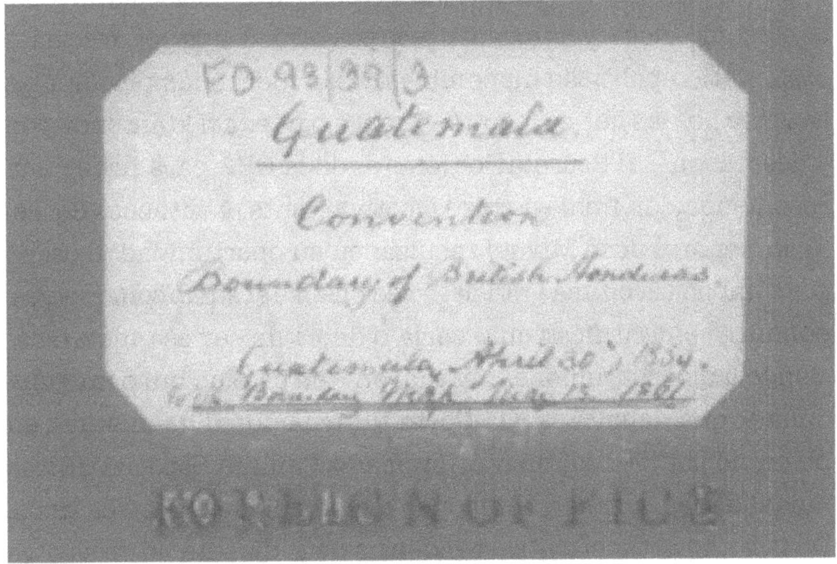

Finalmente y después de un larguísimo y muy complejo camino, se cumplieron los últimos pasos de una extensa y dilatada negociación, la cual previó ab initio, que la disputa —en la que a lo largo de los años siempre insistí, por diversos medios y formas, llamar el Diferendo Histórico—, o sea la solución o acuerdo, nosotros lo llamábamos *definitivo*, en lenguaje extraído de nuestra Ley Suprema, la cual lo norma a través del artículo 19 transitorio, como es ampliamente sabido e innumerables veces reconocido e invocado, sería pues, sometida a una instancia jurisdiccional internacional, para alcanzar la evasiva conclusión, incansablemente buscada, vía todos los medios pacíficos, de solución de controversias, contemplados en todos los instrumentos de Derecho Internacional General Consensuado, tanto latinoamericanos como universales, así como dentro del Derecho Internacional Consuetudinario. Las múltiples formas de negociación directa fueron plenamente agotadas —a pesar de las reservas e incluso oposición, de ilustrados guatemaltecos, que han expresado continuadamente sus dudas, por diversas alternativas y medios de comunicación— y no existían más posibilidades de negociaciones diplomático-políticas disponibles. Esas fueron las principales razones por las que se facultó —ambas partes así lo entendieron y aceptaron— al Secretario General de la OEA para hacer una recomendación final —lo hizo efectivamente el entonces Secretario General José Miguel Insulza, en su oportunidad al darse por cumplida la última gran negociación—, se abstuvo como correspondía, de identificar cuál sería o debía de ser esa instancia, siendo las partes quienes acordaron —en esto no hubo ninguna duda—, que debería ser la Corte Internacional de Justicia en pleno, no por procedimiento abreviado, Cámara Especial u otras modalidades, a saber, arbitrajes o mediaciones de otros tipos. Dada la importancia y trascendencia de la disputa no cabía otra alternativa más que someterse al fallo definitivo, que emitiría y pronunciaría la Corte en pleno.

La aprobación mediante referendo o consultas en ambos países se estableció como fundamental y así se reconoció y fijó en el Acuerdo Especial y su Protocolo, salvo la modificación de la simultaneidad, tema que fue objeto de importantes diferencias, dado que Belice intentó introducir una reforma a su *Acta de Referendo*, donde establecía condiciones plenamente inalcanzables e incurrió incluso en violaciones a normas y prácticas generales del Derecho de los Tratados y del Derecho Internacional General, puesto que mientras se negociaba el Acuerdo Especial, elaboraba y sometía a su aprobación una serie de reformas legales, que afectaban e impactaban no solamente las negociaciones en marcha, sino que establecía también requisitos inalcanzables; a saber, por ejemplo, una participación del sesenta por ciento y otros puntos más, que evidenciaban serias violaciones a la pacta sunt servanda y obligaban tácitamente a Guatemala a no tener más remedio, que invocar la cláusula rebus sic stantivus o dar por terminadas las negociaciones, en virtud no solamente de la evidente mala fe, sino aún más grave, de la modificación de las condiciones existentes, que produciría un profundo daño a lo acordado. Esta situación, simplificada acá, en realidad era más grave de lo que nunca se reconoció, y puso en serio riesgo al mismo proceso. La habilidad diplomática y la paciencia de sus líderes permitió superar la delicada cuestión creada, naciendo así el Protocolo que rompió la simultaneidad y permitió una mayor flexibilidad, tanto en las fechas, como en las convocatorias y la certidumbre, confianza, para seguir adelante, con el proceso y las consultas acordadas.

Una breve cuestión de mis recuerdos del proceso mismo de la negociación, que a su vez sirva de tributo a quienes realmente hicieron posible construir un texto, sin el cual francamente, nada de esto sería viable. La razón por la cual se concibió y estableció la simultaneidad de las consultas, descansaba en la idea comúnmente aceptada y derivada un tanto, de la extensión del principio de igualdad, que aunque tal vez meramente procesal, buscaba evitar eventuales ventajas o generar inequalidades, que afectarían de nulidad al proceso mismo. Concebíamos que se debía evitar influenciar las consultas, en cualesquiera de los dos países, lo cual generaría no solo fuertes dudas, sino las referidas invocatorias de nulidades. Sin buscar caer en un excesivo *procesalismo*, la visión central era cuidar la igualdad más absoluta posible. Se entiende así cómo ante una acción unilateral e inconsulta, no cabía más remedio que suspender la Consulta, ya en pleno proceso de convocatoria y volver a la mesa de negociaciones, para superar la crisis generada. Efectivamente así fue y se logró mediante el conocido Protocolo acordado por las partes. Adicionalmente, Belice modificó posteriormente su Acta respectiva, permitiendo unas consultas en condiciones lo más igualitarias posibles. El resultado final es la aprobación en ambos países, del instrumento necesario para someter de mutuo acuerdo el Diferendo Histórico, ante la jurisdicción de la Corte. Debe destacarse aquí una cuestión, que es de suma importancia —la he acotado anteriormente, en mis otros escritos relativos a esta materia y viene a cuenta repetirlo nuevamente—, la razón por la que se negoció y construyó un Acuerdo Especial, que descansa en las condiciones o normas, establecidas en el Estatuto de la Corte y su Reglamento, para adjudicar o resolver disputas, cuando no exista un instrumento internacional de jurisdicción compulsoria, como es el caso de Guatemala y Belice. Adicionalmente, es una muestra efectiva y real de someter una añeja disputa a una solución definitiva e invocando los mecanismos construidos y contemplados dentro del Derecho Internacional. Guatemala y Belice deben, por estas razones, —nunca está de más destacar, que se recurre a la jurisdicción de la Corte, de manera consensuada y negociada, o sea, en virtud a un Acuerdo laboriosamente construido— actuar de manera civilizada y amistosa; por eso la única forma que debe prevalecer es el sometimiento simultáneo y la comunicación o notificación requerida, de manera conjunta y no unilateral o individual, a pesar que el Acuerdo y su Protocolo así lo permiten; sin embargo, ese es el resultado y el mensaje general, más apropiado y correspondiente. No solo es la voz expresada de ambos pueblos, sino la obligación derivada de las mismas consultas efectuadas, para ambos gobiernos. Esa es la naturaleza del mandato recabado. Es una contundente muestra de un comportamiento ejemplar de dos pequeños países, cuyas historias están íntimamente unidas a esta antigua disputa.

El procedimiento de la notificación está recogido, tanto en el Acuerdo Especial, y, sobre todo, en los artículos 40,1 que se refiere a la incoación de una acción mediante el procedimiento del Acuerdo Especial, adicionalmente en los artículos 39, 40 y 42 del Reglamento de la Corte. Allí se establecen las normas que regirán esta parte del proceso. El plazo para la notificación está inequívocamente expresado tanto en el Acuerdo como en su Protocolo y es de un mes después de haberse efectuado ambas consultas y sus resultados sean ya definitivos y certificados por el órgano controlador. En el caso de Guatemala dos pasos serán absolutamente necesarios; el primero, ya efectuado, de iniciar consultas inmediatas, con las autoridades beliceñas, para coordinar las futuras obligaciones derivadas de las consultas y otra tal vez, más interna, producto de la circunstancia histórica, en la que se llega a este momento. Estamos en las postrimerías de un proceso electoral en su primera ronda; de la misma emergerán dos candidatos, en caso, claro está, que ninguno de todos los contendientes alcance una mayoría absoluta durante la primera vuelta. Pareciera demandar o derivarse, de esta realidad inminente, que se deben iniciar procesos de consultas, informales tal vez, pero consultas de todas formas, eventualmente, para conformar y configurar la manera cómo Guatemala enfrentará el inminente litigio. No olvidemos que derivado del Acuerdo Especial se debe integrar un equipo jurídico, del más alto nivel, que incluya no solo relevantes figuras, dentro del litigio internacional —en esto hay que tener una enorme prudencia. No dejo de pensar en Costa Rica y en su manera de conducir sus asuntos en todos los sentidos y sus impresionantes éxitos en La Haya, sin contar con los recursos y apoyos de una contraparte mucho más afluente, asombrosamente, por cierto, la composición de equipos mixtos, como Perú también demostró, en su oportunidad y a su vez, Chile no lo dejemos de considerar, sino, y esto es sumamente relevante, Guatemala cuenta con varios conocedores profundos del Caso de Belice, quienes han dedicado gran parte de su práctica profesional al Diferendo Histórico, de muchas maneras, desde una enorme discreción y prudencia.

Esperamos y confiamos, que el tratamiento y la manera cómo se ha conducido, todo este proceso se mantenga, me refiero específicamente a la no politización y consideración de ser un asunto de Estado, que involucra a la nación guatemalteca, es decir, un espacio donde su historia trasciende y supera los dominios de la política y sus peculiares prácticas, sobre todo ante los espectáculos a los que hemos asistido en los recientes años. Aquí no caben los narcicismos políticos o los pseudo mesianismos; el sentido e importancia de nuestra historia misma están en juego, se debe resistir la tentación de actuar bajo falsos ídolos y aspiraciones irreales. Esto ha prevalecido hasta ahora, lo he podido constatar a lo largo de mi involucramiento con el Diferendo, aún desde estos últimos años de aparente alejamiento y distancia. Es importante recordar a todos aquellos ilustres guatemaltecos, que han contribuido —muchos bajo una enorme discreción— a que esta disputa llegue al momento de su "solución definitiva". Me consta que la honestidad y profundo interés genuino de algunos de sus hoy en día silenciosos actores, permitió y contribuyó a que este paso histórico se concretara y fuera una realidad efectiva. Sigamos dándole ese mismo tratamiento, que inspirara las acciones de aquellos, quienes dedicaran gran parte de sus vidas a este tan complejo y trascendental capítulo de la historia de Guatemala.

3
BELICE, LA CONSULTA O LA NARRATIVA DE LA DESINFORMACIÓN Y LA CONFUSIÓN

Aunque tal vez corremos el riesgo de continuar repitiendo los mismos temas y argumentos, dada la evolución de las distintas narrativas dominantes alrededor de la Consulta próxima a celebrarse, es oportuno enfrentar algunos de las más graves y puntuales consideraciones, que tienden a confundir y ensombrecer lo que realmente se persigue con el Acuerdo Especial, porqué se construyó y cuáles son las causas decisivas que movieron su negociación y posterior aprobación. El Acuerdo Especial está plenamente aprobado por la arquitectura legal y administrativa del Estado de Guatemala. No existen decisiones, resoluciones, sentencias, que impidan y limiten su plena ejecución. Tal es el fundamento que ha movido al Tribunal Supremo Electoral a convocar la Consulta, bajo el más riguroso apego al derecho y en cumplimiento estricto de un mandato constitucional abundantemente citado.

Guatemala ha pasado por una historia muy compleja y dramática: La Conclusión de los procesos de negociación para alcanzar una paz negociada y acordada, con el fin de dar por terminada una confrontación que causó un enorme dolor, sufrimiento y desesperación en las familias guatemaltecas en ese enorme esfuerzo, por constituirse en una cultura y sociedad abierta, plural y sobre todo, profundamente democrática y poder vivir dentro de un Estado Constitucional de Derecho, que garantizara la convivencia, la seguridad y el porvenir, de todos los guatemaltecos, sin excepciones. Mucho se ha intentado y poco se ha logrado. No toca abordar este tema, aunque el mismo y su más oscuro demonio, el de la inmensa pobreza, flota y cubre todo lo que se hace o deja de hacer, para construir un mejor mundo, para todos, sin marginaciones o exclusiones. Sobre esa transición, del silencio a la expresión abierta y pública, los guatemaltecos intentan salir de las obscuridades del autoritarismo a una realidad franca y transparente. No es nada fácil. Es un proceso sumamente lento. Tal es como podemos ver esos balbuceos, a veces incoherentes, llenos y cargados de la furia y rabia, de los silencios prolongados, traducidos, en andanadas de insultos e improperios, intolerancias a lo diferente, al otro y sus modalidades personales, incapaz al inicio, de construir acercamientos, sino más bien seguir sumidos en las distancias. De habitantes del silencio a habitantes de trincheras. Es desde estos horizontes que acudimos a la experiencia de enfrentar una cuestión que ha vivido con nosotros por varios siglos. Se nos heredó por aquellos, quienes intentaron resolverlo y no pudieron, y es ahora que podemos dar un paso decisivo hacia esa ansiada y buscada solución, que demanda coraje y valentía. Resolución y decisión. Caminamos de la mano del Derecho y de la Justicia, no de la imposición y de la fuerza. Adelante vamos a intentar resumir y responder —repitiendo probablemente— e insistir, en por qué y cómo la Consulta es histórica y sumamente relevante para la nación guatemalteca.

No es sencillo ni instantáneo aprender a hablar. El silencio de mucho tiempo roba miserablemente la capacidad de expresar pensamientos y emociones de manera propia y articulada. Balbuceos iniciales llegan a constituirse en voces profundas y amplias, que inundan todos los espacios que los silencios dejaron vacíos. Así les tocó lentamente a los guatemaltecos abandonar el silencio y el temor, en favor de sencillamente expresarse, decir, hablar. No es ningún secreto que aún hay muchos miedos, la inseguridad recuerda al autoritarismo, es la dictadura de la ilegalidad y del delito. Eso que llamamos corrupción. La Consulta es una forma de hablar, un derecho inalienable y fundamental de opinar; por eso el presente ejercicio ha sido poblado de todas estas expresiones. Son los primeros pasos a formas abiertas de abordar lo que se cree, cómo se ve, cómo se dice. Hay muy pocos ejercicios en este sentido. El debate, la controversia, el diálogo, la simple conversación, la charla y la plática ocupan ahora un lugar central y relevante y no se van a ir. Todo eso y más se está instalando y tomado lugar en Guatemala, tan atormentada por la injusticia y la pobreza. Hablar, analizar, comentar, son las nuevas formas de los lenguajes, expresados de forma contundente y hasta llenos de pasión y emoción. Magnífico. Se está construyendo un mundo diferente. Se lucha contra tanta adversidad y oposición.

En comentarios anteriores, *Belice: la Consulta, Agosto del 2017* y más recientemente *La Consulta, Belice y Guatemala, Febrero del 2018*, donde abordé el tema desde otros ángulos intentando no solamente explicar, sino responder algunas de las preguntas abiertas generadas a lo largo de la controversia, muchas de las críticas proferidas encuentran respuestas claras en esos dos textos. El bloque de argumentos contrarios pueden agruparse desde los que abiertamente hablan de inconstitucionalidad; la defensa del juicio *por equidad*; los que abogan por el arbitraje; la cuestión de la jurisdicción; la pregunta del por qué y qué se vota concretamente y, tal vez, el más preocupante, el que ha construido una densa confusión alrededor de la no definitividad, de la Consulta o, sea que no se ha sometido una solución definitiva, no se ha alcanzado ni se alcanza con el Acuerdo Especial y menos aún, con la consulta misma. Leyendo diariamente textos publicados en diversos medios, la confusión y desinformación campean plenamente. La ausencia de una posición frontal de las autoridades, quienes realizan campañas de divulgación, asumen una neutralidad justificada, en el Decreto de Convocatoria del Tribunal Supremo Electoral, así como las prohibiciones contenidas en el mismo, las cuales van desde el uso de recursos de carácter presupuestario a la prohibición a los distintos funcionarios públicos, de "hacer campaña" en favor de cualquiera de las dos alternativas. Afortunadamente fueron superadas en la modificación del Decreto original en un segundo, el cual supera la referida limitación. Son personas privadas, quienes han asumida la dirección de las dos opciones ya que sobre ellas no privaban las prohibiciones, para involucrarse a favor de cualquiera de las alternativas.

La Cancillería ha referido varias veces que tiene mucho tiempo de estar efectuando una profunda campaña de divulgación sobre la naturaleza del Diferendo, sus orígenes, causas, historia, así como las ventajas que le generarán al país superar esta añeja disputa. Figuras importantes, ex cancilleres y otros ex funcionarios, en su condición de tales, dada su participación pasada, ofrecen sus visiones y perspectivas, la mayoría de ellos a favor del sometimiento a la jurisdicción de la Corte Internacional de Justicia, del Diferendo, o sea, votar a favor del *sí* como vehículo e instrumento para lograr una superación de la misma. Dejemos hablar al texto mismo. El artículo 2 del Acuerdo, fue el más difícil de construir, lo identificamos como *el objeto del litigio* o en algunos casos, *sujeto del litigio*. Los Estados que han acudido ante la Corte, buscando someter una disputa a su jurisdicción y al no tener o ser partes de Convenios internacionales multilaterales, que establezcan jurisdicción compulsoria, han negociado instrumentos similares, como lo contempla el Estatuto de la Corte, en el citado artículo, para acudir y buscar resolver una disputa. El texto es abundantemente claro, contundente: …*toda y cualquier reclamación legal de Guatemala en contra de Belice sobre territorios continentales e insulares y cualesquiera áreas marítimas correspondientes a dichos territorios…*

No hubo nunca renuncia alguna a los derechos históricos de Guatemala. No hubo concesiones de ningún tipo. No se renunció absolutamente a nada. Se va a litigar la totalidad del Diferendo y será la Corte quién decida al pronunciar su sentencia. Sobre lo cual las partes también acordaron, en el artículo 5 del Acuerdo, su aceptación irrestricta del fallo, lo expresa de la siguiente manera el texto del mismo, y dejemos una vez más que el mismo hable: *Las partes aceptarán como definitivo y obligatorio el fallo de la Corte, y se comprometen a cumplirlo y ejecutarlo íntegramente y de buena fe.*

El Protocolo al Acuerdo Especial, en su artículo primero, confirma y reitera lo definitivo de la solución, de la siguiente manera: *…la necesidad de resolverlos de manera total y definitiva en la Corte Internacional de Justicia."*

No hay pues, territorios no disputados, asuntos marítimos parcialmente disputados, concesiones ni renuncias, a lo largo de la negociación y durante la construcción del texto. Hubo extensas consultas internas y externas y se siguieron todos los mecanismos adecuados y legales, para arribar a un texto que ha pasado muchas pruebas y desafíos y se mantiene vigente y estable, a pesar de sus opositores; es la base para alcanzar una solución definitiva, que no se debe mezclar o confundir con un argumento muy peculiar, que abunda en confusión y genera mucha oscuridad. Debe decirse claramente que el texto o el acuerdo no es la solución definitiva, es el medio procesal o vehículo, que permitió e hizo posible el sometimiento de la disputa ante la jurisdicción de la Corte, cuya sentencia dará por cerrado el diferendo. Eso es lo que se votará y no alguna extraña construcción artificial. En cumplimiento del mandato constitucional es la población guatemalteca y no ninguna autoridad, quien decidirá, con su voto, definitivo si es el sí, el cual nosotros creemos y estamos convencidos será de forma afirmativa, para disputar y litigar los Derechos históricos de Guatemala, ante el máximo tribunal internacional, que se haya establecido, dicho sea y aclarando, que los Jueces de la Corte son juristas independientes de un enorme prestigio nacional e internacional, y no representan a sus países de origen, sino a sus extensas y respetadísimas carreras judiciales. Son grandes expertos en el Derecho Internacional General Consensuado y gozan de un reconocimiento pleno de la comunidad internacional. No existe una Corte en ninguna parte que llene estas enormes expectativas, la cual tiene una trayectoria impecable, fuera de cualquier cuestionamiento. Los guatemaltecos deben sentirse seguros que los miembros de la Corte fallarán de acuerdo a los grandes principios del Derecho Internacional General Consensuado y su intocabilidad es absoluta.

4
LA CONSULTA, BELICE Y GUATEMALA

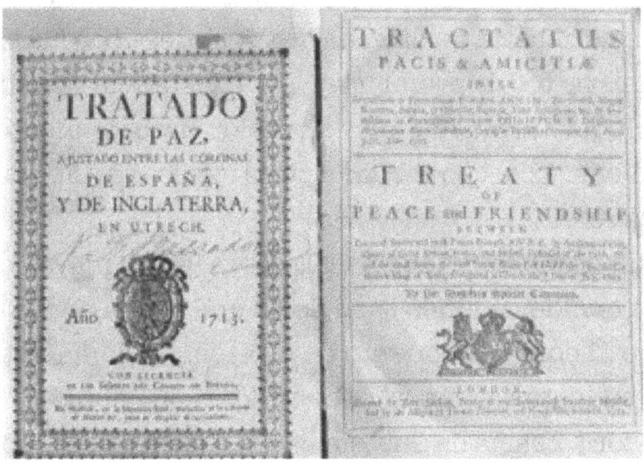

El actual debate, controversia, que se ha abierto en Guatemala, sobre la próxima Consulta Popular, Referendum, que se llevará a cabo el día 15 de Abril del presente año, está produciendo una serie de artículos, publicaciones, comentarios, entrevistas y tomas de posiciones, frente a una cuestión —siempre lo hemos llamado Diferendo Histórico, puesto es de lo que realmente se trata—, los cuales reflejan diversas opiniones y críticas, de todos los tipos, desde las ilustradas, hasta las que son meramente producto del auge de los llamados medios digitales, dentro de la era de las redes sociales, en las que se recogen desde insultos, burlas a expresiones más balanceadas y medianamente informadas. La complejidad del tema hace casi imposible su divulgación. Recuerdo los tiempos en que debatíamos internamente —cuando era el Jefe Negociador del Acuerdo Especial— si incluso no se debería también divulgar no solo el Acuerdo, sino la naturaleza misma del Diferendo, en los demás idiomas de uso amplio en

Guatemala. Espero se haya hecho, solamente así se garantizará la universalidad de la Consulta. A continuación voy a intentar construir una argumentación, sobre por qué se debe votar a favor del sometimiento de la Disputa a la jurisdicción de la Corte Internacional de Justicia, en oposición a quienes abiertamente sostienen no debería ser llevada a la Corte, sea porque favorecen una negativa total, preferirían otra instancia jurisdiccional internacional, arbitraje por ejemplo, procedimiento mixto, procedimiento ex aequo et bono u otros medios de solución pacífica de controversias.

Desde un horizonte general y como gran marco de fondo, hay dos consideraciones esenciales que destacar. La primera se refiere al comportamiento de Guatemala como Estado, a lo largo de su historia —no se debe olvidar, que el Diferendo pasa por la historia misma de Guatemala—, Guatemala en todo momento, con algunas muy breves desviaciones, que obedecen a posiciones individuales de los gobernantes de esos momentos, decía pues, que el comportamiento y el manejo del Diferendo siempre ha estado ceñido al Derecho Internacional General Consensuado, los medios y mecanismos de solución pacífica de controversias, negociaciones directas, conciliación, mediaciones y otras fórmulas más, típicas del espíritu de las búsqueda de resolver de forma amigable la disputa, tanto con el Reino Unido como con Belice. Esto no siempre se destaca y es realmente fundamental. No es un proceso de un gobierno, es una cuestión que se ha llevado adelante por generaciones de guatemaltecos, que han buscado resolver esta difícil controversia. El estado actual que tenemos es el fruto de esas dos clarísimas perspectivas; la una, el apego al Derecho Internacional, y la otra la vocación pacífica para resolver las diferencias existentes. Con ese espíritu actuaron siempre los diplomáticos y negociadores guatemaltecos —contrario a lo que se ha escrito en algunos medios, Guatemala sí tiene y ha tenido estupendos negociadores— para poder arribar al instrumento histórico que hoy tenemos y con el cual contamos para la solución de la disputa y que se puede someter ante el pueblo guatemalteco, para que tome la decisión correspondiente. La segunda consideración se refiere a la no politización de la Consulta. Este asunto no debe ni puede convertirse en un referendum sobre el actual gobierno y sus autoridades.

Lo supera plenamente. El actual gobierno ha sido el vehículo trasmisor y ejecutor de unos acuerdos internacionales, en los cuales han intervenido varios Estados y países amigos, ya sea por la vía de mecanismos de consulta y apoyo, en los órganos multilaterales regionales e incluso vía consultas diplomáticas a otros niveles adicionales y complementarios. Guatemala y Belice se han comportado como naciones civilizadas. Están buscando con su conducta no sólo buscar una solución definitiva, sino cumplir con todo lo negociado, sino también y ante todo, siguiendo sus mandatos internos y ajustados siempre al respeto máximo de sus legislaciones internas en estas materias. No es pues el trabajo de una persona o de un grupo de individuos, es un proceso histórico y más allá de lo meramente generacional o más aún, de las coyunturas temporales, para convertirlo en un valor histórico. Ese y no otro es el propósito que llevó a los dos países a buscar la fórmula adecuada, para llevar ante la Corte el Diferendo y dar así por terminada y superada la controversia.

El Acuerdo Especial tiene una historia conocida. No la voy a relatar nuevamente. Lo interesante acá es la pregunta del por qué fue necesario recurrir a la construcción de un Acuerdo/Tratado, para someter la disputa o el Diferendo a la jurisdicción de la Corte. Sobre esto es importante retrotraer una historia y un caso en particular, el llamado Caso Nottebohm, en que el Principado de Liechtenstein acudió ante la Corte Internacional de Justicia el 29 de Marzo de 1950, para resolver una disputa

sobre derechos y nacionalidad de Friedrich Nottebohm. La Corte
como se sabe falló a favor de Guatemala, por ende no es la primera
vez que Guatemala acude a la Corte. En el caso mencionado, la
adjudicación fue posible sobre la Declaración del 27 de Enero
de 1947, hecha por Guatemala, aceptando la jurisdicción compulsoria, ipso facto, de la Corte para todas las disputas exceptuando
la que se mantenía con el Reino Unido, que se sometería exclusivamente bajo el procedimiento ex aequo et bono, firmada por
el entonces Canciller Eugenio Silva Peña y depositada en la Secretaría General de Naciones Unidas. Acoto la versión en inglés:

*The Government of Guatemala declares that, in accordance
with Article 36 (2) and (3) of the Statute of the International
Court of Justice, it recognizes as compulsory, ipso facto and
without special agreement, in relation to any other State accepting
the same obligation, and for a period of five years, the jurisdiction of the Court in all legal disputes. This declaration does not
cover the dispute between England and Guatemala concerning
the restoration of the territory of Belize, in which the Government
of Guatemala would, as it has proposed, agree to submit to the
judgment of the Court, if the case were decided ex aequo et bono,
in accordance with Article 38 of the said Statute. Guatemala,
27 January 1947.*

Las partes más relevantes de la misma sostienen que tendrá
una vigencia de cinco años —esta fue la principal línea de defensa
en el Caso Nottebohm, argumentando que la misma había expirado
y por ende había cesado la jurisdición de la Corte totalmente,
tal y como se invocó en su momento—, y contiene una referencia
directa a la falta de necesidad de utilizar un *special agreement*
para someterse a la misma y enfáticamente condiciona que el
sometimiento del Diferendo será exclusivamente, si se invoca
el procedimiento ex aequo et bono, citando el artículo correspondiente del Estatuto de la Corte, 38 (2). Aquí se puede ver el

problema existente; el debate sobre el recurso al acuerdo especial ha estado establecido aunque no ha sido invocado, lo cual es una prerrogativa del Estado ya que la Corte lo establece como una de las fórmulas para acudir a su jurisdicción. Dado que Guatemala y tampoco Belice son Estados partes del llamado Pacto de Bogotá, donde se reconoce la jurisdicción compulsoria, de la Corte para resolver disputas, mecanismo ampliamente empleado entre los Estados latinoamericanos, que han sometido disputas, sin acuerdo especial; no quedaba pues otra alternativa que negociar un Acuerdo Especial, así se procedió y como resultado de unas complejas negociaciones, bajo el auspicio y asesoría de la OEA, pudo concluirse felizmente.

Por eso tenemos un Acuerdo Especial y su Protocolo. Como se puede comprender fácilmente, lo que se le pide a la población guatemalteca es pronunciarse vía voto soberano, si autoriza el sometimiento a una administración de justicia; eso quiere decir y significa someterse a una jurisdicción internacional, en este caso, de la Corte y que la disputa sea resuelta de forma definitiva, ante lo cual las partes aceptan el fallo de la misma ya que se ha buscado precisamente la jurisdicción internacional o administración de justicia del más alto tribunal existente en el Sistema de Naciones Unidas, para resolver de forma definitiva el diferendo. Como se apreciará también con claridad, no hay ninguna declaración o pronunciamiento, de ningún tipo, sobre los méritos y contendido del Diferendo como tal, se trata de un mecanismo procesal, plenamente reconocido y ampliamente usado, para la adjudicación de Disputas entre Estados Miembros de Naciones Unidas y de la Corte Internacional de Justicia. Más allá no hay nada y no existen, ni han existido o se han dado, renuncias de ningún tipo y menos aún se ha incurrido en concesiones o negociaciones, que no sean bajo la mediación y observación, acompañamiento, de la Organización de Estados Americanos, sus Secretarios Generales, Testigos de Honor del proceso y todo el sistema de derecho interno guatemalteco, el Acuerdo Especial fue aprobado en todas las instancias, que para la ratificación de un Tratado nuestro sistema y arquitectura legal determinan y, claro está, en pleno apego a la norma constitucional que nuestra Constitución establece.

Así pues, la controversia generada, cuyas características no son tan claras de establecer, giraría alrededor de argumentos tales como los costos de la referida Consulta. Se trata de una enorme suma de millones de quetzales, los cuales bien podrían ser empleados para fines más reales y urgentes, escuelas, salud pública, obra física, todos y ellos, así como otros más, en un enorme déficit de atención e inversión; se ha sostenido incluso que se ha violado la Constitución al convocarse una consulta que no cumple con el mandato de aportar una *solución definitiva*, usando el lenguaje de nuestra Ley Suprema; que la Corte Internacional de Justicia rechazaría el Acuerdo Especial, por no cumplir con ciertos requisitos procesales y no contener una clara redacción, del objeto-sujeto de la disputa y por ende, la Corte decidiría no conocer y preferiría no pronunciarse al respecto; estos son algunos de los principales, temores o contra argumentos que se han ofrecido y planteado, para demeritar e incluso intentar detener la Consulta. En cuanto al costo de la misma, el argumento es altamente sensible. Es demasiado caro y por supuesto que lo es y el litigio lo será también. Y lo que Guatemala hasta ahora ha invertido es inmenso, son muchísimos años de mantener el diferendo presente y vigente; son todos los gobiernos, sin excepción, que han cumplido con la norma, que nuestras distintas Constituciones han mantenido e incluso desarrollado, además de los pronunciamientos de la misma Corte de Constitucionalidad, regulando esta materia y reiterando la obligatoriedad de buscar una solución a la disputa. Son gastos incalculables. Altísimos. Es verdad, en esto va el corazón y la historia de Guatemala y los costos no deberían e incluso no pueden y tampoco deberían limitar los esfuerzos por resolverla. Es más, el mandato constitucional es clarísimo, en el sentido que el Ejecutivo está obligado a buscar una solución.

Y así ha sido. En cuanto a un posible incumplimiento o violación de la norma respectiva al convocar la Consulta, el mismo texto advierte y regula que no hay otra forma más que esa y ese es el espíritu del Constituyente, estableciendo de esa manera que es al final es el pueblo de Guatemala y nunca una autoridad política, quien deberá decidir sobre la solución definitiva de la controversia, si el referéndum es ineludible. Y se está cumpliendo con ese espíritu y esa norma al convocarla. Y en cuanto a un eventual rechazo de la Corte, por supuestos errores en la construcción y arquitectura del Acuerdo Especial, baste decir y repetir que la Corte nunca ha rechazado un caso que haya sido sometido bajo Acuerdo Especial. Eso no ha pasado y ni el Estatuto, ni el Reglamento, contienen cláusula o norma alguna en este sentido. El sometimiento de una disputa bajo Acuerdo Especial es la expresión más alta de resolver una disputa y la expresión de la voluntad de dos Estados, por alcanzarla, de acuerdo a los principios del Derecho Internacional y de manera pacífica y civilizada. Esta es la conducta y el comportamiento de Estados que actúan de la forma más civilizada posible. Guatemala y Belice han dado muestras de ese comportamiento ante la comunidad internacional y el sistema de las naciones civilizadas del mundo. El ejercicio soberano del voto es la forma más precisa en que un pueblo y una nación son convocados, por sus autoridades, para emitir un pronunciamiento final y definitorio. La nación guatemalteca debe votar a favor de resolver definitivamente el Diferendo Histórico.

5
BELICE: LA CONSULTA

En una fecha aún no determinada, Guatemala efectuará la Consulta, que el mandato emanado de la norma constitucional, así lo prescribe. El artículo 19 transitorio, de nuestra Constitución, contiene y expresa sin equivocaciones lo procedente, en cuanto a la llamada solución definitiva o para usar el lenguaje constitucional, *acuerdo definitivo*, Título VIII, Disposiciones Transitorias y Finales, Capítulo Único. La norma referida ha sido objeto de una rigurosa hermenéutica y su subsecuente desarrollo, por parte de la Corte de Constitucionalidad, para lo que se puede consultar la Gazeta número 26 expedientes acumulados 290 y 291-91, página 9, sentencia 03-11-92.

El ejercicio hermenéutico practicado por la Corte se fundamenta en la acepción que los términos tienen y poseen, en el Diccionario de la Lengua Española, de la Real Academia Española de la Lengua. Claro está, en nuestras tradiciones jurídicas e históricas también, ya que se menciona y consideran las fórmulas que en las Constituciones anteriores, 1945, 1956, 1965 y 1985, tenía la norma y sus posteriores evoluciones, modificaciones, adecuaciones o cualquiera sea la conceptualización que aquí quiera emplearse, con lo que se puede inferir que la hermenéutica no es solamente formal, reducida a la acepción y uso de los términos, sino también tiene en cuenta la historicidad y evolución de la norma misma, al referirla y ubicarla en los anteriores textos constitucionales. Hay una hermenéutica no solamente semiológica, sino también deconstructivo-analítica. Las palabras o términos claves son pues, a saber, resolver, solución, realizar, gestionar y definitiva. Y así se ha actuado y actúa. El horizonte es y ha sido siempre, el constitucional, todo lo que se negoció y acordó lo fue, bajo el mandato constitucional, que como muy bien la Corte resalta en la citada referencia arriba mencionada: *el Ejecutivo está constitucionalmente facultado, para realizar las gestiones, que sean necesarias, para solucionar el diferendo con Belice.*

Así pues de manera general tenemos que resolver y solucionar, llevar adelante acciones que resuelvan de manera definitiva el Diferendo. Así como también condicionar la solución definitiva a la Consulta popular, regulada también en la Constitución misma (artículo 173). El Ejecutivo cumplió con esa obligación y agotó todos los procesos y mecanismos de solución pacífica de controversias, desde la negociación directa a las distinta alternativas y modalidades, reconocidas en el Derecho Internacional Público Latinoamericano, como en el Derecho Internacional General Consensuado. Esta es una de las grandes virtudes poco reconocidas de la diplomacia guatemalteca, la antigua y la actual: actuar siempre inspirados en los grandes principios del Derecho Internacional, y a lo largo de la historia del Diferendo se puede apreciar esta constante histórica. Una cuestión que es de enorme importancia es la forma cómo se llega a la decisión de asumir la negociación final, para construir un texto,que faculte a las partes, poder acceder a la jurisdicción de la Corte Internacional de Justicia.

Cuando la negociación marítima concluyó sin acuerdos, en la sede de la OEA, se habían agotado en su totalidad los medios de solución pacífica, las partes habían facultado al Secretario General de ese momento, José Miguel Inzulsa, para emitir una recomendación sobre cómo continuar el proceso y cuáles deberían ser los pasos subsiguientes ya agotadas todas las vías, incluida la negociación directa. En su momento hizo la recomendación de acudir a una "instancia jurisdiccional internacional", no se pronunció cuál debería de ser y como corresponde, quedaban las partes libres de tomar la decisión, y cuál sería la fórmula o mecanismo legal por invocar. El consenso era absoluto, se debería acudir a la jurisdicción de la Corte Internacional de Justicia y someterse a su jurisdicción, aceptando plenamente el fallo que emergiera del proceso y comprometiéndose a su plena ejecución. Dado que no se podían invocar los otros procedimientos, para someterse a la jurisdicción de la Corte, como lo regula el artículo 35 del Estatuto de la Corte, solamente puede accederse vía un Tratado Bilateral o Multilateral. Las partes siguen sin ser miembros del llamado Pacto de Bogotá, no existe un Tratado Bilateral en esta materia, no existe una Declaración actualizada de sometimiento a su jurisdicción y pues solo quedaba el camino del Special Agreement o Compromis y así se procedió.

El resultado es el Tratado —el Acuerdo Especial es un Tratado— conocido como Acuerdo Especial, en el que las partes someten su disputa a la jurisdicción de la Corte, en el lenguaje del Derecho Internacional se le *otorga competencia jurisdiccional a la Corte para resolver definitivamente la disputa sometida.* Se había así llegado al final de un muy largo y difícil camino. Sin embargo, faltaba para Guatemala —Belice no tiene esa obligación realmente— cumplir con la norma constitucional y consultar al pueblo de Guatemala cuál sería su decisión, único camino para alcanzar la *solución definitiva.* Eso es exactamente lo que se está haciendo al convocar a la Consulta. Es decisión exclusiva de los guatemaltecos y la deberán expresar a través de su participación y ulterior voto. No hay otro camino.

En el asunto de la decisión y negociación de someter el Diferendo ante el Pleno de la Corte Internacional de Justicia, creo que no hay realmente mucho que discutir. Sin embargo, hay unos cuantos temas que, dada su importancia, fueron abordados con muchísima seriedad. El llamado procedimiento ex aequo et bono, empleado en algunos procedimiento arbitrales y alguna vez considerado como la vía para someter el Diferendo ante la Corte (Aycinena Salazar y García Bauer), recogido en el artículo 38 de la Corte, demanda aceptación de ambas partes, para que la Corte pueda considerar resolver la disputa de esta forma, las llamadas Reglas de Arbitraje de UNCITRAL, y en su artículo 33 expresa una fórmula similar, aunque también la condiciona a la aceptación de las partes y va más allá al afirmar que si las leyes normativas del arbitraje lo permitieran, podría recurrirse a dicha alternativa. Belice enfáticamente se negó a aceptarlo y aunque fue objeto de consideraciones y análisis se descartó, por ambas partes. El artículo 26 del Estatuto identifica lo que se conoce como el *procedimiento mixto*, acudir ante una Cámara Especial de la Corte y someter la disputa, algunos países lo han hecho, notoriamente El Salvador y Honduras y la famosa disputa por el Golfo de Maine, entre Canadá y Estados Unidos fue sometida a Cámara Especial. Guatemala y Belice no podían someter el Diferendo a ninguna otra modalidad, que no fuera Cámara Plena, y un procedimiento en que cinco jueces y dos jueces ad hoc, decidieran sobre el Diferendo, era francamente inviable. Se descartó plenamente.

La Secretaría General de Naciones Unidas, la Corte Internacional de Justicia, bajo iniciativa de Países Bajos y Suiza, inició un procedimiento, el 24 de Septiembre del 2012, durante el 67 Período de Sesiones de la Asamblea General, que concluye el 24 de julio del 2014, en el que se elaboró y adoptó un manual, para reconocer la jurisdicción compulsoria de la Corte, con apoyo de la Oficina de Asuntos Legales, de la Secretaría General, el manual se completó. Los Estados Miembros que se sumaron a la redacción del Manual son, además de Suiza y Países Bajos, el Reino Unido de la Gran Bretaña e Irlanda del Norte, Lituania, Uruguay, Botswana y Japón. Dicho Manual es un documento público y se encuentra en el sitio de la Corte y de Naciones Unidas. No entiendo por qué causas Guatemala no participó en un asunto que tiene y reviste una enorme y trascendental importancia para el Diferendo.

Para concluir, una reflexión sobre dos elementos que han estado generando controversias entre los formadores de opinión, alrededor de dos asuntos, el primero, costos; el segundo, oportunidad. Personalmente estos temas coyunturales raras veces los abordo, sencillamente el argumento opuesto, expresado de la forma *somos un país muy pobre y tenemos necesidades vitales y apremiantes y no podemos o debemos distraer fondos, para efectuar una consulta no necesaria o urgente* y el otro *existen debilidades institucionales y el gobierno actual no está en condiciones de efectuar una consulta popular, que se puede convertir en un referéndum sobre sí mismo.* No es de restarles importancia. No se trata de devaluar su fuerza y capacidad argumentativa. El tema costo, que puede ser más valioso, que invertir en la historia misma de Guatemala. El Diferendo corta el corazón de Guatemala a lo largo de su historia y ha estado presente, ha ocupado una situación esencial en los actos y devenir del propio país. Esto es incuantificable, no hay forma de medir si es o no muy cara la consulta, se debe hacer y hay que adoptar la decisión del pueblo guatemalteco, que buscará así llevar a la máxima instancia jurídica del mundo, el Estatuto de la Corte fue aprobado inmediatamente después que la Carta de Naciones Unidas. Su condición extraordinaria la convierte en la única alternativa que tenemos para superar esta controversia. Guatemala tiene un caso muy sólido, no debemos discutir en público detalles de la manera y forma como se invocarán los principios del Derecho Internacional General Consensuado, que nos favorecerán, eso es estratégicamente una gran torpeza. Repito, tenemos un caso muy sólido y debemos luchar por los Derechos históricos de Guatemala. En lo atinente a la oportunidad. Debemos y tratemos de evitar politizar la Consulta, es un asunto de nación, la nación entera está involucrada, no es un juego de habilidades políticas o estrategias, de personas y partidos, se trata de Guatemala y de su porvenir.

6
THE SPECIAL AGREEMENT BETWEEN GUATEMALA AND BELIZE

Dados los acontecimientos recientes, tal vez por razones profundamente negativas, se han perdido once vidas y la última, un joven de catorce años, en la denominada Zona de Adyacencia. Una Comisión nombrada por el Secretario General de la OEA presentó un controversial informe, el cual ha sido sujeto de distintas interpretaciones. No extenderé opinión sobre el mismo acá, puesto que mi interés es distinto, y considero que hay varios aspectos, sobre el Acuerdo Especial, como se le denominó en español, haciendo un híbrido del francés compromis y del inglés, special agreement, la expresión francofonizada, Acuerdo compromisorio, no se llegó a adoptar y traducir directamente a la forma anglófona. Acuerdo Especial prevaleció al final. Recuerdo con mucha cercanía aún, todas las discusiones, internas y externas, durante ese complejo período, en el que me tocó ser el Jefe Negociador del Acuerdo, y siempre fui consciente de la complejidad que nos tocaba abordar y hasta ahora me he abstenido de escribir al respecto ya que son muchos amigos y algunos colegas, los que externan opinión continuamente, sobre este tan dramático asunto. El anecdotario y los detalles personales, lo guardo para mis Memorias, las cuales aún no he decidido si ameritan ser publicadas y mantengo en una constante elaboración. Por ello y otras razones, a continuación no daremos nombres. Reitero y enfatizo lo de dramático, porque lo es y lo ha sido. En el pasado he escrito, en informes confidenciales derivados de mis muchos años dedicado al tema, que el Diferendo Histórico —he preferido usar esta expresión constantemente— corta en dos la historia misma de Guatemala. Su historia y solución definitiva, pasan por la historicidad del ser guatemalteco y han definido, en más de un momento, su carácter y condición. Y no digamos de la Diplomacia guatemalteca y de sus mismos diplomáticos. Ha sido el eje y tema central de la misma. Los Cancilleres, en su inmensa mayoría —aunque han habido también viajeros que no han querido acercarse, incluso lo han escondido o postergado, estos son afortunadamente los menos, no se deja ignorar el Diferendo, emerge aunque se le intente sumergir, siempre vuelve a salir, al resurgir lo hace con una fuerza considerable— lo han abordado, han sido sus víctimas también, su elusividad contrasta con la demanda permanente, se rehúsa a ser olvidado y menos aún ignorado. Está allí, patente, presente, reclamando una atención incondicional, impostergable. Hay un drama latente que solo se resolverá al llevarlo a la Corte Internacional de Justicia, como se ha acordado.

El Acuerdo Especial es el resultado de un proceso. No nació de la nada. No es una ocurrencia de alguien o de un grupo de individuos. Fue el resultado de un camino largo y tortuoso, en el que se agotaron todos los medios de solución pacífica de controversias. Se recurrió a la negociación directa, a la Conciliación, a la mediación, son innumerables las reuniones que se sostuvieron, se abordaron todos los temas, bajo diversas estrategias y metodologías. Los esfuerzos no se abandonaron nunca. La OEA estuvo siempre en el centro de la controversia, se había facultado al Secretario General, para que al agotarse todas las formas y alternativas posibles y viables, hiciera una recomendación directa, como efectivamente lo hizo —era el Segundo Secretario General, que estaba directamente involucrado, ahora vamos ya por un tercero-: acudir a una instancia jurisdiccional internacional y someterlo a su jurisdicción, para alcanzar esa solución definitiva, en el lenguaje de nuestra Ley Suprema, en esta materia. Habían dos cosas plenamente claras, una lo era la jurisdicción internacional y la otra era la convocatoria a una consulta popular. Son las condiciones fundamentales para acceder a la Corte. Ni Belice ni Guatemala son Estados partes del Pacto de Bogotá; por ende, no existe la jurisdicción compulsoria para ninguno de los dos. El acceso a la Corte Internacional de Justicia requería de un proceso de negociación final, para crear un instrumento que permitiera someter la disputa a la jurisdicción de la misma, sin renunciar absolutamente a nada, llevando la disputa intacta y total ante el máximo tribunal internacional. La totalidad del Derecho Internacional Público Consensuado está implicado en el Diferendo, disputa territorial, delimitaciones de fronteras, los aspectos marítimos e insulares, la historia de los Tratados Anglo-Españoles, doctrinas y principios, Uti possidetis hasta el Principio de Integridad Territorial, la lista es larga y la Corte tendrá ante sí uno de sus casos más complejos y profundamente dramáticos.

Aunque a riesgo de incurrir en error, me atrevería a identificar tres grandes dudas que se repiten dentro de círculos de juristas, políticos, y la población en general, aunque en realidad es muy difícil aseverar cuál sería la posición del pueblo guatemalteco, si se sabe y reconoce la de ciertos grupos organizados o semi-organizados, otros menos, en el sentido del nacionalismo más fuerte y duro, en el que claramente se detecta un sentimiento adverso y afirmativo, de la posesión total de Belice, que es vista siendo parte integral de Guatemala. Cualquier disputa que tenga varios siglos de mantenerse, tiene una evolución en muchas direcciones, hasta el cinismo puro y pragmático, *nada podemos hacer contra el poder británico, esto ya se consumó,* y otras muestras más de resignación, ante una debilidad profunda e innegable y por otra parte, la demanda expresa de la recuperación y la lucha por los derechos guatemaltecos, usurpados y violados, por una potencia colonial, cuyo comportamiento histórico es más que conocido. Veamos pues, cuáles son esas grandes interrogantes. La primera se refiere a las razones por las que se aceptara acudir a los referendos en condiciones desiguales, o sea, el acto unilateral de Belice, al modificar durante las negociaciones su Acta de Referéndum. La segunda, es el costo y el momento oportuno para efectuar la consulta popular y por último, las ya más que evidentes dudas sobre el papel de la mediación de la OEA. Abordemos las preguntas por separado.

Tal vez aquí es necesario introducir una reflexión relevante. Aunque el mundo de la diplomacia internacional y las negociaciones opera con otras reglas y realidades, Guatemala saltó del silencio a las negociaciones públicas y abiertas. Hasta hoy, a pesar del tiempo transcurrido después de la firma de los Acuerdos de Paz, la cultura del silencio, la desconfianza; en esencia, el temor y el miedo, siguen dominando una transición incompleta y sumamente confusa. Las tendencias al autoritarismo no nos abandonan. La expresión desordenada, caótica y como avalancha incontrolada, que terminó con el gobierno del partido Patriota y del anterior Presidente, es la expresión más radical pensable de rebelión ante el silencio, sobre todo al impuesto, al obligado, al que se carga por instinto y protección. Es el silencio que emergía del temor y del miedo. Sin embargo, esta lucha contra las formas del silencio, que los guatemaltecos asumimos, en eso hay que ser abundantemente claros, las generaciones actuales confrontaron ese silencio y decidieron "hablar", gritar, enfrentar y decirlo, por todos los medios a su alcance, no cabe la menor vacilación, ante la realidad del rol de las redes sociales que fundamentalmente han terminado el monopolio de los dueños, de la palabra escrita.

La prensa escrita tradicional lideró, de alguna manera, esa rebelión ante el silencio; sin embargo, son las voces de todos los que decidieron hablar y no continuar y aún lo hacen, con el silencio ese vetusto, enraizado, en el horror de un pasado aún no resuelto.

Guatemala no ha podido reconciliarse. No ha podido hacer su paz real e interna. Los políticos no quieren enfrentar eso. A diferencia de la transición española, que al salir del autoritarismo, vivió lo que ellos llamaron, en su momento *el destape*, con excesos o sin ellos; sin embargo, nosotros no lo hemos podido hacer. Las razones para eso son distintas y no las vamos a abordar acá. Nos es imprescindible acotar este hecho esencial porque eventualmente los guatemaltecos tendrán que hablar, esa es la voz del referéndum o consulta popular —el "constituyente" previó esta cuestión, por eso nuestra Constitución "humanista" le impuso el límite al autoritarismo: esto no lo resolverá un poder electo y pasajero, lo va a hacer el pueblo mismo, una nueva virtud de nuestra Ley Suprema—, nos tendrán que decir, si vamos o no a resolver definitivamente el Diferendo Histórico y lo vamos a poder someter a la jurisdicción de la Corte. No hay otro camino de hacerlo, existen mecanismos no considerados, empero la Constitución es determinante y contundente en esta materia, sin consulta no hay solución definitiva.

Aquí la pregunta inicial es por qué se generaron condiciones desiguales, cómo sucedió eso si la intención era regirse por el principio de la igualdad procesal, no establecer ventajas procesales, para ninguna de las partes y acudir de mutuo acuerdo a un consenso cuidadoso y laboriosamente construido. Las negociaciones para construir el Acuerdo Especial se llevaron a cabo bajo una estricta y meticulosa mediación internacional. La OEA no solo fue la sede donde se efectuaron, sino que prestó y facilitó asesoría a las partes, designó un experto muy prestigioso y reconocido —quien lamentablemente falleciera hace algunos años—, para que apoyara, en todo momento, a las delegaciones, con el fin de trabajar la arquitectura del Acuerdo. En lo personal, enfrentamos una doble negociación, una interna y otra externa. Ambas de una enorme complejidad y dificultad. No era fácil alcanzar acuerdos, en ninguno de los dos niveles. Belice lo tenía relativamente más sencillo. Asumió la negociación con las mismas personas que lo han hecho y lo continúan haciendo. Construyeron acuerdos políticos internos, no del todo sólidos y definitivos, aunque aceptaron sumarse a la arquitectura del texto y a que se generara uno.

Nosotros debatimos hasta por los *"modelos"* del texto. Hubo incluso acusaciones e insinuaciones de varios tipos. El hecho es que la Corte ha recibido varios casos, bajo la fórmula del Acuerdo Especial, por cierto aquí es muy importante destacar que nunca ha rechazado ningún sometimiento o adjudicación de una disputa, presentada ante la misma, bajo un Acuerdo Especial. Léase bien, ninguna disputa ha sido rechazada por la Corte o calificado o negado el trámite, y menos en función del Presidente de la Corte, *decidir o calificar a priori*, sobre la disputa. En ese momento procesal, lo que ocurrirá es la notificación sin más, del sometimiento de la disputa, mediante el mecanismo construido, el Acuerdo Especial. El Reglamento de la Corte contempla la posibilidad que sea una de las partes la que notifique al Registrador de la misma el Acuerdo y una nota explicativa, en las que se relacionarían las razones y se expresarían también los consensos y acuerdos construidos para acudir ante la Corte. Esto es especulativo puesto que cuando llegue el momento deberán idealmente ponerse de acuerdo ambas partes y comparecer conjuntamente en el acto de sometimiento del Diferendo. La Corte lo recibirá y actuará de acuerdo a sus procedimientos reconocidos y ampliamente establecidos. Aquí es importante destacar un elemento muy sensible dentro de este camino. Guatemala ha evidenciado abundantemente, de manera congruente y sostenida, su vocación de solución del Diferendo, por los medios del Derecho Internacional Consensuado.

Lo ha hecho saber en todos los foros internacionales pertinentes, ante la Corte, ante los Jueces, algunos han terminado sus tiempos y otros aún continúan sirviendo en La Haya. En su momento nosotros llamábamos a este proceso Diplomacia Jurídica. Belice debe acompañar en todo momento este caminar. No hay otra opción, titubear o entorpecer, ese camino puede colocar al de este modo actuante, ante la duda de su verdadera intención y convicción de apego al Derecho Internacional General y a sus formas. No es nada aconsejable fomentar dudas. Por eso no comparto los titubeos de someter el Acuerdo a la consulta popular. Puede generar incertidumbres potenciales sobre los verdaderos propósitos, al actuar de manera dubitativa y secreta. La decisión es del pueblo y de nadie más. Sea la que fuere debe respetarse. Como también se debe actuar dentro del respeto total y pleno a la Constitución y lo que en esta materia norma. La solución definitiva será únicamente posible, mediante los referenda y las consultas.

En el delicado tema de la modificación de las condiciones existentes, en el lenguaje del Derecho de los Tratados, el Acuerdo Especial es un Tratado, esto hay que tenerlo siempre presente; pues bien, al radicalmente cambiar la legislación vigente, el Acta de Referéndum, sin informar a Guatemala o a la OEA, como también correspondía, Belice introduce elementos que pueden generar la nulidad de lo acordado y del Tratado Mismo —aunque hay que recordar que el mismo no está plenamente vigente, puesto que no se han efectuado las consultas y no se ha resuelto de forma afirmativa lo consultado—, eso se ha debatido, aunque se ha preferido reiterar y sostener la vigencia del Acuerdo. De manera expresa tanto Guatemala como Belice así lo han sostenido, de forma enfática, ante foros internacionales, al Secretario General mismo y ante sus poblaciones. Sin embargo, la duda prevalece. Se violó la pacta sunt servanda y se actuó de mala fe. De eso no cabe duda alguna. Causas más que contundentes, para invocar la nulidad del Acuerdo. Ahora bien, no tendría ningún sentido y no generaría ninguna ventaja a las partes disputantes, volver de nuevo al principio de la disputa e iniciar negociaciones totalmente nuevas, aunque hay quienes preferirían una acción de este tipo. No creo ni veo sino enormes desventajas y la consiguiente pérdida de credibilidad internacionales, para ambas partes. Belice debería dar una muestra de buena fe y compromiso, para someter la disputa ante la Corte, si unilateralmente regresara a las condiciones previas y ambas consultas se hicieran, sin las diferencias hoy existentes. Veo muy difícil que esto suceda y me genera serias dudas sobre las verdaderas intenciones al efectuar esas modificaciones. Claro, es un asunto interno y soberano; empero, sería un gesto expeditorio de una gran trascendencia. Guatemala debería responder aprobando el Protocolo que ambos firmaron y en el cual aceptarían las partes, efectuarían las consultas en fechas distintas. Nunca vi las ventajas especiales de esta modificación, cualquier elemento que requiera aprobación por parte del Congreso de la República corre graves riesgos, no solo de un eventual rechazo, sino de una politización, de una cuestión, que requiere tratamiento de asunto de Estado y no de coyuntura o de agenda partidaria.

Incluso ya ha pasado demasiado tiempo para su aprobación, evidentemente se buscan momentos de mayor oportunidad, los cuales hoy día son muy elusivos. Creo que Guatemala enviaría una señal muy poderosa a la Comunidad Internacional y los Amigos del Proceso, al aprobar el Protocolo, expeditando aún más el camino hacia las consultas. Dicho sea de paso, no hay que dejarse seducir o engañar por el argumento de costos exorbitantes de la Consulta, inabordables dadas las carencias y limitaciones financieras dominantes. La consulta debería efectuarse mediante una papeleta adicional, en el momento en que se sometieran a consulta las Reformas constitucionales proyectadas, nada más. Al romperse la simultaneidad, Guatemala debe asumir sus obligaciones adquiridas y cumplirlas, demostrando su total voluntad histórica y política, de resolver definitivamente el Diferendo, por los medios acordados. Debemos comparecer ante la Corte y someter la disputa a su jurisdicción, es la mejor herencia de nuestras generaciones, para el porvenir de Guatemala y las futuras generaciones. Esta y no otra debe ser la respuesta a la segunda pregunta, ante los eventuales colosales costos elevadísimos de semejante proceso. Mi criterio siempre ha sido que aquellos quienes señalaban esos colosales costos, empleaban ese argumento para demorar y posponer las consultas indefinidamente. Mantener el status quo no generará nunca certeza jurídica. Todo lo contrario, alimenta la inseguridad y limita enormemente, la normalización de unas relaciones que deben pasar a un nivel más estrecho y dejar atrás la desconfianza prevaleciente. Eso no es un asunto de costos. Está en juego la historia misma de Guatemala.

En cuanto a la última interrogante abierta, el rol de la OEA y sus Secretarios Generales, Testigos de Honor del proceso, por cierto, estamos ya ante un tercer Secretario General, que asume esa mediación y la organización ha continuado esa tarea de amigable componedora. Las condiciones actuales, bajo las que se opera no son del todo favorables para Guatemala, de eso no cabe la menor duda. Nunca antes hubo un Secretario General Adjunto, que hubiera sido actor relevante en las negociaciones, un diplomático beliceño, este hecho es real y trascendental. No puede ni debe soslayarse o disminuir su importancia. El Informe y el tratamiento en general al incidente en la Zona de Adyacencia, no ha contribuido sustancialmente a superar o despejar estas y otras dudas. No se trata de dudar de la honorabilidad de nadie y menos aun de su profesionalismo y de la eventual neutralidad

requerida y demandada, para un proceso de esta importancia.
Guatemala debe y está obligada a proteger sus intereses, de esto
no cabe la menor vacilación. Si se optara por otra alternativa a
la intermediación existente, habrá que contar con la anuencia
de Belice, muy poco probable que la aceptara; una eventual
mediación Papal/Vaticana, que rindió éxitos entre Chile y la
Argentina —no sé si podría darse, en este momento, personalmente
la veo como muy interesante, dado el altísimo nivel de la diplomacia vaticana, sino además y esto es muy importante, sus
contribuciones al Derecho Internacional son notables y plenamente reconocidas—. No creo, eso sí, que llevarlo a una mediación
de Naciones Unidas, pueda rendir frutos, mi visión es que esta
es una disputa más histórico-jurídica, que política —no afirmo
para nada que no haya elementos políticos en el Diferendo, claro
que los hay y los hubo—, pero Guatemala busca el reconocimiento
de sus derechos históricos y eso solamente será posible al reducir
al mínimo el rol político de las partes actuantes, las ocultas y
las que aún no emergen, lo cual harán, en el momento de la
adjudicación de la acción. Los países pequeños y con notorios
límites de influencia o peso internacional, debemos recurrir ante
todo al Derecho y a la presentación de nuestros argumentos,
eso sí, en los foros adecuados. Y la Corte Internacional de Justicia
es el más adecuado de todos los foros posibles. El artículo 41 del
Estatuto de la Corte la faculta, para emitir Medidas Cautelares.
Una vez iniciado el proceso, Guatemala debe inmediatamente
solicitarlas, con el expreso fin de salvaguardar la llamada Zona
de Adyacencia, las personas, sus vidas y sus bienes, así como
cualquier otra cuestión que lo requiera, protegiendo de esa manera
los intereses históricos de Guatemala y de su población.

CHAPTER V
IN MEMORIAM

1
IN MEMORIAM MARCELO DASCAL

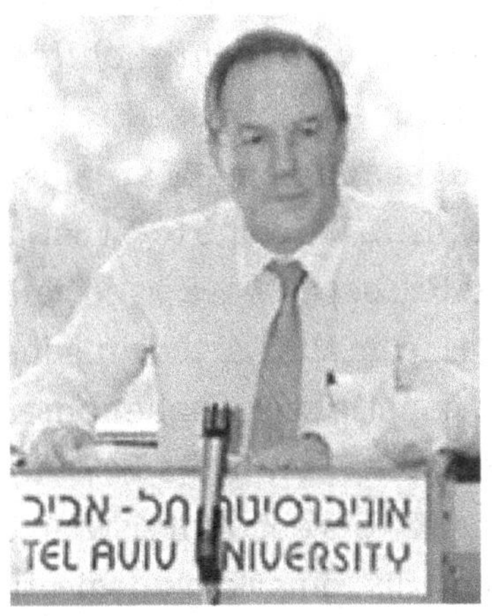

When the recent passing of Marcelo Dascal took place my memories gather around a simple thought: one of the most brilliant minds, not only in the Jewish world but everywhere, and Marcelo was known all over the world. Not only did he travel constantly, his work and lifelong dedication to Philosophy and more specifically, to the Theory of Controversies, Pragmatics, and the study of knowledge guided his entire work. The world at large will miss this extraordinary human personality. We all that have the privilege and honor of meeting and calling him a friend, will miss him dearly. We met in Israel while I was serving as the Ambassador of my country and immediately established a connection that lasted since. We were introduced by another extraordinary Israeli intellectual, Professor Nahum Megged, whose enormous body of work brought him closer to the Latin American world, where is admired and loved. This was the nineties and Israel was involved in the now almost forgotten *"peace process"*

hope bloomed from every corner, peace was a possibility and Yitzhak Rabin was the Prime Minister, then tragedy stroke, and dreams were shattered and broken.

Our friendship remained close throughout the years. Although we came from different philosophical traditions, mine is what is described by the term *continental philosophy* —I dislike its usage and connotations— as opposed to *analytical thinking*, also an unfortunate terminology. Marcelo's thinking went far beyond logical positivism. We came together through our mutual interest in Edmund Husserl's work especially the late Husserl, the one that emerges from the Cartesianische Meditationes und Pariser Vortraege, constitutional phenomenology and methodological Intersubjectivity, presents Leibniz idea of the Monad and Monadology meant his encounter with the Leibniz work. I had a strong glimpse at his remarkable dedication to the publishing of the Leibniz Complete Works and we had frequent contacts while in Berlin, Marcelo introduced me to the group working on the edition and publication of the Leibniz immense body of work. Controversies were of course, at the center of the process, Leibniz no stranger himself to the matter. An array of books, essays, symposia, and articles bloomed around the endeavor. I was fortunate enough to begin to move slightly from my Heideggerian roots, deeply embedded in my thinking. So then, Pragmatics but not as a linguistic phenomenon exclusively, not to forget that analytical philosophy deals also, with "ordinary language" to use Austin's concept, Marcelo pragmatics was not supposed to substitute semantics, it is grounded not on algorithmic rules but on heuristic ones. The question of the language uses. A long tradition stands in the framework and Marcelo devoted his life and work to these complex ideas and developed his now well-known Theory of Controversies. Much has been studied and written on this challenging subject and much more to come.

What we are lacking at the time is a precise and organized edition of his complete work so the reflection and analysis are maintained and strengthened.

The frequent meetings change to a new venue. I was posted as Ambassador to The Kingdom of the Netherlands, and Marcelo came frequently so we enjoyed frequent meetings. His publications with the prestigious *John Benjamins Publishing Company*, based in Amsterdam developed into a series of very important contributions, both as author and editor. The number of outstanding and leading scholars whose articles and essays can be found in all the books of this remarkable series is highly impressive. The Theory of Controversies became an essential school of thought. Since my attachment to International General Consensual Law intensify and gained in-depth, not exclusively as my diplomatic postings demanded, but also my involvement with "conflict resolution and negotiations", required the development of skills and certain tools, Marcelo's thinking and work became a part of my insights and conceptions as well as my heuristical methods. The analysis of language is fundamental to understanding and

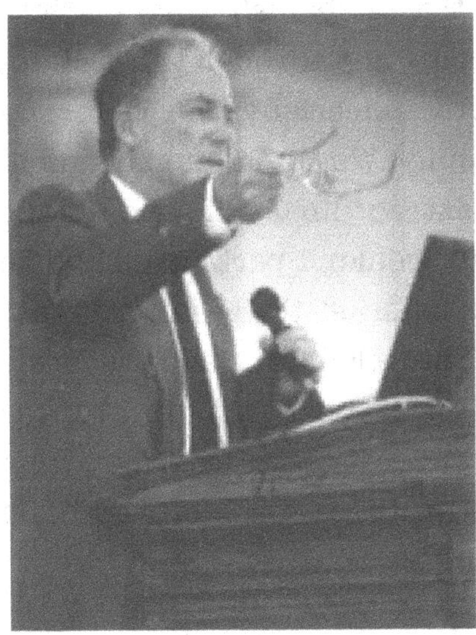

solving disputes which to me became controversies —the current concept goes beyond the usage within the realm of International Law as traditionally employed— and was able to build a crucial innovative approach.

One extremely important point is that the movement around Marcelo's work and life has produced a long list of contributions by many leading Philosophers, Linguists, and Philologists all over Europe, Latin America, and beyond. The Theory of Controversies has found fruitful grounds in other disciplines and to some extent, the spirit of the mathesis Universalis as envisioned by Leibniz is present at the core of the research and thinking. Leading, scientists, academics, scholars, and intellectuals amongst many more, Sir Geoffrey Lloyd, Professor Rodica Amel, Professor Fernando Gil, Professor Eduardo Rabossi, and especially Professor Giovanni Scarafile, Vicepresident of the IASC, should foster and maintain the spirit and legacy that Marcelo created throughout his remarkable life and work. We all know that Varda, Marcelo's beloved wife and now his widow, permanent support and source of inspiration during his entire life, is suffering immensely as well as his children, to use a very special german word, that stems from Max Scheler's axiology and was later employed and referred to by some other great philosophers, in the Spanish world, Ortega y Gasset comes to mind instantly, attempted to render a translation for the word —Einfühlung— as *empathy*, empatía in Spanish, meaning *feeling-with-the-other*, padecer con el otro, in Spanish, what matters here is that we all feel the suffering and through this *feeling-with-the-other* we might understand briefly, her pain and suffering as well as the entire family. We stand humbly and in admiration to honor Marcelo's extraordinary life and unique work. Probably for most of us who couldn't participate and be present at the mourning process in Israel, the best words that can be uttered, come from the Hebrew language and the forms of mourning amongst Jews, which is no other than to remember the suffering ones and us all that comfort comes from mourning "with all of Zion and Jerusalem" as is said in Hebrew: המקום מילשוריו ויצ ילבא ראש דותב מכתא מחני.

CHAPTER VI
ADDENDA

1
LOS LIBROS DE ALFONSO PORTILLO

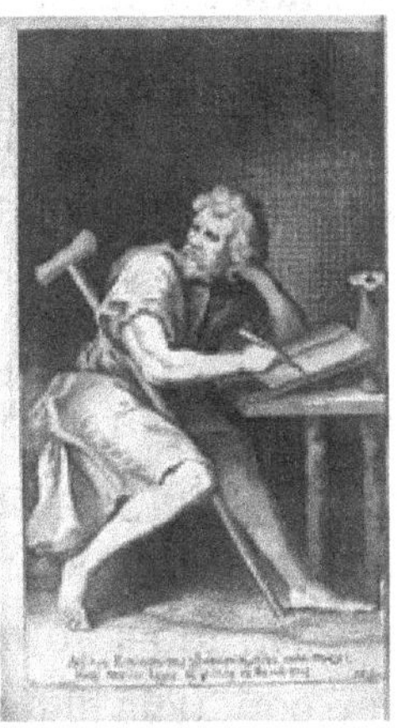

Epictetus con su bastón

Hace unos años se hizo pública una lista de lecturas que Alfonso Portillo recomienda a los políticos guatemaltecos y en general, a todo aquel en busca de alcanzar una mayor instrucción o desarrollar mayores conocimientos en el Arte del Gobierno y manejo de la Cosa Pública —uso deliberadamente un lenguaje que no sea común al de los analistas políticos contemporáneos—. Y es que la lista de referencia es sumamente interesante y aunque incluye algunos títulos de lectura observada y practicada por estudiantes de muchas disciplinas afines, tiene una característica muy especial: hay un gran peso en autores clásicos; son, sin lugar a equivocarnos, no todos por supuesto, pero sí importantísimos textos de la gran tradición humanística; forman parte fundamental de aquellos que recibieron o fueron parte de una formación casi totalmente olvidada, por siglos y generaciones. Muchísimos fueron aquellos educados bajo la guía y el espíritu del mundo clásico. Llama aún más la atención, y cito los autores latinos en este momento, Séneca, Plutarco, Aulo Gelio, Cicerón, Suetonio y Marco Aurelio, el emperador romano autor de los Soliloquios y quien fuera el penúltimo emperador de los Antoninos. Boecio forma parte de la tradición latina también. En el siglo VI compuso De Consolatio, en la cárcel de Pavía y posteriormente fue ejecutado por órdenes de Teodorico. El debate sobre el humanismo y la religión, quedó abierto a partir de aquel trágico momento y se repetiría a lo largo de los siglos, en muchas ocasiones y bajo diferentes circunstancias.

En los textos clásicos, una de las condiciones fundamentales para el hombre de poder, el emperador o el rey, es la presencia de un formador, a saber, Aristóteles y Alejandro; Seneca, el maestro y educador de Nerón, una paradoja autentica, dada la manera irracional en la que Nerón conducía el Imperio y más. La forma como su vida termina, se suicida ante la terrible realidad que le toca observar. Otro caso extraordinariamente notable, es la conflictiva relación entre Cicerón y Julio César, el Senador y gran retórico, orador de oradores, quien conspira contra Julio César y es parte central del grupo de amigos e incluso familiares de Julio César, que lo asesinan miserablemente en la sede misma del Senado romano. Epictetus, a quien el Presidente Portillo cita, en su lista, en el parágrafo XLIII, del Enchiridion, sostiene que, *Todo tiene dos asas, una por la que puede ser llevado y otra por la que no...*, más aun, en el famoso Prefacio, I, *Hay ciertas cosas que dependen de nosotros y otras que no....* Sin intentar agotar el tema, imposible para los modestos limites de este comentario, lo que se nos hace evidente al leer estos textos, es que en la tradición humanista existía una relación ontológica irrompible entre ética y moral, con el uso del poder, el emperador y el rey, que debían actuar de acuerdo a un conjunto de principios, los cuales los obligaban, los mantenían ligados a un cierto comportamiento que debían seguir y respetar.

Los fracasos son más que evidentes y la historia está llena de ellos, aún en el mundo de las religiones. Su administración de la mundanidad o de los asuntos terrestres, históricamente es una autentica catástrofe. Hay demasiados ejemplos en este sentido, pensemos solamente en el Infierno de Dante y la galería de los habitantes de los círculos infernales. Sin embargo, el recurso a los textos clásicos tiene un poderoso efecto formativo, hay un elemento esencial en la lectura y formación clásica, al conocer la historia podemos aprender de ella. Y esto de hecho ha pasado. No todos los hombres de poder han sido esencialmente malos o totalmente amorales; incluso en el mundo clásico hay algunos ejemplos extraordinarios. Y creo que por eso es la referencia a Marcus Aurelius, que hace el Presidente Portillo. Y viene a cuenta, al inicio de los Soliloquios, Marco Aurelio nos dice, en el III, que aprendió de su madre *...la generosidad y la abstención no sólo de obrar mal, sino de incurrir en semejante pensamiento....* Sabemos del respeto y profundo afecto que tiene a su señora madre, de esto no cabe duda ninguna. Podríamos así seguir extendiéndonos más. La vida política del Presidente Portillo no ha terminado y para nada se ha agotado, está entrando en una nueva etapa, creemos que se ha estado preparando, con serenidad y meditación, desde la adversidad. Lo cual no es extraño para los políticos realmente importantes, los que no se desvanecen en el olvido o en el anonimato aquel, producto del rechazo total y absoluto, que resulta de una gestión dudosa o carente de responsabilidad pública. Lamentablemente es la inmensa mayoría. La política ha dejado de ser un arte, para convertirse en una oportunidad. Concepto este extraño al mundo clásico.

Unas palabras finales sobre el resto de la lista, que solamente se refiere a tres grandes autores latinoamericanos, Jorge Luis

Borges, Carlos Fuentes y Octavio Paz. Suficiente o no es otro asunto; tanto Fuentes como Paz son grandes ensayistas, reflexionan alrededor de una realidad inmediata y muy cercana a todos nosotros. Estamos ya muy lejos del mundo clásico, este es el tema de la realidad del poder en la región y en nuestros países, ligadas a otros paradigmas. Borges es universal. Se refiere a lo más profundo de la naturaleza humana. A fin de cuentas es el hombre *la medida de todas las cosas*, el metron, μέτρον al que Protágoras se refiere es el estin ἔστιν, griego, o sea el ser lo que es, según la antigua experiencia de la lengua griega; por ello, en realidad el texto griego o la sentencia original debe leerse como *el hombre es la medida (metron) de todo lo que es*. Homo omniunrerum mensura est, según Diógenes. Y la formación y educación del hombre es pues la tarea mas importante a la cual se puede dedicar el ser humano; de eso dependerá esencialmente la condición de los hombres que nos dirijan o gobiernen, y, es a esto, fundamentalmente, a lo que la lista del Presidente Portillo se refiere.

2
CORRUPTIO OPTIMI PESSIMA

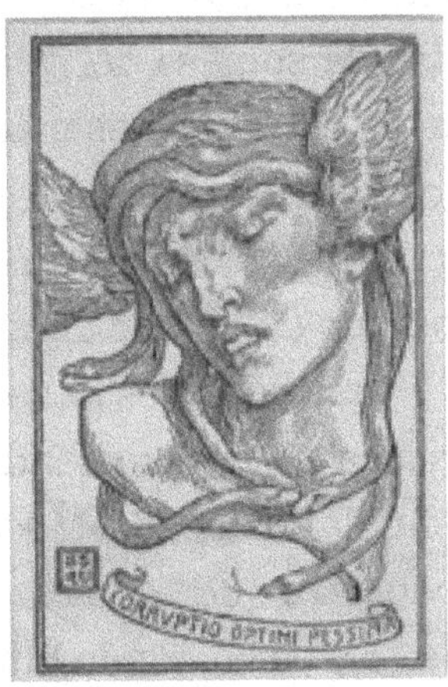

Simeon Solomon, print 1893, The British Museum

Un sistema roto. Reformas imposibles de llevar adelante. Cuando la administración de justicia se ve amenazada o limitada por fuerzas ocultas o poderes, que desde la oscuridad maniobran, para protegerse y mantenerse al margen, de la responsabilidad ante la ley, el país sucumbe ante la más terrible de las amenazas: la imposibilidad de la justicia. Lentamente la erosión se come las esperanzas de las personas, una sociedad profundamente enferma, con patologías diagnosticadas y cuyas posibilidades de sobrevivir, se están volviendo escasas, muy escasas. Divisiones y confrontaciones, que no se han cerrado. Odios abiertos o disimulados. Mundos paralelos que coexisten sin intentar tocarse, la reiteración y repetición de lo mismo. Atrincheramientos, posiciones irreconciliables, renuncia fáctica a la posibilidad de construir consensos. Acuerdos parciales tal vez si alguien o algunos se benefician. La muerte camina, entre nosotros, diariamente y sin ninguna preocupación, a eso lo llaman algunos impunidad, para otros es el regreso a la barbarie. A las formas más primitivas de la naturaleza humana, retroceso al abismo del horror. La noche oscura. El cinismo se ha convertido en la mejor forma de sonrisa, la sonrisa del que se burla de todos y de todo. No hay quien imponga limites más.

Los pensadores o filósofos creen que el arte de construir preguntas es más importante, que más que la capacidad misma de responderlas, debemos aprender de nuevo a formular las preguntas correctas, y pareciéramos haber perdido esa virtud. El horror cotidiano por la monstruosidad nos impide ver con los ojos de la razón. Refundar el Estado. Modificar la Constitución Política. Cambiarlo todo para que nada cambie. Ante la enorme Galería de Cínicos, que nos mira con la burla de la sonrisa, del que desprecia todo lo que no sea el mismo y sus beneficios. ¿Cómo podemos enfrentarlos, si nos han quitado las armas, con las que se puede enfrentar al demonio de la corrupción y del cinismo? Algunos valientes aún denuncian, escriben en los medios, que mantienen independencia y credibilidad. Son más de los que podemos creer. Rebelarnos, sí, pero de qué manera, la época de las revoluciones violentas ya terminó, busquemos a todos aquellos, que en silencio, saben que debemos derribar la Galería de Cínicos. Y hay más de lo que imaginamos, no se han rendido todos. Aquellos se opondrán a que los mismos u otros, iguales, dueños de sonrisas burlonas y ambiciones personales, continúen burlándose de nosotros. Debemos terminar con la pseudo cultura, de malgastar lo poco que hay y queda, bajo el cinismo y el nombre de la explotación y el abuso de una autoridad que se cree ilimitada, eterna y perpetua. Aquí es donde el pensador debe levantar esa pregunta: ¿dónde están aquellos, que escaparon al cinismo y al abuso?

Ese es pues el sentido de la terrible frase, *corruptio optimi pessima*, los que verdaderamente están afuera del cinismo y del abuso, son los que no han hablado tal vez, deben salir de su silencio, para salvar lo que aún queda del Estado guatemalteco, para evitar su caída total y salvar del precipicio al que la están lanzando. La corrupción de los mejores es la peor forma de corrupción, nos quita la esperanza y nos deja a la merced de la Galería de los Cínicos.

3
LA NUEVA GUATEMALA, LA QUE LOS POLÍTICOS NO PUDIERON VER

Desde lejos y tal vez con más distancia, he seguido con una enorme minucia y atención los acontecimientos que han estado sacudiendo a mi país, repito: sacudir; no es para menos, hay un despertar de un largo letargo o tal vez más bien, ha llegado el momento,que las cosas cambiaron, se decidieron a romper un viejo silencio, un silencio múltiple, complejo, a veces prudente y a veces sencillamente cobarde y cómplice, dirían algunos de los que se han alzado con la voz. No pasó ni hoy ni ayer, se vino gestando precisamente dentro de ese mismo silencio. No pasó de pronto ni de improviso. Llegó como las lluvias, con la contundencia y la fuerza de los ciclos eternos, circulares, que se repiten constantemente en nuestro país. Siempre me asombró ese silencio, no es que no pudiéramos hablar, habíamos elegido no hacerlo, porque nos habían obligado a callar; sin embargo, el silencio es una elección, es una decisión. En nuestro caso fue siempre la respuesta del miedo, del temor. En nuestras generaciones hemos sufrido demasiadas muertes y hemos visto demasiado dolor y sufrimiento. Ya no era posible seguir callando. Estaban destruyendo Guatemala y no se les podía permitir que lo siguieran haciendo. Ese silencio era un reclamo. Siempre estuvo allí, presente, inmutable, tenía la mirada de la incredulidad y la serenidad de la espera.

Hoy todo ha cambiado. El antiguo silencio ha dado espacio y tiempo a la voz, es una voz múltiple, aunque claramente audible empieza lentamente a constituirse. Se articula a través de la protesta, tiene el encanto de lo sagrado, de lo que no apela ni a la fuerza o a la violencia, o a los demonios feroces, que han asolado sin misericordia a Guatemala. Es más bien diversa, plagada de formas nuevas, de lenguajes renovadores, habla de una nueva realidad, que está por venir y que se desea construir. No se trata de cambiar el viejo orden por uno nuevo, más bien aquí se está hablando, del establecimiento de un mundo nuevo, más justo y más humano, donde los monstruos atávicos del pasado sean expulsados definitivamente. Y la voz se convirtió en grito...

No me interesa reconstruir y nombrar a aquellos que han convertido esta voz múltiple en una realidad total. Eso escapa a mis deseos e intenciones de singularizar y destacar personas o grupos; lo fascinante es su condición colectiva, general, profundamente amplia, al principio casi anónima, en un sentido diferente al de meramente no tener nombres, lo ha ido gestando después, hoy empezamos a reconocerlos, emergen desde el movimiento mismo, que han generado al tomar voz. Convocan y acuden, casi llevados por una espontaneidad natural, no siguen consignas, o son el fruto de una estrategia política o de alguna organización semioculta, su no pertenencia y adhesión es una de sus mayores virtudes. Solo así se puede invocar una honestidad y dignidad, que el mundo de la política guatemalteca no podría jamás reivindicar. Mas bien, esta rebelión con voces diversas ve a esas figuras políticas como uno de los objetos de su rebelión. De allí que es muy claro ese divorci, entre viejas dirigencias, políticos profesionales y más o menos dedicados a la misma, como negocio e inversión. Desnuda los errores y limitaciones de un sistema, no solamente cuestionado, sino canibalizado a sí mismo. Y allí yace la extraña incapacidad de escuchar esa voz, no digamos sus múltiples tonalidades.

Los más recientes datos ofrecidos por el Tribunal Supremo electoral hablan de una demografía, la respuesta está en su composición y la absurda incapacidad de tomarla en cuenta. En los rangos de edad, establecidos en la metodología, de tabulación de las cifras, se establecen intervalos por edades, 18-25, 26-30, 30-35, 41-45, 46-50, 51-55 y sigue. Se reconocen unos 8 millones de guatemaltecos aptos para ejercer el voto. Lo fascinante son los porcentajes, en los intervalos de 46 en adelante, apenas se recogen cifras de un dígito, entre 18 a 45 todas son de dobles dígitos, y los más altos se concentran entre los 18 a 35 años de edad. Y se encuentra el olvido. La mayor parte de los políticos nuestros, exceptuando una minoría muy notoria, así como probablemente los más relevantes candidatos a la presidencia, han sido incapaces de articular un mensaje orientado a entrar en un dialogo, con todas estas voces —estoy convencido que nadie está en este momento en condiciones de predecir quién la ganara, por estas razones-; se reconoce un grupo de candidatos cuyas edades están en los límites donde se encuentra la mayoría de la población votante; otros están muy por encima, lejos de estos niveles. Sirva esto para decir que el lenguaje de la política guatemalteca ha ignorado esta realidad. Si entre esos rangos se concentra un sesenta por ciento de los votantes, aproximadamente, y si agregáramos el 8% de los que están, entre los 46 a 50 años de edad, tendremos que se trata de una mayoría abrumadora, enorme y no más silente. El germen del cambio ha florecido y no está dispuesto a ser ignorado.

La vieja costumbre de adoptar el lenguaje jurídico como el único lenguaje político se ve aquí plenamente superada. Es un error intentar identificar estas voces con estructuras jurídicas o visiones particulares y muy individuales, de ejercer hermenéuticas constitucionales. El derecho tiene un limite, es su misma naturaleza, en nuestro caso esta ante sus limites. Las voces múltiples hablan un lenguaje no audible, para los que exclusivamente ven y hablan desde la juricidad. Un país, una cultura, una sociedad, son mucho más que sus leyes; mas bien aquí están en duda esas mismas leyes, unos marcos jurídicos, que conceptuales y abstractos, están exquisitamente formulados, aunque no siempre, en la mayoría de los casos. Este no es un problema de leyes o de nuevas y mejores leyes. La crisis de la administración de justicia guatemalteca no se engendra en la falta de las mismas, sino en su constante incumplimiento y violación. De esto no cabe duda. Necesitamos reformas constitucionales, mas no así una nueva Constitución. Ese camino es una trampa. Destruir es muy fácil. Conservar y cambiar es muchísimo mas difícil. Esta enorme crisis es de personas, de instituciones corrompidas por personas, no hay que equivocarse en esto. Por eso y para cerrar estas reflexiones, quiero referirme al tema de los lenguajes y las voces.

Las generaciones mayoritarias de guatemaltecos hablan un lenguaje, el cual es incomprensible, inaudible, para la mayoría de los políticos; por eso esta rebelión o revolución, de redes virtuales o sociales, del mundo digital y de la ultra velocidad, de su articulación y concreción, los ha tomado no preparados. No han sabido responder. Los símbolos son tan distintos, que no existe posibilidad alguna de acercamiento. Horizontes irremediablemente distanciados. Sistemas de valores antagónicos, en conflicto. Visiones del mundo tan radicalmente distintas, que hace imposible se puedan reconocer. Las respuestas no vienen de interminables discusiones, sobre artículos constitucionales o de cualquier otra ley ordinaria, sino de escuchar lo que piden y buscan. Los pontífices de la juridicidad seguirán insistiendo en todo lo que no se puede hacer y es violatorio, cumplen su sagrada misión sacerdotal de la defensa de un orden, del cual han perdido su sentido de finitud y límite. Si el mensaje que se envía a esos jóvenes no es otra cosa más que todo lo que no se puede hacer, que deben entender bien esto, serían excluidos, porque no hablan o poseen ese lenguaje; la imposibilidad del diálogo o de la mera y elemental comunicación queda cerrada totalmente. Conceptos como honra-

dez, dignidad, respeto, desbordan las definiciones contenidas
en códigos o leyes, tienen un origen en algo más profundo y eso
es a lo que se está apelando. Se buscan hombres nuevos y que
hablen otro lenguaje, uno que responda a esas voces múltiples
y diversas. Y lo mismo es válido para el lenguaje de la economía,
aunque este no ha penetrado tanto como en otros países, donde
la existencia de un verdadero estado de derecho, no hace necesario debatirlo y si más bien, se debate sobre los modelos económicos
con más amplitud. El lenguaje de la economía ha llegado tangen-
cialmente a los discursos políticos. Hablar de empleo, mercado,
competitividad, inversión, crecimiento económico y desarrollo,
ha quedado semi suspendido ante la avalancha de la juridicidad
del discurso político. Sin embargo, ambos carecen de lo mismo,
no responden a las voces, no invocan y menos aún, convocan, a
una reunión, a ese gran encuentro y ese gran diálogo, que desde
la calle se los está pidiendo una voz, que se ha convertido en
grito.

4
LA SILLA DEL QUETZAL
Y LA CERCANÍA DEL ÁGUILA

Cuando Carlos Fuentes pensaba en *La Silla del Águila*, reflexionaba sobre el misterio del poder. "Se dejó retratar en el dinero", nos recuerda Fuentes, tal vez el escritor latinoamericano que más mereció ese elusivo Nobel, que a algunos les llegara por razones muy complejas y largas de discutir aquí. Los presidentes mexicanos se sientan en la Silla del Águila, los nuestros, vecinos esencialmente unidos a México, de una manera indisoluble y de un entramado metafísico, mas que meramente dinerario, casi podemos hablar de una historia compartida; decía pues, los presidentes guatemaltecos se sientan en la Silla del Quetzal. El Quetzal es un tipo distinto de ave, me cuesta llamarlo animal, el corrido mexicano se refiere al Águila *como siendo animal, que se retrató en el dinero*. El Quetzal también se retrata en el dinero; es más, la divisa guatemalteca lleva ese nombre. Lleva ese color, el verde del Quetzal. Sin embargo, son totalmente distintos.

El Quetzal es elegancia pura, casi etérea, semi invisible, hay que buscarlo, fundamentalmente se le avista, en ocasiones se deja ver. Es pura sutileza. No es un depredador, observa y reposa en su más profunda intimidad. La majestuosidad y poder del Águila es mas que evidente, su mera presencia la instala en la tierra sin dejar dudas y, sobre todo, guarda las alturas. Vigila. El Quetzal observa. Mantiene una vinculación ontológica con los habitantes de sus dominios, su secreto le recuerda a estos, nosotros, que se nos ha permitido vivir y habitar aquí, solamente siempre y cuando, se respeten las reglas que él nos ha revelado, desde su sabiduría silenciosa. No todos los que se han sentado en la Silla del Quetzal han sabido escuchar esa sabiduría y menos aun, la han podido siquiera entender. El Quetzal ha decidido volver a hablarnos. Nos recuerda cuál es y debe ser la forma de respetar esas viejas reglas, no escritas aunque tantas veces traicionadas.

Neruda nos hablaba de *unas tierras de bosques, sin números, donde bajaba el viento*, es donde habita El Quetzal. La niebla y la transparencia, la luz y la claridad, la sabiduría antigua y milenaria, que se encontró con otra, también milenaria, iniciando un diálogo aún no completado, tantas veces interrumpido. La serenidad es una de las condiciones para vivir con esas reglas, hoy más que nunca la necesitamos, hemos podido hablarnos y decirnos muchas cosas, sin que la violencia, ese atávico demonio, que camina libremente, por nuestras tierras, empañe este extraordinario y muy poco común ejercicio de sabiduría. Tradicionalmente no nos hablamos, no nos decimos las cosas, tenemos temor y nos cuidamos más de la cuenta, nos obligaron a callarnos. Por eso no todos saben hablar o quieren aprender a hacerlo. Hoy día el vuelo del Quetzal está llenándonos de inspiración, queremos decirles a los que han sido los compañeros de la oscuridad, del demonio de la violencia, que ya no queremos mas engaños y mentiras. Que es el momento de abandonar *los negocios*, por el bien común, por la justicia, por salir de esa miseria a las que nos han querido condenar, sin ninguna justificación. Es fundamental volver la mirada hacia el otro, a aquel que no tiene nada, que se le ha negado todo, no se puede seguir robando y saqueando todo lo que es nuestro, con el sencillo propósito del más cruel de los egoísmos y el más monstruoso de los vicios, esa avaricia interminable de un grupo de personas que han desnaturalizado la más digna de las actividades humanas, el servicio.

La política siempre ha caminado con el hombre. Lo seguirá haciendo. No hay duda alguna. Pero el poder, en su misterio, es a pesar de todo, una herramienta, algunos la saben usar, para construir belleza y justicia, con un poco de verdad; otros, sencillamente, la usan para destruir y castigar, llenos de intenciones torcidas y poco claras, con ese narcisismo patológico de muchos enamorados de sus propias mentiras. La Silla del Quetzal no es para narcisistas, es para los llenos de la generosidad y la sabiduría, impregnada de la condición esencial, que le impone el Quetzal a aquel que aspira a sentarse en ella, y que sepa cómo respetarla, defenderla y, sobre todo, recibir con una enorme modestia, el privilegio de haber sido invitado a sentarse en ella. Nadie es dueño de la Silla del Quetzal. Será siempre alguien escogido, para temporalmente ocuparla, a quien se le permitirá, por un tiempo, llenarse de esa dignidad. Esa es la primera regla que El Quetzal le impuso a los invitados a la Silla. Temporalidad y servicio. Altruismo y honestidad.

Para terminar, los guardianes de la Silla no son los que creen serlo. Somos todos los habitantes de esta tierra de sol y de montañas, desde sus costas hasta sus bosques, desde sus arideces a sus exuberancias. Y en cualquier momento pueden pedirle la Silla especialmente a los que no la han sabido respetar y la han ultrajado, olvidándose que la Silla es de todos y no de algunos pocos. Es un privilegio extraordinario haber sido invitado a sentarse en ella. Y los dueños de la misma le están recordando estas viejas reglas, a todos los que desean sentarse en ella; mientras El Quetzal desde arriba observa vigilante, que se respete esa antiquísima sabiduría no escrita y que define la condición misma de los pobladores de este extraordinario mundo de sol y de montañas, que llamamos Guatemala.

CHAPTER VII
FROM THE ORIGINS OR THE ETERNAL RETURN OF THE SAME

1
THE SAN FRANCISCO GIANTS

It was the year 1962, and the New York Yankees were playing the Giants in the World Series. A young boy growing up in Guatemala was being introduced by his father to the World Series, he was a Yankee fan the boy hardly understood baseball but was curious enough to pursue his father's path, funnily in the opposite direction. There was this magical centerfielder by the name of Willie Mays, he could do it all: hit for power, run, playing probably the best defense ever witnessed and he ended his career in NY with the Mets, the same city where it started before the Giants moved to the City by the Bay. Mays is one of the most revered baseball players for many generations and amongst Giants fans, he is simply the greatest player ever to play the game. The Yankees won that series despite Willie McCovey's shot catching Bobby Richardson's glove. The boy became a lifelong Giant fan and has fowled his beloved time through many joys and sad moments. The boy isn't any more a boy his life has taken him to many places but the Giants remained always his team and escape from the sadness and despair, the irrationality and cruelness he has faced throughout his life. Eugen Fink called "game" an oasis of happiness in many ways it's been that and in many ways a fantastic learning process.

The boy while growing up in a non-English speaking country, was surrounded by English books which eagerly devoured but his passion for the Giants took him to the daily following of the Season and of course the Giants games, two sources were at his disposal, one the American Club in the city, just a block away from his only men school, they had a library and the New York

Times carried the box scores of all the games and the boy for years, went through those magical squares that carry the line-ups and how each player performed. He knew all the players' names and their daily performances throughout the season. The other source was the radio. The Arms Forces and Television Services broadcasted live some of the games and a few times a month, there was the Giants who were regularly competing for the title. This became a habit. After the radio, came the television, sports channels, the direct broadcasting of every game, and now the Apps, the At-Bat, but the radio remained loyal the boy still listens many times to the live broadcast of the Giants games where names such as Jon Miller, Mike Krukow, Duane Kipper and others bring the magic of the Giants games, the boy now enjoys very much when Jon Miller calls a home run with his familiar Spanish expression, ticked with the heavy American accent, "adios pelota". Brings back memories of something called "La cabalgata deportiva Gillette", which broadcasted in Spanish the World Series and the annual All-stars Game under Buck Canel and other memorable Spanish legends.

The Giants have won their third World Series in the last five years. They also lost some other memorable ones where a terrible earthquake stroke San Francisco during the World Series and the Giants lost or in baseball language were swept by the Oakland A's four cero. Painful but tragic at the same time. Lives were lost and huge damage caused to this beautiful and incredible city showed once again that life is above the game and the oasis has its limits. The second time Bobby Bonds was a leading part of this team, lost to the Angels —notably again to another Californian team— in game five where the great Dusty Baker proved that sometimes the wrong decision will hunt some managers for life. While watching in my home in Virginia, late at night, when Bruce Bochy brought Madison Bumgarner in relief of Jeremy Affeldt couldn't avoid the thought, will Bochy be haunted by another wrong decision, he was not. He made the right call. Even to my disbelief having MadBum pitched the ninth inning without Casilla and Romo warming up in the bullpen and after looking eyes-wide shut Gregor Blanco and Juan Peres desperately chased a ball that was eluding them and playing with them, fortunately for the Giants Peres has a great arm and Brandon Crawford also has a proven great arm, which at the end was the reason why Alex Gordon was stranded at third base without daring or attempting a suicidal chase of an impossible dream which the reality of the strong arms of the Giants players, would have prevented to happen for the great Royals team. The Giants beat a great team fair and square. Like they swept the Tigers with Miguel Cabrera and his Triple Crown. For the boy who grew up in a non-English country the oasis of happiness that the Giants represent brought this great illusion and joy of achieving the ultimate dream. They became a dynasty.

INDEX

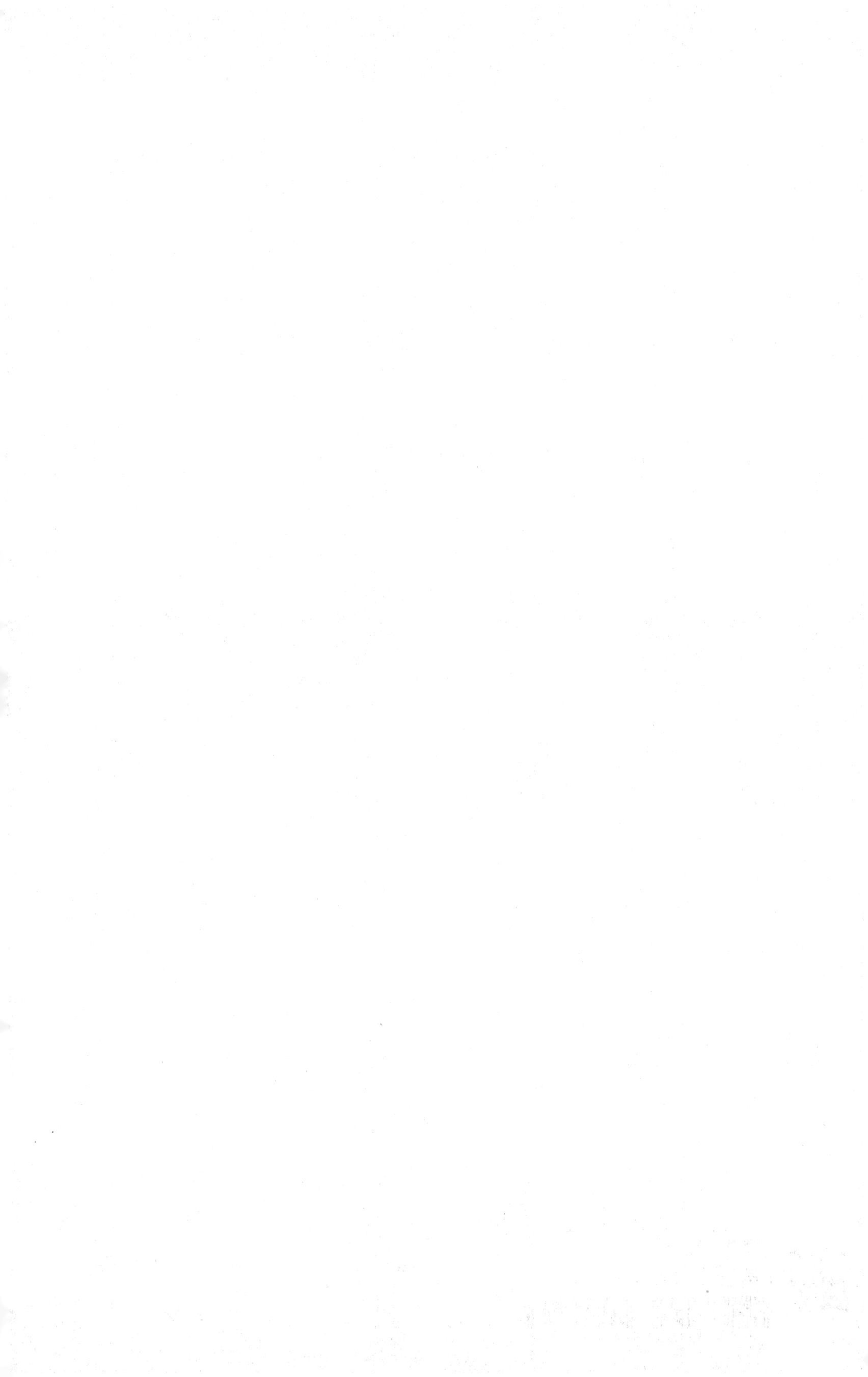